D1714771

(

The Critical Turn

Rhetoric and Philosophy in Postmodern Discourse

Edited by
Ian Angus and Lenore Langsdorf

Southern Illinois University Press
Carbondale and Edwardsville

Library of Congress Cataloging-in-Publication Data

The Critical turn : rhetoric and philosophy in postmodern discourse /
edited by Ian Angus and Lenore Langsdorf.
    p. cm.
    Chiefly papers presented at the annual meetings of the Speech
Communication Association and the Society for Phenomenology
and Existential Philosophy.
    Includes bibliographical references and index.
    1. Rhetoric—Congresses. 2. Communication—Philosophy—
Congresses. I. Angus, Ian H. II. Langsdorf, Lenore, 1943–   .
P301.C75   1993
808'.001—dc20   92-9398
    ISBN 0-8093-1843-1 (cloth). — ISBN 0-8093-1844-X (pbk.)   CIP

The paper used in this publication meets the minimum
requirements of American National Standard for Information
Sciences—Permanence of Paper for Printed Library Materials,
ANSI Z39.48-1984. ∞

With love and gratitude
to
Viviana Elsztein Angus and *Vernon Lee Crawford*

Contents

Acknowledgments

We (the coeditors) began talking about the theme of this book in Toronto in 1984. Continued conversation was punctuated by sessions we organized at the annual meetings of the Speech Communication Association and the Society for Phenomenology and Existential Philosophy; most of these essays were originally presented at those meetings. As editors, we acknowledge with thanks the participants' sustained interest and collegiality.

As contributors, we all thank James VanOosting (chair of the Speech Communication Department, Southern Illinois University) for his support of the project, and Mariangela Maguire (doctoral student in speech communication, SIU) for her especially valued contribution as editorial assistant.

Contributors

IAN ANGUS (Ph.D., York University, 1980) is an associate professor in the Department of Communication, University of Massachusetts at Amherst. He is author of *Technique and Enlightenment: Limits of Instrumental Reason* and *George Grant's Platonic Rejoinder to Heidegger*, editor of *Ethnicity in a Technological Age,* and coeditor (with Sut Jhally) of *Cultural Politics in Contemporary America.*

JAMES W. HIKINS (Ph.D., University of Texas at Austin, 1985) is an assistant professor in the Department of Communication at Ohio State University in Columbus. He is the author (with Richard A. Cherwitz) of *Communication and Knowledge: An Investigation in Rhetorical Epistemology* and has contributed numerous essays on rhetorical theory and criticism to such journals as *Quarterly Journal of Speech, Philosophy and Rhetoric,* and *Communication Studies.* His research focuses primarily on the relationships among the concepts of human communication, rhetoric, and knowledge. Most recently, he has been exploring the application of contemporary notions of rhetoric as epistemic to methods of rhetorical criticism.

MICHAEL J. HYDE (Ph.D., Purdue University, 1977) is an associate professor of communication studies in the Department of Communication Studies at Northwestern University and is the editor of, and a contributor to, *Communication Philosophy and the Technological Age.* His numerous essays and critical reviews appear in such academic journals as *Quarterly Journal of Speech, Man and World, Communication, Rhetoric and Philosophy, International Journal of Oral History,* and *Visible Language.* He is a past national Fellow of the W. K. Kellogg Foundation and a recipient of national and university research grants for his work in the rhetoric of medicine.

LENORE LANGSDORF (Ph.D., State University of New York at Stony Brook, 1977) is an associate professor of the philosophy of communication in the Department of Speech Communication at Southern Illinois University at Carbondale. Her published work has appeared in several journals, including *Human Studies* and *Informal Logic,* and in several edited collections. She is coeditor (with Andrew R. Smith) of *Recovering Pragmatism's Voice: The Classical Tradition, Rorty, and the Philosophy of Communication* and editor of the SUNY Press series in philosophy of the social sciences. Her research focuses on hermeneutic phenomenology, argumentation and rhetorical theory, and issues in the philosophy of the social/human sciences.

RICHARD L. LANIGAN (Ph.D., Southern Illinois University at Carbondale, 1969) is a professor of the philosophy of communication in the Department of Speech Communication at Southern Illinois University at Carbondale. He has been a postdoctoral fellow in philosophy at the University of Dundee, Scotland, and at the University of California at Berkeley. His books include *Semiotic Phenomenology of Rhetoric, Phenomenology of Communication, Speaking and Semiology,* and *The Human Science of Communicology.*

RAYMIE E. MCKERROW (Ph.D., University of Iowa, 1974) is a professor of communication studies in the Department of Speech Communication at the University of Maine. He edited *Explorations in Rhetoric* and is coauthor of *Principles and Types of Speech Communication.* His published work has appeared in several journals, including *Journal of the History of Ideas, Church History, Rhetorica, Philosophy and Rhetoric, Quarterly Journal of Speech,* and *Communication Monographs,* and in several conference proceedings and edited collections on argument theory and criticism. His research areas include nineteenth-century rhetoric, the history of contemporary argumentation, and critical theory.

DAVID JAMES MILLER (Ph.D., Purdue University, 1991) is an assistant professor of philosophy and communication in the Department of Humanities at Michigan Technological University. He is the author of "Immodest Interventions" (*Phenomenological Inquiry*, 1987). His research focus is on the philosophy of communication.

CALVIN O. SCHRAG (Ph.D., Harvard University, 1957) is the George Ade Professor of Philosophy at Purdue University. He is the author of many articles and five books, the most recent of which are *Radical Reflection and the Origins of the Human Sciences, Communicative Praxis and the Space of Subjectivity*, and *The Resources of Rationality: A Response to the Postmodern Challenge*.

CRAIG R. SMITH (Ph.D., Pennsylvania State University, 1969) is the director of the Center for First Amendment Studies and chairman of the Department of Speech Communication at California State University, Long Beach. He has published many books and articles focusing on rhetorical theory and first amendment issues.

KENNETH S. ZAGACKI (Ph.D., University of Texas at Austin, 1986) is an assistant professor in the Department of Speech Communication at Louisiana State University. He has published philosophical and critical articles in such journals as *Quarterly Journal of Speech, Philosophy and Rhetoric*, and other regional journals. His research focus is on rhetorical theory and criticism and the relationship between philosophy and rhetoric.

The Critical Turn

Unsettled Borders

Envisioning Critique at the Postmodern Site

IAN ANGUS AND LENORE LANGSDORF

WE ARE ALL LATECOMERS: WE BEGIN QUESTIONING IN THE midst of situations already marked by the questioning and answering that came before. What we decide to do, what we think we know, the answers we are likely to hear, the actions we are disposed to perform—all bear the imprint of layers of discourse and action, challenge and response. And even more than the explicit questions we ask, the unthematic background of everyday practices is, in large part, formed through the history of human inquiry. In a sense, the topic of this book is the nature of questioning itself and, specifically, the centrality of critical reasoning to questioning. These essays inquire into the shape and practice of inquiry and communication within the institutionalized divisions of work and authority that comprise our intellectual tradition. They are united by the claim that such inquiry comprises a critique of received knowledge and its institutions.

More particularly, this book suggests that human inquiry has entered a new situation—which, along with many others, we are willing to call postmodern—such that the settled answers concerning its rhetorical and philosophical aspects no longer suffice. The convictions and orientations that have traditionally marked the separation of rhetoric and philosophy—

1

the concern for truth and the focus on persuasion—have begun to converge on a new space that can be defined through the central term *discourse*. The crossing of boundaries that we take as the beginnings of convergence are clear: rhetoric has come to focus on the process of inquiry, often with an epistemic interest. In ceasing to be defined as the epistemological legitimation of truth, philosophy begins to seek an interventionist role within the intellectual conversation over which it used to presume a queenly, dispassionate rule from above. A redrawing of the borders is already underway, with far-reaching implications for both disciplinary authority and the procedures of specialized research. The essays collected in this volume make different contributions to mapping the territory that has emerged through the interrelation of philosophy and rhetoric in this new situation. Such maps can no longer presume the dichotomy of a factual field of objects standing over or against its descriptive representation. Mapping simultaneously constitutes the territory mapped. The following descriptions and discussions are also agonistic interventions in the discursive field.

In this introduction to the volume, we want to stress the postmodern unsettling of traditional boundaries in order to point to the territory that the essays explore. We do not attempt a totalization of the various contributions, since such an attempt presupposes precisely the notion of an epistemological metanarrative that the turn toward discourse undermines. A traditional introduction that settles the place of each contribution within the editors' presumed totality presupposes that each contribution is a chapter in an unfolding, self-subsistent, and harmonious story of knowledge that the editors have had the foresight to orchestrate. To the contrary, we wish to acknowledge that these essays are more than nodes on our preordained map, that there are tensions between them, and that this is itself a part of the agon of rhetoric and philosophy in contemporary discourse. Our introduction can thus only be a similar mapping, though it is oriented more toward describing a point from which the contributions take off than toward engaging with them in mapping the territory.

Perhaps, then, we can begin our task of introduction with a story that illustrates the traditional territory that rhetoric and philosophy occupy. This territory goes back to the ancient Platonic polemic against the Sophists, where the main issue was between two competing ways of life—political and philosophical. This divergence has thrown its shadow over subsequent history, though it has now again become debatable. But the main issue in more recent times has been determined by the distinction between specialized sciences and a (more) universal, critical reason that is characteristic of modern, post-Renaissance civilization. Sorting out this ancient/modern/postmodern issue of periodization is a key aspect of a contemporary theory of discourse (Angus, 1992). Since the contemporary convergence of rhetoric and philosophy has been made possible by critiques of the assumptions of the modern representational scheme of knowledge, we will begin there. But, as we will argue below, the contemporary postmodern situation reformulates this issue in terms of discursive practices and, to that extent, returns the issue to one of the ways of life—political—though perhaps no longer as a competition.

At the outset of a sociology of religion course that one of us took as an undergraduate, the professor stated that the course would not consider whether any given religion was true. Rather, consideration would be limited to the social consequences of belief in the various religions. The student was scandalized; it seemed impossible to discuss religion, or even its social consequences, without facing the question of its "truth"—its ability to disclose the proper conduct of human life. But then, the student was a beginning questioner who had not accepted—really had not even understood—the necessary abstraction that distinguishes sociology of religion from philosophy of religion, theology, or the social gospel. Surely there is something of value in that naive view. For it, religion matters, in the way many things matter to living beings who must make decisions. When those decisions relate to religion's role in the conduct of life, our interest is quite different from that of the scholar for whom the sociology (or the politics or epistemology, etc.) of religion is a circumscribed subject matter.

It is probably inevitable that knowledge be divided if there is any substantial headway to be made along the many

3

possible paths of inquiry. Such intellectual divisions of work and authority would pose no intractable problems if the necessary abstractions that undergird each separated inquiry could be redeemed by resituating those inquiries in relation to a larger whole. In other words, the ultimate role of a given specialized inquiry can only be adequately determined with reference to the complete architectonic of knowledge that clarifies its valid contribution and suggests its inadequacies. This may well be an adequate answer and self-defense for the specialized scientist, even though it does pose the difficult problem of who, in an age marked by the immense accumulation of specialized researches, can be capable of undertaking the vast survey that such a synthesis demands. If this task were itself to demand a division of labor—an army of philosophers, perhaps—the goal of synthesis would retreat another step and perhaps continue to retreat ad infinitum. On the other hand, the task of synthesis could be terminated pragmatically with the requirement that it include only as much, and see only as far ahead, as the present practical purpose demands. Such a pragmatic realism would be a rhetorical rejoinder to the seemingly impossible task of philosophical synthesis. Given the post-Renaissance, modern systematic division of knowledge, the opposition between philosophy and rhetoric stems from these two gestures toward synthesis, their ultimate goals, and their practical effects.

Philosophy and rhetoric, within this representational tradition stemming from the notion of a specialized science, have been concerned with what lies outside the boundaries that delimit specialized domains—with a (more) universal human reason understood as critique. From this perspective, the crucial issue pertains to the wider context in which science functions and effects. In contrast to the positive specialized sciences, critique begins with a negative moment. The foundation of critique is as much in what we recognize that we do *not* know as that of science is in what we claim (or believe) that we *do* know (Langsdorf, 1991b). This indicates a basic relation between rhetoric and philosophy in contrast to science. These are disciplines that share the peculiarity of being everywhere and nowhere, of transcending the special sciences through an ongoing and unending reflective venture.

4

It is this question of a (more) universal, critical reason that rhetoric and philosophy seek to address within the modern age. Inquiry within the Western scientific tradition demands a delimited subject matter and methodical investigation procedures that can be specified and applied by any competent researcher. What is not demanded, and may even be discouraged, is ongoing reflection and reassessment of the stipulations of both content (subject matter) and method (procedures) employed within a particular research domain. Abstractions from the complexity of human experience are made in order that progress within boundaries can occur, and research within these abstracted domains becomes institutionalized. Certainly there is a sense in which this practice is unobjectionable: we cannot simultaneously and uniformly investigate the entirety of our environment. But in this scientific practice itself, there is no justification of the boundaries that include and exclude, or of the methodological prescriptions that serve to specify how we are to investigate and what is to be investigated. Nevertheless, due to their institutionalization, specialized sciences compete with each other for resources and prestige. In this sense, there are continuous and pervasive boundary disputes. To the extent that the sciences defend their boundaries in this manner, they are forced to enter the domain of philosophy and rhetoric. For this reason, the actual progress of specialized sciences has required mobilization of the resources of rhetoric and philosophy.

The modern parameters of the debate between rhetoric and philosophy (as competing versions of critical reason) are instituted by the relation of both members back to the prior notion of a specialized science. Philosophy has oscillated between a commitment to an architectonic of knowledge and a skeptical denial of generalizable knowledge-claims. In being divided between these two extremes, philosophy has tended to evacuate the space of practical action that rhetoric has claimed—usually with reference to a pragmatic criterion of truth. Within the representational paradigm of modernity, the debate between rhetoric and philosophy revolves around these respective emphases of critical reason. Once again, perhaps we can illustrate with a story, an allegory, these boundaries in which the modern version of the relation between rhetoric and philosophy occur—boundaries that are becoming unsettled in the postmodern condition.

If sciences are plural, they must have a ruler: a queen of the sciences who builds the architectonic, guards against its crumbling, and designs new apartments to keep accommodations up-to-date. This ruler needs a servant who can explain to the beginner and generalist that abstractions are necessary, although their partial and transitory nature can be admitted: in time, the wisdom of those who came before will be evident to the latecomer. After sufficient primary reflection, within a universe differentiated into specialized domains, reflected by the university's many departments, and arranged in accord with the architectonic, a second reflection will leap over those abstracted parts. Only then will the whole of knowledge cohere with the beginner's or nonspecialist's need to know: only then will the relation of developed theory to everyday practice be clear. Philosophy is the grand representation of the plural representations of the special sciences.

Coming after the sciences (so such a story might continue), philosophy needs rhetoric to reach those who must be persuaded to be patient and yet to embark upon one or another of the specialized domains of science. The authority of the architectonic is cited by the rhetor (who is not obliged to understand it): the road to knowledge begins with a belief, inculcated by those who are supposed to know, that delaying the desire for knowledge useful in the exigencies of life will lead to satisfaction in time.

But, as is often the way with servants and rulers, the servant may come to be so capable, and the ruler may come to be so distant, that the queen of the sciences seems unnecessary. The less we are concerned with second reflections and architectonics, the closer we seem to be to the field of action. Furthermore, that field appears to be broad enough to allow everyone the right to speak and persuade. Thus emerges the vision of a new, queenless regime populated by liberated servants. The second reflection that reveals coherence and perhaps also the first reflection that reveals delineations now appear to be just like the servants (though with more pretentions) schooled in techniques of persuasion that (unlike the more honest servants) they try to keep secret.

The lesson to be learned (so such a story might conclude) is that we make the most of the plurality of roads of inquiry, and that we are most faithful to the pluralities of the human condition, if we declare openly the persuasions that each of us practices and do not pretend to engage in them in the service of esoteric knowledge. The beginner and the generalist do not have to wait; they can be assured of prompt, piecemeal gratification of their epistemic and ethical needs to know. Delay for developing second reflections that might accomplish integrated, even systematic, insight into the whole now appears as a conceit—even a deceit. However (as another conclusion to the story would go), the fact that the previous second reflections have been shown insufficient does not warrant the inference that one cannot be found. And there has just been discovered a new principle for second reflections, a new theory of representation. This time we will not be left wanting.

The history of rhetoric (as we can glimpse through this allegory) is composed of squabbles between obedient and rebellious servants. There have been rhetorics that served their queen by accepting the architectonic on faith and delaying judgment in the name of a promised coherence. And there have been rhetorics that served plurality by denying the possibility of coherence and thereby shifting inquiry closer to the decisions made in the middle of life, without final justification. The history of philosophy has had its dissidents too: there have been many who were never purged of the impatience of the beginner, and who doubted the welding of inquiry to architectonic. Often, they recalled one who had paid with his life in the unsatisfied pursuit of knowledge.

And here the story has languished for some time—two basic positions, each with complications to sort out, much clarification to do, and always new material to integrate: rhetoric as the obedient servant of philosophical architectonic providing the persuasion to initiate and conclude inquiry at the moments when it cannot be known to the participants; rhetoric as the liberated servant, skeptical of the final edifice of knowledge, providing less glorious and more practical motives to the beginner; philosophy as stern and ultimate justification, complete to itself and unconcerned with those who do not understand the whole (or with those moments of initiation and conclusion when the whole is not apparent); philosophy as ultimate justification, but sagely requiring the dulcet tones of rhetoric to smooth the moments of knowledge's absence with the comforts of reasonable belief. The boundaries of this modern debate remained fixed by the prior distinction between specialized science and a (more) universal, critical reason. As Chaim Perelman puts it, rhetoric pertains to "every discourse which does not claim an impersonal validity" (1982, p. 162). Philosophy, by way of contrast, is concerned with just such impersonal validity—not with what is true for you or me but with what is true for everyone, without restriction. The core notion from which philosophy as representation emerges is such a scientific domain of impersonal validity. Rhetoric is delimited by what is left over.

But, as we have intimated, the borders illustrated by the above allegory no longer sufficiently outline the territory of contemporary debates between philosophy and rhetoric. The boundaries that were fixed by their relation to the core modern notion of a specialized science have shifted. We will, in dialogue with other contemporary writers, call this shifting of boundaries "postmodern." While this term has been used to indicate almost anything and everything about contemporary culture (Gitlin, 1988; Hebdidge, 1986), it can, nevertheless, be given a specific meaning in the context of a given topic. In the case of a new convergence between rhetoric and philosophy, this specific meaning consists in a shift of the third term used for comparison from *science* (modernity) to *discourse* (postmodernity).[1] Let us introduce this shift from modernity to postmodernity through what we regard as a key transitional work—Edmund Husserl's *The Crisis of the European Sciences and Transcendental Phenomenology*.

The crisis of the sciences, as Husserl identified it, is not a crisis of theory or method *internal* to the sciences, which are understood as impressive bodies of fact and explanation that constitute the specialized domains of our intellectual environment staked out during that period that we now name, retrospectively, "modernity." It is rather a crisis brought on by what we may term a tension between specialization and critique: between our ability to abstract domains within which we develop propositional knowledge and our inability to re-

flect on the multiplicity of these domains so far as they inter-
penetrate and transform the whole sociohistorical environment that phenomenologists call the "lifeworld." Indeed, the
key point is that the larger inability with respect to the civiliz-
ing power of human reason as such is brought forth precisely
by the development of specialized domains. In this respect,
Husserl's diagnosis intersects with that of Max Horkheimer
and Theodor Adorno, who argue that the "great discoveries
of applied science *are paid for* with an increasing diminution
of theoretical awareness" (1972, p. xi, emphasis added). The
lifeworld includes ourselves and our practical everyday life as
well as the sciences and their practical effects. In Husserl's
words, there is "a general lament about the crisis of our culture
and the role ascribed to the sciences" that "concerns not the
scientific character of the sciences but rather what they, or
what science in general, has meant and could mean for human
existence" (1970, p. 5). The model of science that has given
rise to success within specialized domains has simultaneously
undermined the capacity of reason to theorize the lifeworld
as a whole. Thus the crisis is not internal to the sciences but
pertains to their meaning for human life.

Husserl sought to address this crisis through the restitu-
tion and reconstitution of a comprehensive conception of reason that could address the question of the "meaning" of human life. But what form can such a concept of reason take?
Husserl proposed phenomenology as a "theory of theory
forms," or a theory of scientific forms, that would be both
comprehensive and "material"—content oriented rather than
merely formal. Phenomenology should be a universality capable of encompassing specialized sciences, on the one hand,
and capable of articulating a conception of the meaning of
human life with definite content, on the other. Husserl proposed "an *essential, endlessly reiterated, reflexive bearing* of transcendental phenomenology upon itself, in which the essential
sense of an ultimate justification by itself is discernibly included, and that precisely this is the fundamental characteristic of an essentially ultimate science" (1969, p. 268).

The difficulty is this: Can such a content oriented theori-
zation of human meaning claim the status of science, or definite knowledge, in any manner comparable to the specialized

sciences that it transcends? The tension here between human reason as critique and as specialized science extends into Husserl's proposal for remedy. He reforms the concept of truth to situate it always "within horizons," and he argues that the "systematic explication" of these horizons is the task of phenomenological philosophy (1969, p. 279). But so assigning that task is all too easily understood or, as we would argue, misunderstood as deeming philosophy an ultimate science with a priviliged method that enables final justification. While the diagnosis begins in critique, it terminates in a synthesis that would seem to make critique unnecessary. Alternatively, the call for "explication" could be (mis)understood as specifying the task of philosophy as mere commentary—perhaps similar to Richard Rorty's notion of "useful kibitzing" (1979, p. 393). The Owl of Minerva might become something of a carping parrot, or even a parasitic buzzard. We would, instead, place emphasis on philosophy's "reiterated, reflexive" character. Its ever-renewed vigilance necessitates a common ground with a rhetoric for which procedure and justification occur in constant engagement with the particular object of criticism. Such a concretely situated reflection delineates "material universals" (in phenomenological terminology) that resonate with the centrality of "topics" in rhetorical theory.

Husserl's diagnosis of the crisis of the sciences begins, then, with the tension between specialization and critique that marks modernity. But his proposed solution dissolves that tension into an uneasy—and perhaps untenable—synthesis. Together with a specificity of method and topic (a situation of "truth within horizons") reminiscent of rhetoric, he would hold a universality of vision (an "essential sense" of "ultimate justification") reminiscent of philosophy. We argue that, when it is properly understood, the result is a common ground, inevitably experienced from two perspectives, but scarcely noticeable from interests rooted in the counterposing of specialization and critique.[2] It cannot be defined as the territory of either philosophy or rhetoric. Rather, this ground constitutes a new (postmodern) situation for the project of a (more) universal reason that radicalizes the notion of critique. Within the modern representational scheme, critique is counterposed to specialization and terminates in synthesis—

whether understood as architectonic or pragmatic action. In the postmodern site, critique is even more radically homeless since it serves no interest derived from specialized science and cannot contribute to its progress (Langsdorf, 1991a). The contours of this site require reformation of both traditions, and their relation, in ways that can be startling and even unwelcome.

Let us return for a moment to our initial story of the student dissatisfied with a class in the sociology of religion. Typically, it is the meaning or larger import of, for example, the question of religion that is of interest to both the beginning student and the member of the larger community. For both those interests, a difficulty appears: the second reflection that overcomes the division of labor and power—the abstractions accomplished in the first reflection—is too far down the road of inquiry to be visible to one still trying to turn out of the driveway. How can the necessary separation and ultimately transient nature of these divisions be made accessible to those who are beginning a first reflection in the middle of their lives? Are specialized inquiries of any use at all to those whose interest in knowing does not extend to the construction of syntheses? In this case, the institutionalized divisions seem to block any inquiry at all, or to imply that more general conclusions drawn from separate studies become entirely eccentric.

To put the point more technically: If the interest in the communal pursuit of knowledge through specialization becomes problematic through an orientation to practical wisdom, the conception of critique must be radicalized. In the postmodern situation, the problem of scientific specialization cannot be adequately answered with reference to synthesis—a reference that remains within modernism's assumption of the primacy of the question of knowledge. In contrast, features that define scientific specializations as institutionalized practices with internal legitimations that produce wider social effects appear much more significant.

It is this set of issues that is thematized under the heading of *discursive formations*. This is the first half of the postmodern question concerning knowledge, and it is at this point that the convergence of rhetoric and philosophy emerges. The second half of the question has to do with what resources for orientation can be expected and utilized in this situation. Any thought that would attempt to justify a contemporary divergence between philosophy and rhetoric—in method, aim, or result—must begin from their initial convergence on discursive practices. The beginning point here is not the division of knowledge but the public, generalized discourses that construct the common places of our common sense.

One way to recognize the extent of reformation required is through reconsidering from a more basic angle the earlier question of scientific specialization: How is the boundary drawn that delineates a domain for methodological investigation? More generally, how is science separated from the cultural, linguistic, and practical complex of everyday life? Within the tension of modernity's representational schemes, the issue is one of investigation from beyond the boundaries of delimited domains. Within this reformed and radicalized notion of critique, the process of delimitation is itself questioned: How is a "pure internality" constructed? Husserl's work, as well as that of Horkheimer and Adorno, is situated at the point where the initial modern issue turns over and into this postmodern reformation of the question. Since justifying a (more) universal reason is undermined by the delimited concept of science from which it emerges, the reformed question must be how is delineation itself—and thus delimitation—possible?

Pursuit of this question reveals that specialized science begins in valorizing the *development* of knowledge within the reasoning *mind*, alongside a correlative depreciation of the *communication* of knowledge in the cultural *world*. This duality of reason and language, of knowledge and intersubjectivity, of truth and persuasion, has characterized modern philosophy and rhetoric as diametrical. The notion of the mind as a self-contained representation of the world, capable of truth, assumes and promotes divorce between that representation and its subsequent dissemination and effects. Understanding truth as (internal) correct description implies and reinforces understanding communication as (external) plurivocal transmission. There is one meaning, held internally, although there are many broadcast messages. What is internal, possessed (universal truth), is valued more highly than what is external, disseminated (local opinion). Metaphorically speaking, science and philosophy are concerned with the discovery and justification of an internal and immaterial product—truth—written on the pages of a letter. Rhetoric is concerned with the external process of dispatching and delivering those sealed-up (and so sealed-off) pages. Once delivered, the message on the pages will revert to its (properly) immaterial status.

It is precisely this diametrical duality that has been effaced in both the "linguistic turn" in philosophy and in the turn toward a "rhetoric of inquiry" in recent rhetoric (Langsdorf, 1990). Once philosophy turned toward language as the fundamental phenomenon, its distinctiveness became difficult to defend—the poetic and rhetorical resources of traditional philosophical texts are too obvious to overlook (Baynes, Bohman, & McCarthy, 1987, pp. 5–6). Similarly, the traditional claim of philosophy to arbitrate other discourses fell prey to the plurality of language games and to the antireductionist message of that philosophy (West, 1985, p. 263; Bernstein, 1985, pp. 79–108). With this end of the presumption of a sovereign language, it becomes possible to imagine, in Calvin O. Schrag's words, "that when philosophy comes to an end it becomes rhetoric. . . . Philosophy emerged out of rhetoric. We thus seem to become spectators of a rather remarkable homecoming" (1985, p. 166). All of us—rhetoricians and philosophers—may begin to read *all* of Plato. From the other side, through its turn toward the rhetoric of inquiry, rhetoric has begun to throw off its subordinate status by rejecting the distinction between inquiry and advocacy and demonstrating the polemical and persuasive components of scientific discourses. Herbert W. Simons sums it up in this manner:

> The general point is that no system of logic is ever self-validating; it depends, rather, on some other system for its support, and that system must be validated by another, and so on, in an infinite series. By this reasoning the very idea of a logical system—a logic of logics—is itself rhetorical . . . rhetoricians of inquiry are thus

prompted to speak of conventions of logic, with the understanding that these too are human inventions. (1990, p. 14; see also Nelson, Megill, & McCloskey, 1987)

Thought together, the critique of representation in philosophy (largely through the linguistic turn) and the development of rhetorics of inquiry (based on the viewing of scientific discourse as always already an advocacy) initiate a postmodern discursive philosophy/rhetoric that is dialogically, rather than diametrically, delineated. Rather than each limiting and devaluing the other, both extend into and require the other. The very means for conceptualizing dualities of reason and speech, knowledge and persuasion, truth and opinion—in short, mind and body—are annulled.

Within this reformed situation, we find ways of talking that blur and transgress traditional distinctions between rhetoric and philosophy. The strange use of the word *theory* in contemporary discussion, noted by Frederic Jameson (1984), is an instance. Neither the "theory of" anything nor the most general theory was traditionally called philosophy. Likewise, the word *discourse* refers to scientific, political, and institutional dimensions. Any attempt to confine it to just one of these undermines what is emphatically new in its usage: it encompasses at once both knowledge and power in their institutional forms. That the term *postmodern* is itself lacking in positive content is instructional, and even more so when that lack is criticized. It designates discourse that comes after modernity, but it recognizes that it cannot name itself without falling again into modernity's presumption of an external vantage point that delimits and designates—that is, that limits even as it gives a sign by which the discourse will be known.

The notion of critique plays a key role in the postmodern situation, and it does so in ways that may be especially disturbing to those who adopted its practice within modernity's boundaries. It now tends to fall either toward mere description of practices (as if that were enough to condemn them) or toward mere condemnation (as if analysis were not necessary). But critical reason, as reflection within the boundaries of modernity, was supposed to synthesize both these dimen-

14

sions through concrete description with evaluative content. In this sense, the new dualistic tendency cannot simply be brushed aside. It indicates a new intellectual situation whose emergence demands a rethinking of both analysis and evaluation. Both require delineation and delimitation—and those are the very (rhetorical) activities and (philosophical) concepts that have become fundamentally problematic. The specific contribution of this book to the wider conversation is situated at this juncture. As critique, both philosophy and rhetoric resist institutionalization. Both are homeless so far as they now unsettle the boundaries of modernity.

Now, institutional homelessness translates all too readily into intellectual disenfranchisement—that is, into voicelessness (no classrooms, no publication sites, no research grants) and economic death (no corporate sponsors, no government subsidies, no paying consumers). There is, however, a way to avoid this fate—to present oneself as doing another specialty alongside the rest—that must be reckoned to be an endemic tendency in an environment that institutionalizes a representational view of knowledge. Contemporary philosophy and rhetoric, understood as disciplines, have identified their subject matter and methods more on the basis of economic power and political usefulness than on the basis of intellectual exigency and the demands of the environment as a whole. Our own critical turn, directed initially at the process of delineation of a specialized science, leads also to some uncomfortable questions (and conclusions) directed toward the subject matter of our own traditions, especially as they are recast within a new condition. Both philosophy and rhetoric have too often, and too predictably, succumbed to the tendency of institutions to define specialized system-maintaining research domains, to the detriment of their historic role of investigations "outside the boundary."

Despite this domesticating tendency, some rhetorical and philosophical tendencies continue to operate within the postmodern reformed situation in order to clarify it. Most characteristically, discourse analysis takes up philosophy's traditional concern with the internal coherence of knowledge-claims. Examination of those claims can reveal that an argument has been carried to conclusion more by domination of particular persons, positions, or strategies than by the strength of reasons acknowledged as good by all actual and potential participants in the discussion. Reflections of this sort typically focus on identification of suppressed voices, unjustified boundaries, obscure consequences, vested interests, or reified concepts. Such identifications are themselves claims and must be open to recursive critical inquiry. Thus, internal coherence passes beyond the status of an internally unquestioned standard. As it implicates the unnoticed and unsaid, it turns itself outward toward the political and institutional ("good") reasons for "bad reasons."

Correlatively, rhetoric's traditional concern with discursive effectivity directs it more easily to these political and institutional dimensions. But, increasingly, it uncovers epistemic implications and claims rooted in those practices, and with this inward turn, converges with philosophical tendencies headed outward. Thus we have a shared focus on tendencies in communicative events, modes of discourse, and institutions, with a shared attention to implicit patterns that emerge from those practices and the ways in which they form us, their participants and observers. Surely the key term in this convergence is *discourse*, which names the common ground from which rhetorically and philosophically oriented interventions proceed. This new commonality institutes a new relation, for within the intellectual and political structures of modernity, the third term was *science*—more precisely, *specialized science*—in contrast to philosophy's attunement to the universal and rhetoric's attention to the particular. In the reformed situation of postmodernity the third term is *discourse*, rather than *science*. Intrinsically and explicitly, then, postmodern critique focuses on a process (discourse) that subdues, and even conceals, institutional forces at least as successfully as science did. Surely one task for the convergence of rhetoric and philosophy that these essays describe, then, is the uncovering of the institutional patterns that inscribe knowledge and power within discourse.

Reassessment of the dualities of modernity has not brought with it dissolution of, or extrication from, the crisis

16

of rationality that Husserl and the Frankfurt School described. But the crisis can no longer be analyzed based on the opposition between specialization and critique. We now recognize that the very ideas of delimitation, specialization and internality—in themselves and in their interconnection—are problematic. That brings us to recognize that the very foundations of the diagnosis of crisis (as Husserl, Adorno, and Horkheimer identified it) are not beyond analysis and justification—in short, not beyond critique. The reformed situation has deepened the crisis, for as the end of traditional modes of rhetoric and philosophy become imaginable in a postmodern situation, their institutionalization often becomes, paradoxically, more entrenched. Yet our capacity for reflective critical thinking beyond that horizon—for identifying issues and articulating alternatives—becomes more confident.

Notes

1. It is possible, of course, to place this specific shift within the larger context of cultural history. By *modernity*, defined as the focus on (specialized) science, we mean the period from 1637, with the publication of *Discourse on Method*, to 1914 and the beginning of World War I. These parameters encompass an era dominated by the focus on the human subject as the center of knowing and acting and a concomitant concern with epistemology—the justification of knowledge—and autonomy—the principle of free action (Angus, 1988a, 1988b).

2. We may note here that this critique, or rather clarification, of Husserl is not the same as the "error" attributed to Husserl's work by Jurgen Habermas. He argues that the concept of theory in Husserl's phenomenology is composed of two incompatible factors: cosmological intuition based on the ancient Greek notion of theory, and the modern notion of science as directed to infinite horizons (Habermas, 1971, pp. 304–306). Habermas thus misses the radical rethinking of the concept of theory in Husserl as truth within "systematically explicated horizons." The present account argues that this new concept of theory cannot be properly characterized as science without undermining its difference from everything that has gone under that name. Husserl's sense of theory instigates a radical reformulation of philosophy that overflows the assumptions of modernity.

References

Angus, I. (1988a). Circumscribing postmodern culture. In I. Angus & S. Jhally (Eds.), *Cultural politics in contemporary America* (pp. 96–107). New York: Routledge.

Angus, I. (1988b). Displacement and otherness: Toward a post-modern ethics. In I. Angus (Ed.), *Ethnicity in a technological age* (pp. 107–128). Edmonton: Canadian Institute of Ukrainian Studies.

Angus, I. (1992). The politics of common sense: Articulation theory and critical communication studies. In S. Deetz (Ed.), *Communication yearbook 15* (pp. 536–571). Newbury Park, CA: Sage.

Baynes, K., Bohman, J., & McCarthy, T. (1987). General introduction. In K. Baynes, J. Bohman, & T. McCarthy (Eds.), *After philosophy: End or transformation?* (pp. 1–18). Cambridge: MIT Press.

Bernstein, R. (1985). *Beyond objectivism and relativism: Science, hermeneutics and praxis.* Philadelphia: University of Pennsylvania Press.

Gitlin, T. (1988). Postmodernism: Roots and politics. In I. Angus & S. Jhally (Eds.), *Cultural politics in contemporary America* (pp. 347–360). New York: Routledge.

Habermas, J. (1971). *Knowledge and human interests* (J. Shapiro, Trans.). Boston: Beacon. (Original work published 1968.)

Hebdige, D. (1986). Postmodernism and "the other side." *Journal of Communication Inquiry, 10*(3), 78–98.

Horkheimer, M., & Adorno, T. (1972). *Dialectic of enlightenment* (J. Cumming, Trans.). New York: Herder and Herder. (Original work published 1944.)

Husserl, E. (1969). *Formal and transcendental logic* (D. Cairns, Trans.). The Hague: Martinus Nijhoff. (Original work published 1929.)

Husserl, E. (1970). *The crisis of the European sciences and transcendental phenomenology* (D. Carr, Trans.). Evanston: Northwestern University Press. (Original work published 1954.)

Jameson, F. (1984). The politics of theory. *New German Critique, 33*, 53–66.

Langsdorf, L. (1990, October). *Placing the rhetorical horse in front of the postmodern cart.* Paper presented at the annual meeting of the Speech Communication Association, Chicago, IL.

Langsdorf, L. (1991a). Critical thinking: Both rhetoric and philosophy. In D. W. Parson (Ed.), *Argument in controversy* (pp. 27–32). Washington, DC: Speech Communication Association.

Langsdorf, L. (1991b). In defense of pure cogitation: A reinterpretive endeavor. *Inquiry, 7*, 3–5, 17.

Nelson, J. S., Megill, A., & McCloskey, D. N. (1987). Rhetoric of inquiry. In J. S. Nelson, A. Megill, & J. N. McCloskey (Eds.), *The rhetoric of the human sciences: Language and argument in scholarship and public affairs* (pp. 3–18). Madison: University of Wisconsin Press.

Perelman, C. (1982). *The realm of rhetoric* (W. Kluback, Trans.). Notre Dame: University of Notre Dame Press. (Original work published 1977.)

Rorty, R. (1979). *Philosophy and the mirror of nature.* Princeton: Princeton University Press.

Schrag, C. O. (1985). Rhetoric resituated at the end of philosophy. *Quarterly Journal of Speech, 71*(1), 164–174.

Simons, H. W. (1990). Introduction: The rhetoric of inquiry as an intellectual movement. In H. W. Simons (Ed.), *The rhetorical turn: Invention and persuasion in the conduct of inquiry* (pp. 1–31). Chicago: The University of Chicago Press.

West, C. (1985). Afterward: The politics of American neo-pragmatism. In J. Rajchman & C. West (Eds.), *Post-analytic philosophy* (pp. 259–272). New York: Columbia University Press.

Words of Others and
Sightings/Citings/Sitings of Self

Lenore Langsdorf

DURING THE MIDDLE YEARS OF THE TWENTIETH CENTURY, sustained and diverse critiques of the egoic self as knower and of knowledge as representation have dissolved those allied foundations of philosophical discourse. From within rhetoric during this same time—and especially from the lines of thinking known as rhetoric as epistemic, rhetoric of inquiry, critical rhetoric, and dialogical rhetoric—have come alternative conceptions of self and knowledge.[1] These reconceptions of rhetoric at the end of modernity respond to inadequacies in philosophical and common sense assumptions about the knowing self and encourage the revival of classical rhetoric's emphasis on the primacy of practice. The result can be a realignment of both rhetoric and philosophy in our time that enables an understanding of human beings as preeminently practical rather than theoretical; as developing in the reflective, critical activities of moral and political discourse rather than coming to that discourse as egoic selves.

The homophones of my title provide a means for envisioning this understanding of human being through a comparison of several extant traditions of theorizing the self. I have in mind the words of those who have discerned the self as an entity constituted in vision, in language, and in action; that is, by what may be observed, by what may be spoken, and by what may be done. Three individuals may be associated with these orientations: René Descartes, Benjamin Lee Whorf, and Alfred Schutz.[2] None of these discerners of the self was a rhetorician by trade, and only Whorf is identifiable as engaged in communication theory. Yet the traditions they embody (philosophy, linguistics, and sociology) seem to me determinative of much of twentieth-century rhetoric. The turn to discourse in contemporary intellectual inquiry gives us an expanded conception of rhetoric as extending throughout cultural production. This expansion renews social criticism through an emphasis on the performative dimension of language. Yet this emphasis on the performative grows at the expense of a traditional conception of the rhetor as one who observes, reflects, and instigates the performance that is discourse.

Now rhetorical criticism of science, institutions, and politics has the positive value of taking separate discourses out of their isolation, revealing relations of domination embedded in them, and yoking them to a general discourse on the good life. Yet this breadth of rhetorical criticism carries a subtext, which I summarize as a tendency to collapse the rhetorical and philosophical moments of critical discourse analysis. Critical recall of discourse properly concerns how we might say, while philosophical recall seeks a more pervasive critique of the conditions in lived experience for saying or not saying, acting or not being able to act. The convergence of these two moments—if the result is conflation rather than mutual enhancement—may be unhealthy not only for rhetoric and philosophy but for that broader cultural activity that I characterize as the cultivation of the self in the course of diverse acts and plannings for action.

In what follows, I will examine how this activity fares within Cartesian, Whorfian, and Schutzian conceptions. My thesis is a dual one. First, I believe that Schutz's way of understanding human being as situated in social action provides a plausible basis for a rhetoric and a philosophy that lean upon, but do not collapse into, one another. Several contemporary scholars have developed that basis in directions that I will discuss briefly. Second, this contemporary group of philosophers and rhetoricians provides an alternative understanding of the self that bypasses difficulties in Descartes' understanding (based in seeing) and Whorf's understanding (based in saying).

In speaking of Descartes' understanding of human being as based in seeing, I do not mean to ignore or dispute the strong current of Platonism in Descartes' thinking. That deep and broad stream of thought is crucial to Cartesian rationalism and is anything but hospitable to the evidence of the senses—including, especially, sight. It seems likely that Plato's anti-incarnationist prescriptions for ratiocination were motivated by the pervasive shift from orality to alphabetic literacy that was accomplished in his time. A good deal of scholarship during these past twenty-five years has argued that pre-Platonic thought was dominated by what Eric Havelock (1963, p. 198) summarizes as a "Homeric state of mind." This same period, of course, was the age of classical rhetoric. Formulation and retention of information, as well as critical reflection on what was known, was accomplished orally in performances that required that reason function through ongoing and recalled deeds that embodied principles and maxims.[3]

The new alphabetic literacy depended upon the eye as much as orality had depended upon the ear. Yet the nature of the seen was quite different from the nature of what had been heard: principles and maxims were now stated in propositional form, quite apart from the lived experiences (ongoing and recalled deeds) that had been the medium for epistemic endeavors as well as theoretical and moral teaching in oral cultures. Learning became a matter of separating mind from sensory involvement in the world, and the philosopher's life of conversation with the Forms was extolled as superior to the rhetorician's life of conversation with fellow members of the polis. Furthermore, the eye engaged in reading does not see the page as it would see the face of another who tells of deeds, events, and things. The seeing that occurs in reading is quite removed from actually seeing those deeds, events, and things about which the rhetor tells. Thus we already have, in Plato, the clear and distinct *seeing* of *ideas* that is the distinguishing characteristic of good thinking in Descartes. Seeing in the mind's eye, for Descartes even more than for Plato, is best accomplished away from the marketplace—and even away from the classroom.

We are all familiar with the circumstances Descartes (1980) recounts at the very start of the *Discourse on Method* and refers to again, briefly, at the start of the *Meditations*: he retreated from public life, both military and scholarly, and resolved to set aside all that he had learned from others (both in his formal schooling and in the travels that instructed him after he left the classroom and library), in order to reflect upon the stock of knowledge resident in his mind. He constructed, in that solitary reflection, a method for increasing his knowledge by relying only on those ideas he could see, clearly and distinctly, in his mind's eye. He knew, as we all do, that the nonmetaphorical eye—the embodied eye that discerns events, things, and deeds—can be irretrievably mistaken by virtue of insufficient clarity of seeing and indistinctness of the seen. However, Descartes argued that much of what we think we learn through embodied seeing is actually a judgment of the mind: witness our tendency, noted in the ball-of-wax and passersby examples of the "Second Meditation," to credit our seeing for what we know on the basis of our thinking. Those examples brought Descartes to this conclusion: "What I believed I had seen with my eyes, I actually comprehend with nothing but the faculty of judgment which is in my mind." He went on to ratify the conflation of embodied and mental vision in a reference to the cogito: "But it could not happen that, while I see or think I see (I do not now distinguish the two) I who think am not something" (1980, p. 66).

Vision in this sense (what I "think I see") is the fundament and proof of the self for Descartes. This is not a departure from Plato so much as a more firmly engraved impression. I choose that metaphor in order to remind us that Descartes was *writing* the *Discourse* and *Meditations* in a historical moment during which the printed text was supplanting the holograph. During the period of technological revolution symbolized by invention of the printing press in the fifteenth century, the shift from ear to eye that occurred as alphabetic literacy supplanted orality in Plato's century was completed. Furthermore, the particular sort of vision that founds and confirms the Cartesian self requires a separation of the knowing self from the actual, spatiotemporal context of whatever that self would know. Both reading and reflection—seeing the page and introspecting the soul—require disengagement from conversation, in the broad sense of embodied interaction with the environment (including other human beings).

Descartes' inquiry into the nature of this "I, who think" literally substantiated his abstraction of the thinking self from lived experience, and thus from applying that self's cognitive powers to reflective criticism of that experience. He formulated an understanding of human being in terms of selves that are thinking substances. Each was knowable only privately— by itself—yet with the certainty that was (for Descartes) the mark of knowledge. That knowing was even so private as to occur without the help of cultural or spiritual support, such as language and God. But that knowing did not in itself (without God's help) include information about the extended substances comprising that self's environment. The full title of the *Meditations* includes the claim that it is a work in which *"The Existence of God and the Real Distinction Between the Soul and the Body of Man are Demonstrated."* Although the "demonstration" is debatable, the heritage of this understanding of human and divine being is clear: a human being is a substantial self discoverable in introspection rather than in reflective criticism of its institutions and encompassing environment. The nature of human being, in other words, is such as to be accessible to a mental vision that is indistinguishable from thinking.

Although the correlative understanding of divine being is not directly relevant to the theme of this chapter, one aspect of Descartes' "demonstration" of God's existence is germane. The mental vision that comes to know the self as thinking subject cannot know anything (with certainty) about the extended substances that comprise that self's environment. Nor can everyday lived experience, guided by embodied vision as well as by institutions that embody oral tradition, be relied upon for knowledge. For Descartes, our knowing is validated instead by a supermundane source: we can only know the environment (extended substance) by means of clear and distinct ideas that we "see," and the veracity of those ideas is guaranteed by God—not by practical engagement in the deeds, events, and things that comprise our lived experience or by reflective critique of that engagement.

The vicissitudes of Cartesianism in general and this understanding of self in particular are well known. The notion of a knowing self that encounters a world quite other than itself—of a mind that sets out to know matter—was conceptualized in John Locke's empiricism as an "empty cabinet" in which, or "white paper" on which, experience "writes" the characteristics (primary and secondary "qualities") of things (1939, pp. 22, 42, 66–67). Within that same tradition, and quite rapidly, Bishop Berkeley (1939) suggested that embodying mind and ideas as slates and qualities (or any other spatiotemporal items) was quite superfluous. David Hume (1978) instituted further economies: he could identify only experiences, whether conceptualized as things or ideas. "There are some philosophers who imagine we are every moment intimately conscious of what we call our self," he notes at the beginning of his considerations "Of Personal Identity." But he goes on to dispute that claim: "It must be some one impression that gives rise to every real idea. But self or person is not any one impression, but that to which our several impressions and ideas are supposed to have a reference." He adds experiential evidence to this conceptual difficulty: "For my part, when I enter most intimately into what I call myself, I always stumble on some particular perception or other . . . I never can catch myself at any time without a perception, and never can observe anything but the perception." It may well be, Hume concludes, that among "some metaphysicians" there is someone who can "perceive something simple and continued which he calls himself"; but he affirms "of the rest of mankind that they are nothing but a bundle or collection of different perceptions, which succeed each other with an inconceivable rapidity and are in a perpetual flux and movement" (1978, pp. 251–252). The Cartesian notion of a self discoverable in introspection and cognizant of its environment by means of ideas—even knowing the events, things, and deeds of its environment by virtue of clear and distinct ideas supported by an all-seeing God—could not survive a thoroughgoing determination to think economically about conceptual structures.

This austerity diet may be responsible for the eventual death of philosophy (in its traditional, institutionalized form, at least). There were other intellectual endeavors, however, that continued in what now appears to have been fortunate independence from philosophy's overreliance upon a visual metaphor for understanding the nature of cognition and identification of ideas as the proper object of cognition. Rhetoric, for one, was already pried loose from philosophy when Plato was writing the Socratic dialogues. We have there a portrayal of the Sophists—and by extension of rhetoric as a practice in general—as opposed to philosophy. The crux of the opposition is the rhetorician's concern with communicative interaction in political contexts in contrast to the philosopher's concern with the intellectual content of that interaction. Philosophy's tendency to understand human being in terms of intellectual content in the mind's eye eventuated in Hume's dissolution of the self within experience. We need now to consider the fate of the rhetorical counterpart of that endeavor. Thus far, I have considered only the *sighting* of self, which is implicated in intellectual activity that proceeds from literal or metaphorical grounding in *seeing*. Does the *citing* of self, within intellectual activity that proceeds from literal or metaphorical grounding in *saying*, eventuate in a comparable dissolution of the self within experience?

At first consideration, there seems to be a vital difference between seen and spoken objects. Our everyday assumption is that what is seen does, in some sense, exist without the presence of the self who sees. I do not mean to deny that there have been, and still are, long and complex philosophical struggles over this issue. But I want to focus on this difference between the seen and the said in the domain of everyday knowledge, which tends toward an epistemological attitude that some philosophers call "naive realism." Within that attitude, the seen is there to be seen, whereas the said must be said. Furthermore, all animal life looks at the environment and sees what is available to it. But only human beings speak, in contrast to signal. (Here again, there is debate among scholars as to the appropriateness of the speaking and signaling differentiation, and some are convinced that animals have language. For my purposes here, I continue using the everyday belief that linguistic activity is proper to humankind.) The domain of speech would seem to be more promising than the domain of sight when the issue is the province wherein the self may ground its being. Yet the self has fared no better in diverse forms of intellectual inquiry based on linguistic practice than it has in disciplines that are based (literally or figuratively) on visual practice. A particular hypothesis seems to me to be responsible for the fate of the self in inquiry into verbal practice. Although this hypothesis, named after Edward Sapir and Benjamin Lee Whorf, dominates contemporary rhetoric, is widely accepted in current philosophy, and is almost pervasive in modern linguistics, I want to consider it here in abstraction from those disciplines.

The core of the Sapir-Whorf hypothesis is the idea—ranging from a hunch to a conviction—that our language determines our being. Often, that is put in terms of language limiting world. The crucial point (for our interests here) is that the thesis of language as limiting or determining includes, explicitly or implicitly, belief in a limited or determined being of the language-using self, and particularly in a limited ability of selves to use language to criticize institutions. "Language speaks man," as a currently popular slogan expresses the point; thus, "man" cannot speak language critically, cannot question or deny its power or the inevitability of its institutions. The prevalence of this belief throughout contemporary scholarship, in a variety of strong and weak forms, may encourage us to neglect the fact that it is not similarly prevalent in everyday rationality.

In our everyday understanding, the presumption is that seen objects exist independently of their being seen, whereas said objects gain existence only through their saying. By extension, then—although this is not a deduction elicited in everyday thinking about human being—the speaker has priority over the said, is even *responsible* for the existence of the said, and can reflect upon and speak critically of what is said. If we perchance even think about which determines what—whether self determines language or vice versa—in the course of our everyday thinking, the evidence provided by our conduct would be that people determine what they want to say. More generally, the self uses language to carry out its purposes; those purposes, and that self, are independent of modes of articulation. Although speakers may be frustrated by the linguistic tools available to carry out their wishes and needs—and especially to articulate possibilities that cannot be ostensively presented—we muddle through by creating and changing words and modes of speech to suit our needs. To summarize this basic difference between our everyday thinking and currently predominant theorizing, everyday conceptions of human being incorporate a set of beliefs about the relationship between self and language that is quite opposite to the linguistic determination of experience and self posited by the Sapir-Whorf hypothesis. Earlier I referred to Whorf, rather than Sapir, as understanding human being to be based in saying. That specificity indicates not simply a difference in opinion between two individuals but a theoretical difference crucial to the dissolution of the self in contemporary rhetoric.

There is considerable textual evidence to support the claim that Sapir, the academic linguist, only slowly came to hold a mild version of the hypothesis that includes his name. His early work proceeded from the position that "the essence of language consists in the assigning of conventional, voluntarily articulated, sounds, or their equivalents, to the diverse elements of experience" (1921, p. 11). Although he recognized "some tendency" for "racial and cultural lines of cleavage to correspond to linguistic ones," he argued at length that culture and language "are not necessarily correlated." "Culture," he went on to say, "may be defined as *what* a society does and thinks. Language is a particular *how* of thought" (pp. 215, 218, Sapir's emphasis.) Throughout his early work, there was a consistent conception of language as a means by which experience is expressed. But there is no hint that this "most significant and colossal work that the human spirit has evolved" is itself instrumental in forming, much less determinative of, that "human spirit" (p. 220). In other words, Sapir did not find that the speaker is an epiphenomenon of speech; he did not hold that language determines experience. It seems, then, that Sapir did not entertain the possibility that a speaker's language determines the nature or character of that speaker's self.

Even in Sapir's late work (1931), his sense of the connection between language and experience remained congruent with everyday belief about the priority of self in regard to language. However, he became increasingly aware of the extent to which language, an accomplishment of the "human spirit," can dominate its creator:

> Language not only refers to experience largely acquired
> without its help but actually defines experience for us
> . . . because of our unconscious projection of its implicit
> expectations into the field of experience. . . . [Its] catego-
> ries . . . are not so much discovered in experience as im-
> posed upon it because of the tyrannical hold that linguis-
> tic form has upon our orientation in the world. (p. 578)

We still have here the attitude of everyday rationality in regard to language and self: human experience is at least in part nonlinguistic, and language refers to that experience. It can come to dominate our actions within the "field of experience"; but experience remains distinct from the "tyrannical hold" that is "imposed" by "linguistic form."

Whorf called that "field of experience" the "macrocosm" and contrasted it to what he called the "microcosm"—the interior " 'thought world' which is more than simply language": "In brief, this 'thought world' is the microcosm that each man carries about within himself, by which he measures and understands what he can of the macrocosm" (1956b, p. 147). Although Whorf and Sapir first met in 1928, they did not work closely together until after 1931, when Sapir moved to Yale University. Whorf was working throughout Connecticut as a fire inspection engineer—the work by which he earned his living after completing a degree in chemical engineering in 1918. It was in the course of that work, he tells us, that he came across numerous examples of fires caused not by "a physical situation qua physics, but [by] the meaning of that situation to people . . . through the behavior of the people" (1956b, p. 135).

There seems to have been several factors that brought Whorf, in stages that are quite perceptible when reading his collected work in chronological order, to beliefs about the relation between self and language that are quite at variance with everyday attitudes. His analyses as a fire inspector and his studies of Hopi and other indigenous American languages are obvious contributions. But the behaviorism that pervaded the social/human sciences of his day may well have been the crucial factor, for it encouraged treating the self as nothing more than a back-formation (so to speak) from behavior. I understand behaviorism, as a theoretical orientation, as a paradoxical offshoot of Cartesianism that grants evidential status only to what can be (clearly and distinctly) observed, and that explicitly rejects unobservables—such as meaning and self—in favor of observables—such as behavior. In the context of Whorf's work, that meant conceiving of self—or, as closely as he came to that term, conceiving of "consciousness"—as a linguistic construction. That is, in effect, the strong version of the Sapir-Whorf hypothesis, as Whorf stated it in a paper written shortly before his death in 1941 (Sapir had died in 1939):

> Every language is a vast pattern-system, different from others, in which are culturally ordained the forms and categories by which the personality not only communicates, but also analyzes nature, notices or neglects types of relationship and phenomena, channels his reasoning, and builds the house of his consciousness. (1956a, p. 252)

Although the linguistic turn in contemporary scholarship occurs on a variety of paths and is marked with the names of various scholars who practice the habits of various disciplines, this remark epitomizes a remarkable common pattern. Across the disciplines, we can find this same movement from noting the influence of language on human being to upholding the principle that language specifies the speaking being, or "builds the house" of "consciousness." In speaking, and then in the cognition inferred as the interior of that speaking, a personality is indicated, referred to, mentioned, even summoned. The product of this linguistic activity is the self, constituted by words about it. In sum, the self is cited in language; it owes its being to its being said.

The difficulty with this understanding of human being is paradoxically similar to that which troubles an understanding based in sight: if the self lives in and by means of what it sees or says, we have no way of understanding how it can perceive and speak what is not to be seen but is possible; that is, possibilities envisioned in critical reflection on what is in fact seen and said. The sensory world does indeed delineate the self by providing a variety of content—the things, events, and deeds that are the visual content of our lives. We catch sight of the self, almost literally, as it is reflected and perhaps even reified in the objects it sees. Likewise, language does indeed delineate the self by providing a grammar, syntax, and vocabulary that permits and limits our ability to speak about anything—including, especially, our ability to cite the self. We speak and we see in terms of sameness and difference. Each item in the environment is an object to us only so far as it is somewhat similar to, and somewhat different from, every other. And we first come to discern ourselves in the same terms: I speak of myself as born in a certain place, but not in others; as growing up in a certain historical period, but not in others; as taking up a certain vocation, but not others. In all of this, I really am identifying only an aspect of myself, for I am speaking of what is already accomplished and can be recognized and talked about in its similarity to, and difference from, other items of the same type. What is missed in this way of speaking is that aspect of the self that engages in the very activity of identifying itself by speaking of its own present and by anticipating other, future similarities and differences.

The difficulty with ways of understanding human being that proceed from seeing and saying is that they require a mode of discerning the self in its paradoxically weakest moment—in precisely that aspect of it which, upon further reflection, dissolves. The dissolution may be into successive moments of seeing (in the literal, Humean sense or the figurative, Cartesian sense). Or the dissolution may be into the categories of a linguistic structure, as in the variety of contemporary theories that adopt the Sapir-Whorf hypothesis in one or another form. I speak of this as a paradoxically weakest moment because we habitually think of what is accomplished as more stable than what is now being accomplished or what is anticipated as being accomplishable. That is, we typically construe "the past" as an object of investigation along something of the same lines as a tree, stage play, or chemical substance. We really know better: there is no such object as "the past." Yet we persist in identifying the self in terms of its past. Thus we center our understanding of human being in an apparently accessible entity that disintegrates as we search for it. To some extent, we also identify our selves in terms of our futures. That reliance may well be more enabling in a psychological sense. But it impoverishes us epistemically and ontologically, for we can know nothing of our actual selves in the future; we cannot even know that a particular self will exist as a future mundane actuality.

This line of thinking implies that there is another aspect of the self that is not linguistically or visually dissolvable, and that may be able to sustain the understanding of human being I mentioned at the start of this chapter. I noted that I find Alfred Schutz's focus on certain performances that are social actions a more plausible basis for a rhetoric that rejoins philosophy in an understanding of human beings as preeminently practical and emergent in the reflective critical activity that is moral and political discourse. In order to state the case for Schutz's alternative, I need at last to define the "self" that is at issue throughout this chapter. The aspect of self upon which Schutz's understanding depends, and which I propose as basic for reconceptualizing the self, cannot be seen or said. In a sense, it *is* not, for it does not have a content that we can identify in terms of similarity to, and difference from, other aspects of the self. Although we cannot identify it (so far as identification depends upon similarity and difference), we can evoke it by a rather roundabout look at Schutz's procedure as it contrasts with Descartes' and Whorf's.

Descartes placed the content of his knowledge into doubt. More precisely, he placed major categories of his knowledge in doubt; theological and formal domains were explicitly excluded. Thus he was able to continue using logic and believing in God's nature as nondeceptive. But he did not focus his analysis on the very process of initiating doubt. He noted that there was thinking going on, but then he quickly turned to analyzing the nature of thinking's accomplishments. Thus his method is attuned to investigating self along those lines I mentioned earlier: like but unlike a tree, a stage play, or a chemical substance. His formulation of the self's nature as a "thinking substance" provides an understanding of self in what I have called its weakest moment, as both like and unlike other items in the environment. Missing from that analysis is recognition of the self's unique moment as instigator and anticipator of inquiry; as reflective actor who performs the cogito. Descartes set out to investigate the nature of "consciousness" without noticing that he was accomplishing that "consciousness" (or self) in that very investigation. Not surprisingly, the moment of accomplishment eluded his search. The noticing itself—the "I am" that instigates the "I think"— evades notice.

Whorf's methodology was almost opposite to Descartes'. He sought a broader inclusion of elements, while Descartes sought to exclude what lacks certainty. More precisely, Whorf developed a sensitivity toward the extent to which language influenced the thinking of individuals within his own culture. He went on to conclude, from evidence given in linguistic and nonlinguistic behavior in other cultures, that linguistic structures limit the way of thinking accessible to each language group. These reflections eventually brought him to the conviction that language "builds the house of consciousness" (1956a, p. 252). In other words, he came to believe that language forms the self. What remained unnoticed in that progression was his own role, as speaker, in the theory he formulated. How could he recognize and articulate modes of being that were novel to (merely possible for) his own language and culture? Unless he was to be an exception to his theory—and he provides no account or justification for considering himself as transcendent to the processes he describes—he must exemplify a consciousness formed in the categories of what he called "Standard Average European." Thus, according to his theory, his comprehension would be limited to the ontological and cosmological orientations embedded in that language group and specified in the institutions within it—and especially in his own education. Yet his practice contradicted that theory.[4] He was able to recognize, appreciate, and even articulate radically different ontological and cosmological assumptions. Whorf, in sum, set out to investigate language without noticing that he was using it in ways that his theory decreed impossible.

Whorf and Descartes both instituted a reflective, critical

attitude in relation to what they discerned. But in neither case did the critical turn go full circle. They reflected upon their subject matter (language or linguistically formed thinking), but not upon how they themselves, as constituted in and by their language (or thinking), could theorize that subject matter. Thus the notions of self that they developed were read out from what the self had accomplished: all that it doubted, and all that it spoke, became the foundation for their ways of understanding human being. Schutz's reflection had to be a more radical one, because he chose to use a phenomenological procedure.

Phenomenology is (at least) a determination to study the human condition from a locus in consciousness engaged in a variety of activities, including human interaction.[5] Thus Schutz developed an understanding of the self as constituted in social action, which he understood as the sort of performance that proceeds from a motive that takes another self into consideration. This may seem paradoxical, especially when juxtaposed to conceptions that proceed from seeing and saying. Those conceptions start from two abilities of human beings (language and vision) and seek to understand "the self" on that basis. Schutz's notion, however, requires other actual selves for there to be the one self who seeks understanding:

> I am born into a world which is inhabited by others who will confront me in face-to-face situations. My experiences of particular human beings as well as my knowledge that there are other human beings—only some of whom I have experienced directly as fellow-men—originate in this a priori given by my birth. Scheler rightly maintains that the We-experience forms the basis of the individual's experience of the world in general. (1964, p. 25)

This basic "We-experience" is formed in interaction, rather than in seeing or saying:

> In the community of space and time our experiences of each other are not only coordinated but also reciprocally determined by continuous cross-reference. I experience

myself through you, and you experience yourself through
me. The reciprocal mirroring of Selves in the partners' experience is a constitutive feature of the We-relation in
face-to-face situations. . . . not grasped reflectively but directly experienced. . . . My experience of the ongoing
phases of my own conscious life and my experience of
the coordinated phases of your conscious life is unitary.
(1964, p. 30)

Schutz situates the self in these "directly experienced . . .
ongoing phases of . . . conscious life." They constitute the
elusive—and I propose basic—aspect of the self that is missing
in Whorf's and Descartes' analyses. We can borrow George
Herbert Mead's (1934) terms in order to label these two very
different aspects as the "self as I" and the "self as me." But
we must guard against a danger in this convenient labeling:
it carries considerable risk of rending a unified act into an
instigating force and a reified accumulation of effects of that
force. If that tendency toward sundering the inseparable can
be resisted, however, we gain a convenient way to distinguish
that weakest aspect of the self—"self as me," which is the only
moment theorized by the seeing and saying traditions—from
the usually unnoticed, although continually instigating, moment of the self—"self as I."

I have sought to evoke, or direct us toward, a notion of
self that has no need for foundation in linguistic and perceptual givens. A good deal remains to be said about the virtues
of this starting point for understanding human being.[6] But I
will conclude this evocation with a brief indication why siting
the self in the performances of social interaction seems to
me especially appropriate for a contemporary realignment of
philosophy and rhetoric. Schutz's focus on social interaction
gives us a starting point for a nonegological understanding of
the self, which may then be developed in terms of certain
themes pursued by contemporary rhetoric and philosophy.
But that is not to claim a one-way dependence; for Schutz's
discussion of social interaction may be enriched by those
themes. Interweaving Schutz's starting point and these more
recent themes gives us a commodious location for a philosophy and rhetoric realigned about the possibility of critique—

indeed for siting a self that can further the critical practice of both rhetoric and philosophy. A concise formulation of Schutz's conception may be helpful before joining it to discussions of "communicative praxis" and "narrative rationality" as intrinsic to the "space of subjectivity."

Schutz develops a conception of human being that withstands theoretical dissolution of the self and reduction of its critical abilities into linguistic and conceptual frameworks. He sites human being at those "ongoing phases of conscious life" (1964, p. 30) in which the self-as-I instigates and anticipates action. The reductionist path, from noticing the prevalence of linguistic activity in human interaction to proclaiming all of human interaction as linguistic action and so governed by the structures of language (in general or in a particular language), is circumvented if we adopt Schutz's conception as our starting point and go on to focus on rhetoric as performative of self. This is a course of theoretical choices that enables us, first, to replace citing of human being by language with Schutz's siting of human being in social action and, then, to identify the crucial role that communicative activity plays in the self's emergence from contexts that make human being possible, as well as its ability to institute criticism of those contexts.

Siting the self in Schutz's way—within the space of social action that I call, following phenomenological tradition, the lifeworld—realigns our attention from abstracted epistemic issues to the diverse difficulties that human beings actually encounter in coping with exigencies of nature and society. We engage in communicative interaction in order to respond to these demands; those responses are the "why" (the intrinsic telos) of social action. Anyone who acts in response to exigencies has a grasp, however tacit and unclarified, of the advantages of responding in concert with others who can provide additional strategies or strengthen those in use.[7] Communicative interaction is thus impelled by the recognition that "two of us could do (x) better than one." A variety of institutions (including language) come to be in order to ratify and improve these strategies. Thus, this intrinsic telos includes both axiological and epistemic dimensions. "Good action" is action that responds to exigency as well or better than alternative ways of responding. And a basic model for "true assertion" is discourse that affirms or denies the goodness of an action so that all appropriately informed actors can agree. Adopting Schutz's starting point reminds us, however, that communicative agreement implies prelinguistic action, for action that is justifiable (by its outcomes) precedes discursive claims concerning the goodness of that action.

In order to continue from Schutz's starting point in social action and consider communication's role within that action, I borrow Michael Hyde's (1983) provocative expansion upon Martin Heidegger's locution: "Rhetorically, man dwells." All too easily, attention to this rhetorical dwelling place reduces to defining self in terms of its real estate. In the words of my earlier discussion, this means defining the self in terms of its accomplishments. But this certainly is not the case in Hyde's discussion, for he defines human being in terms of a virtual, and so, irreal, moment that is realized (made known) by rhetoric: "I will argue," he says at the start of his analysis of the functions of both poetry and rhetoric, "that rhetoric's primordial (i.e., ontological) function is the making-known of Being in and through discourse" (1983, p. 202). Hyde goes on to rely upon both Heidegger and Hans-Georg Gadamer, proposing that a human being exists as a "historical entity that understands, interprets, and formulates meaning in and through language" and "thereby 'dwells' in a world of language founded on the *projective* saying of poetry" (1983, p. 210, emphasis added).[8] This projective (rather than reportorial) function is poetry's primary "making-known" function: "Poetic discourse teaches humankind to authenticate its existence by grasping and sharing its *potential* (i.e., its understanding of what is) in and through the word" (1983, p. 210, emphasis added).

Rhetoric actualizes this potential by communicating what has been projected: "When a person attempts to assert an interpretive understanding of something that was first made-known poetically in the discourse of thought, the something must be 'pointed out' by 'predicating' it in a definite way," so that it "can be communicated and 'shared' with others" (Hyde,

1983, p. 211). But this is not to say that rhetoric performs a merely referential function within interpersonal communication. Rather,

> rhetoric must be seen to show itself originally in and through the various ways understanding is interpreted and made-known *intrapersonally*: What the 'as' of a perceived object is chosen to be when a linguistic possibility is actualized in a person's thought marks the primordial occurrence of rhetoric . . . once Being is revealed in a moment of truth, in a poetic disclosure, it becomes the task of rhetoric to 'preserve' the meaning of this revelation by making-known this meaning both to oneself and to others. (1983, pp. 213–214, Hyde's emphasis.)

The crucial point of Hyde's analysis, for my argument here, appears when we ask why intrapersonal preservation is needed. It is necessary, I would argue, because there is as yet no self to possess poetry's "projective saying." Rather, the "person" is a site of communication with Being. Within that space, self is enacted in that blend of progress without chaos and stability without inertia that Hyde identifies as the achievement of poetry's and rhetoric's disclosive performances: "Progress without stability eventually leads to chaos; stability without progress eventually leads to inertia. To achieve progress, people must learn to dwell poetically; to achieve stability, they must learn to dwell rhetorically" (1983, p. 216). If there is to be stable progress at the site of self's emergence, then, we need some way of organizing rhetoric's preservations and poetry's (and perhaps also philosophy's) projections for use by critical analysis.

I would argue that the rationale of this organization is narrative and heuristic rather than formal and algorithmic. Once again, there is a danger of reducing an ongoing activity to its accomplishments. Specifically, understanding the self's rationality as formal and algorithmic encourages construing the self as the product of a narrative structure imposed upon poetry's projections and read out of rhetoric's already accomplished preservations. That construal would blunt the self's critical capacity, for it would reduce projective endeavor to reportorial function, envisioning the potential to sheltering the established, and poetic progress to rhetorical preservation. That construal can be subverted by identifying three distinct levels of narrative organization: narrative as *intrinsic* to lived experience, narrative as the structure of *oral* discourse, and narrative as specific to *written* discourse. Differences between oral and written narrative structure are discussed only tangentially in the wealth of recent scholarship on narrative, and the possibility of a distinct dimension of lived narrative has hardly been noticed. Although it is narrative as an organizational mode of lived experience that is crucial to my argument here, we need to look briefly at all three levels of narrative organization.

Two scholars, Paul Ricoeur (1984–1988) and Walter Fisher (1987), have written extensively about narrative in recent years. Since Ricoeur writes from a philosophical orientation while Fisher's basis is in rhetoric, they provide useful variations in emphasis. Common to both, however, is a tendency to derive their understanding of narrative from written text. Michael Presnell (1989) finds this tendency in Fisher's explication of the "narrative paradigm" and contends that it is strengthened by "current attempts to refine Fisher's proposed narrative paradigm" (p. 118). "Researchers developing narrative as a paradigm for communication," he maintains, "typically ignore the oral/literate distinction, equivocating storytelling and conversation with narrative in general" (p. 130).[9] So far as "narrative in general" is understood on the model of written narrative, current scholarship tends to dismiss the intrinsic narrative that organizes the site of self-emergence. Much as behaviorism encouraged treating the self as nothing more than a back-formation from behavior, contemporary theories that contend "language speaks man" dismiss the possibility of intrinsic narrative in favor of theorizing structures of lived experience as back-formations from the self's verbal (whether oral or written) accomplishments.

Carroll Arnold (1980), in a discussion that seeks to show that "oral rhetoric differs fundamentally from that which we normally call literature and differs significantly from other rhetoric that is not oral" (p. 170), stresses that "orality—the act or the anticipated act of speaking to alter another's perceptions—is itself meaningful . . . for mutually influential interaction or the expectation of it is inescapable in speaking and being spoken to" (p. 161).[10] Meaningful organization at this level of activity builds upon organization at the most basic of the three levels of narrative I mentioned earlier: narrative as intrinsic to lived experience, as the endemic organization that enables meaningfulness, even in an "anticipated act."

David Carr (1986) develops this notion in some detail. He argues that narrative

> is our primary way of organizing and giving coherence to our experience. . . . it is not as if 'our experience' existed somehow independently of it [i.e., of narrative organization] and that our capacity for storytelling somehow intervened to impose a narrative structure . . . What we have been arguing, by contrast, is that narrative form is not a dress which covers something else but the structure inherent in human experience and action. (p. 65)

With reliance upon a broadened version of Ricoeur's discussion of emplotment, Carr develops a conception of daily life as constituted in ongoing engagement that weaves events together as an organized structure.

Carr is careful to point out that he is not claiming universality for, for example, modern, Western versions of narrative time. Rather, he argues that at both the "social" and the "individual" levels, "narrative, far from originating externally and *imposing* a story-line on what was previously a mass of unrelated facts, is *inherent* in the process in the first place" (1986, p. 177, emphasis added). Such structures as "departure and arrival, departure and return, means and end, suspension and resolution, problem and solution," Carr argues, "inhere in the phenomena from their inception"; they provide "a 'logical' air . . . in the midst of experience and action, not in some higher-level linguistic construction or reconstruction of the experiences and actions involved" (pp. 49–50). What Carr does, then, is "shift the focus 'backward' from the literary products . . . to the historical experience that lies behind and precedes" both "the author's creative act" and "the historian's scientific procedure" (p. 9). I take his analysis even further "backward" by attending to the "creative act" in which the "author" is projected as a potential telos, implicated in those structures Carr lists, rather than instigating them. In so doing, I take Carr's analysis as descriptive of the site at which the self (author) comes to be in the midst of events that are narratologically organized.

A second intrinsic mode of organization of these events is suggested in my earlier discussion of coping with exigencies originating in both nature and society. I suggested that we engage in dialogue in order to *respond* to those demands, which constitute an intrinsic telos for social action. Bruce Wilshire (1982) finds that "mimetic response" of active bodies— not cognitive recognition between consciousnesses—is at the core of this dialogue: "Cognition presupposes expression which presupposes mimetic response. The other person is with me from the beginning of me" (p. 170). Selves, then, are evoked within organized interaction:

> We introduce a sliding scale of individual identity. We
> must speak of greater and lesser degrees of individuation
> of a human self. One becomes more and more individu-
> ated as one makes more and more of one's experience
> and activity experienceable by one *as* mimetically induced
> and yet *also* one's own. It follows from this that we can-
> not tell exactly when the individual human self arises,
> nor even in many situations when it ceases to be. (p. 197,
> Wilshire's emphasis.)[11]

Thus the site of self is not clearly delineated. It is in fact describable in terms of capacities for particular activities ("induced" by another and yet "one's own") rather than in terms of what we might see or say.

"To be a self," Wilshire concludes, "is to be a human body that is mimetically involved with other such bodies, but that nevertheless has a capacity to distinguish itself consciously from others and to regard its history and its prospects as its own" (1982, p. 226).[12] The moment at which that "capacity" for self comes to actuality is the one at which a partner in responsive activity can "distinguish" its role as mimetic, and so in a sense not "its own," thereby constituting "its own," its self, in that very distinguishing. In other words, we can identify a critical moment of responsive interaction—of specifying the self in reflection on the not-me—as a second intrinsic organizational structure occurring at the site of daily life and taken up again in our seeing and saying. In everyday communication, this moment may be most familiar to us in the lived experience of conversational turn-taking between the "me" and the "not-me."

Calvin Schrag (1986) names this intrinsically organized site the "space of subjectivity" that is "woven" by events of "communicative praxis." He stresses the *creative* power of "praxis" by pointing to its "verbal root" in "related senses of doing, acting, performing, and accomplishing" (p. 19). What is performed is not, Schrag argues, an exteriorization of what had already been in a performer's mind or consciousness. Rather, what is performed is "consciousness as a happening or an occasion" that is "given birth in the dialogic and actional encounters with other subjects and is able to sustain itself only within such encounters" (p. 171).[13] The basic insight here is George Herbert Mead's: "It is the social process itself that is responsible for the appearance of the self; it is not there as a self apart from this type of experience" (1934, p. 142).[14]

In full awareness of contemporary scholarship's decentering and deconstruction of all notions of consciousness, subject, and self, Schrag sets about the "recovery and restoration of the subject within the folds of communicative praxis" (1986, p. 11). Perhaps the most concise way to indicate the direction of that recovery is to reflect upon the contrast between Schrag's metaphors and those more usually employed in talking about the self, for he is explicit about the importance of metaphor for his task: "Metaphor does not simply adorn our discourse; it *carries* it" (p. 3, Schrag's emphasis). The metaphorical domain that "carries" his "recovery and restoration" project is that of weaving a textured fabric:

> We want to set forth the *texture* of communicative praxis. . . . this may be the most important term because it indicates the bonding of communication and praxis as an intertexture within their common space. . . . The metaphors of horizon and field are visually weighted. . . . In

our shift to the metaphor of texture a somewhat different
range of indexical associations is called forth as one slides
away from the privilege of seeing and the centrality of
the eye. The texture-metaphor appears to enjoy a wider
scope of playfulness. There is the texture of woven tapes-
try, the cellular texture of plants, the texture of wood and
the texture of soil, muscle texture in the human body,
harmonic texture, and the texture of poetry and prose.
(p. 23, Schrag's emphasis)

Schrag goes on to stress the "processual" sense of this
metaphor in the course of commenting on John Thompson's
(1981) conception of a "critical hermeneutics":

The expressivity of action does not congeal into a universalized essence. . . . the plurivocity of descriptions move
about within the *open texture* of communicative praxis as
an amalgam of discourse and action. . . . Communicative
praxis as the ongoing process of expressive speech and
expressive action has neither an interior nor an exterior,
viewed as separate domains. Expressive meaning is woven into the fibers of verbal speech acts, gestures, body
motility, personal goals, social practices, institutions, and
historical trends. Never coming to rest as an essential feature of this and that, meaning is stitched into the global
and processual texture of communicative praxis. (1986.
pp. 46–47, Schrag's emphasis)

The weaving metaphor allows Schrag to bypass issues of the
priority and hierarchy of these several "fibers." One simply
cannot weave with one strand, and predominance can only
be a function of an overall design that is contingent upon
ongoing and (to some extent, at least) contingent choices of
discourse and action.

When Schrag instigates "a shift of focus of attention" so
as "to address the 'who' of discourse and the 'who' of action,"
he finds that the communicative praxis formed by discourse
and action "not only delivers a hermeneutical reference to the
world, it also yields a hermeneutic *implicature* of a *situated*
speaking, writing, and acting subject" (p. 15, emphasis
added). In other words, when Schrag turns to consider who

43

chooses and decides how the "weaving" will look, and what meanings it will speak, he finds not an "epistemological space of a lonely ego seeking commerce with an external public world" but a "wider space of communicative praxis that provides the proper parameters for a transvalued subjectivity . . . implicated in the discourse and action that limns communicative praxis" (pp. 120–121). The weaving (as both verb and noun) is where the weaver must be; critical analysis of that texture shows and tells it as the site of self.

We can now draw together the strands of the reflection upon extant notions of the self that I have endeavored to weave here. At the outset, I noted that I wished to evoke a notion of self that is not founded in linguistic and perceptual givens, and that Schutz's work suggests an alternative that bypasses certain difficulties in the perceptual and linguistic models that have dominated our cultural history. I went on to present brief discussions of work by several rhetoricians and philosophers who develop good continuations of the pattern explored by Schutz. The result is an understanding of the self as sited in the space of communicative activity, understood as a conjoining of *doing* and *saying*, in which our *seeing* is constituted. This portrayal responds to exigencies of the contemporary intellectual conversation in regard to the efficacy, and even the very possibility, of the self. We could instead respond to those exigencies by calling upon philosophical or rhetorical conceptions of the self that are woven from the seeing or saying of bygone polities. But that would be an attempt to realign rhetoric and philosophy by repeating—rather than critically reflecting upon—historically evident patterns. Such a realignment would be, at best, a forfeiture of human beings' creative capacity for actualizing possibilities that may be recognized in critical reflection on the past and present. Furthermore, it would be an attempt to ignore the very clear sense of postmodernity: both philosophy and rhetoric, in those historically evident patterns, have reached their end.

Instead of attempting to recall those patterns, I have proposed here that we consider anew the extent to which (rhetorical) saying and (philosophical) seeing are intertwined in a critical praxis—a creative, intrinsically organized doing—that weaves novel possibilities into a narrative of self. This reconsideration takes up Schrag's (1985) response to talk of the end of philosophy and rhetoric. Rather than "cessation or elimination"—much less, "fulfillment"—he identifies this direction:

> End is here understood as a perpetual 'thinking beyond,' an ongoing dissemination of sedimented metaphysical and epistemological position-taking. It defines a task rather than a state of affairs. (p. 166)

> The point of it *all* is that in thinking to the end of philosophy and the end of rhetoric we perpetually take up the history of both disciplines, using them against themselves in an effort to think beyond their stock categories and their systems of classification. (p. 169)

In this chapter, I have sought to "think beyond" just one of those "stock categories": the self. The alternative I propose enables (even requires) understanding our philosophical and rhetorical endeavors as occasioned not by an egoic self but by a critical practice that instigates and anticipates in concert with others.

The self I have been describing here, then, dwells comfortably in the realignment of rhetoric and philosophy necessitated by postmodernism's rejection of traditional (and especially Cartesian) notions of self. In reflective critical response to the realities of the environment, by conceiving and enacting novel proposals and practices, a realigned philosophical and rhetorical practice calls the realm of possibility to the site of the self.

Acknowledgments

I thank Ian Angus, Lynn Bauman, Erazim Kohák, and Kenneth Pike for many conversations that have found their way into this chapter. Responsibility for what I have done with their insights remains, of course, my own.

Notes

1. The publication trail of epistemic rhetoric is marked early on by Scott (1967) and in mid-journey by Scott (1976) as well as Leff (1978). For a spectrum of views on the current situation, see Brummett, Cherwitz, Hikins, & Farrell, 1990.

   Rhetoric of inquiry came to general notice by virtue of a 1984 conference at the University of Iowa. Thus the best overview of that orientation may be the volume resulting from that conference (Nelson, Megill, & McCloskey, 1987). See also Simons, 1985, 1989; Lyne, 1985; Nelson & Megill, 1986.

   For critical rhetoric, see McKerrow, 1989, 1981. For dialogical rhetoric, see McGuire and Slembek's (1987) discussion of Helmut Geissner's work.

2. These three orientations and scholars are not the only ones I could choose for a discussion of dominant models of the self. Most obviously neglected are traditions and scholars in psychology, philosophy, and rhetoric (e.g., Freud, Jung, Cassirer, Langer, and Burke) for which or whom human being is primarily symbolic rather than "seeing" of "saying." The very richness of that tradition precludes discussing it along with the three I do consider here. In another context, I plan to contrast that tradition, construed as emphasizing *poiēsis*, to the "siting" tradition that emphasizes praxis.

3. See Langsdorf, 1989, for extensive discussion of this notion of rationality.

4. Thomas Kuhn (1970) has the same difficulty. He argues that the "disciplinary matrix" (one sense of "paradigm") limits and determines what a researcher may "see." Thus he cannot account for how he was able to develop his nonconventional history or theory of science in the course of his "fortunate involvement with an experimental college course treating physical science for the non-scientist" (p. x). A more rhetorically informed reflection could propose that setting out a taken-for-granted story for a different audience is an instance of a rhetoric of discovery. For a further discussion of this difficulty, see Langsdorf, 1992.

5. I expect that I owe this formulation to Richard Zaner or Maurice Natanson. If this is an instance of citation without reference, I ask the neglected author's forbearance and correction.

6. These remarks owe much to the discussions of Maurice Natanson (1970) and Richard Zaner (1970). For a more detailed discussion of Schutz's theory, see Langsdorf, 1991, which is an earlier and briefer version of the present essay.

Words of Others

7. I argue that much of the interaction that occurs prelinguistically is informed by what Michael Polanyi (1962) calls "tacit knowing."
8. Graeme Nicholson (1984, pp. 48–49) argues that Heidegger's crucial term, *Verstehen*, should be translated as "projection":

> Normally, this term is translated 'understanding,' but based on the thesis of Heidegger that *Verstehen* has the power of projecting (*Entwerfen*, I propose that 'projection' is a more accurate translation of the word. . . . it is plain from the start of Heidegger's discussion that by *Verstehen* he means a basic, pervasive constitutive factor in human existence. It is not a faculty that is employed merely in the reading and understanding of written material, nor is it even restricted to cognitive situations. It is, rather, an ontological notion . . . defined essentially by its relation to the possible. It is precisely an orientation toward possibilities—not that of merely entertaining them, contemplating them, or speculating on them, but rather a being-toward possibilities, prior to any reflective thought, which he calls projection or projecting (*Entwurf*, or *Entwerfen*.

9. Presnell focuses on a particular consequence of this tendency: neglect of differences between orality and literacy in relation to the significance of differences between women's and men's narrative predilections. (In arguing that position, he may well overestimate Fisher's relative inattention to differences between oral and written narrative.) My bypassing that theme here should be taken not as denial of Presnell's thesis but as a setting aside (bracketing) in order to focus on lived narrative, which would precede both oral and written narrative forms (although it does seem closer to oral narrative). If Presnell is correct, the structure of lived narrative would be closer to women's typical patterns for forming and interpreting experience than to men's typical patterns. In Western culture, at least, the latter may well depend more on written narrative structure.
10. Arnold's remarks on oral rhetoric seem to assume an already constituted self that can engage in interaction with other selves "in consequence of the unique human relationships that constitute the conditions of orality" (1980, p. 170). I cite his discussion of orality in order to support the importance of moving our focus from writing to speaking, and then into still more basic levels of

47

lived experience—his "conditions of speaking." I argue that
these last are the very conditions that enable emergence of the
self in communicative interaction. But I do not mean to imply
that Carroll would agree with my proposal that there are structures of a narrative nature that are responsible for the very
formation of the self in the acts he describes.
11. Importantly, mimetic involvement, interaction, and attachment
are aspects or stages of enactment rather than of impersonation. "Enactment" is acting as the other by using "the universal which resonates within each": "Impersonation is a form of
mockery; enactment is a form of love" (Wilshire, 1982, pp. 6–
7).
12. Calvin Schrag (1986, p. 155) quotes this remark in his portrayal
of the communicative context in which self emerges.
13. Schrag notes his dependence here on Ricoeur and Gadamer, as
well as his differences from both of their conceptions.
14. Schrag quotes this remark in the context of developing a "portrait
of the subject as an ensemble . . . whose identity is an acquisition
rather than a given, achieved within the play of difference . . .
a postured response to the ongoing conversation and to the prior
action . . . a base of operations . . . but neither a metaphysical
nor an epistemological center" (1986, pp. 148–149).

References

Arnold, C. A. (1980). Oral rhetoric, rhetoric, and literature. In E. E.
White (Ed.), *Rhetoric in transition: Studies in the nature and uses
of rhetoric* (pp. 159–173). University Park: Pennsylvania State
University Press.
Berkeley, G. (1939). Principles of human knowledge. In E. A. Burtt
(Ed.), *The English philosophers from Bacon to Mill* (pp. 509–579).
New York: Random House. (Original work published 1710.)
Brummett, B., Cherwitz, R. A., Hikins, J. W., & Farrell, T. B. (1990).
Forum: The reported demise of epistemic rhetoric. *Quarterly
Journal of Speech, 9,* 69–84.
Carr, D. (1986). *Time, narrative, and history.* Bloomington: Indiana
University Press.
Descartes, R. (1980). *Discourse on method* and *Meditations on first philos-
ophy.* D. A. Cress (Trans.). Indianapolis: Hackett. (Original work
published 1637, 1641.)
Fisher, W. R. (1987). *Human communication as narration: Toward a
philosophy of reason, value, and action.* Columbia: University of
South Carolina Press.

Havelock, E. A. (1963). *Preface to Plato*. Cambridge: Harvard University Press.

Hume, D. (1978). *A treatise of human nature* (2nd ed.). L. A. Selby-Bigge (Ed.). Oxford: Oxford University Press. (Original work published 1740.)

Hyde, M. J. (1983). Rhetorically, man dwells: On the making-known function of discourse. *Communication, 7*(2), 201–220.

Kuhn, T. S. (1970). *The structure of scientific revolutions* (2nd ed.). Chicago: University of Chicago Press. (First edition published 1962.)

Langsdorf, L. (1989). *Reasoning across the media: Verbal, visual, and televisual literacies*. Montclair: Montclair State College, Institute for Critical Thinking (Resource Publication, Series 302).

Langsdorf, L. (1991). The worldly self in Schutz. *Human Studies, 14*, 141–157.

Langsdorf, L. (1992). Realism and idealism in Kuhn's philosophy of science. In L. Hardy & L. Embree (Eds.), *Phenomenology of Natural Science* (pp. 173–196). Dordrecht: Kluwer.

Leff, M. C. (1978). In search of Ariadne's thread: A review of the recent literature on rhetorical theory. *Central States Speech Journal, 29*, 73–91.

Locke, J. (1939). An essay concerning human understanding. In E. A. Burtt (Ed.), *The English philosophers from Bacon to Mill* (pp. 238–402). New York: Random House. (Original work published 1690.)

Lyne, J. (1985). Rhetorics of inquiry. *Quarterly Journal of Speech, 71*, 52–64.

McGuire, M., & Slembek, E. (1987). An emerging critical rhetoric: Hellmut Geissener's *Sprechwissenschaft*. *Quarterly Journal of Speech, 73*, 349–400.

McKerrow, R. E. (1989). Critical rhetoric: Theory and praxis. *Communication Monographs, 56*, 91–111.

McKerrow, R. E. (1991). Critical rhetoric in a postmodern world. *Quarterly Journal of Speech, 77*, 75–78.

Mead, G. H. (1934). *Mind, self, and society*. C. W. Morris (Ed.). Chicago: University of Chicago Press.

Nathanson, M. (1970). *The journeying self*. Reading, MA: Addison-Wesley.

Nelson, J. S., & Megill, A. (1986). Rhetoric of inquiry: Projects and prospects. *Quarterly Journal of Speech, 72*, 20–37.

Nelson, J. S., Megill, A., & McCloskey, D. N. (Eds.). (1987). *The rhetoric of the human sciences: Language and argument in scholarship and public affairs*. Madison: University of Wisconsin Press.

Nicholson, G. (1984). *Seeing and reading.* Atlantic Highlands, NJ: Humanities.

Polanyi, M. (1962). *Personal knowledge: Towards a post-critical philosophy.* Chicago: University of Chicago Press.

Presnell, M. (1989). Narrative gender differences: Orality and literacy. In K. Carter & C. Spitzack (Eds.), *Doing research on women's communication: Perspectives on theory and method* (pp. 118–136). Norwood, NJ: Ablex.

Ricoeur, P. (1984–1988). *Time and narrative*, 3 vols. Chicago: University of Chicago Press.

Sapir, E. (1921). *Language.* New York: Harcourt, Brace, World.

Sapir, E. (1931). Conceptual categories in primitive languages. *Science, 74,* 572–581.

Schrag, C. O. (1985). Rhetoric resituated at the end of philosophy. *Quarterly Journal of Speech, 71*(1), 164–174.

Schrag, C. O. (1986). *Communicative praxis and the space of subjectivity.* Bloomington: Indiana University Press.

Schutz, A. (1964). *Collected papers, II. Studies in social theory.* A. Brodersen (Ed.). The Hague: Nijhoff.

Scott, R. L. (1967). On viewing rhetoric as epistemic. *Central States Speech Journal, 18,* 9–16.

Scott, R. L. (1976). On viewing rhetoric as epistemic: Ten years later. *Central States Speech Journal, 27,* 258–266.

Simons, H. W. (1985). Chronicle and critique of a conference. *Quarterly Journal of Speech, 71,* 52–64.

Simons, H. W. (1989). *Rhetoric in the human sciences.* Newbury Park, CA: Sage.

Thompson, J. B. (1981). *Critical hermeneutics: A study in the thought of Paul Ricoeur and Jurgen Habermas.* Cambridge: Cambridge University Press.

Whorf, B. L. (1956a). Language, mind, and reality. In J. B. Carroll (Ed.), *Language, thought, and reality* (pp. 246–270). Cambridge: MIT Press. (Original work published 1942.)

Whorf, B. L. (1956b). The relation of habitual thought and behavior to language. In J. B. Carroll (Ed.). *Language, thought, and reality* (pp. 134–159). Cambridge: MIT Press. (Original work published 1939.)

Wilshire, B. (1982). *Role playing and identity: The limits of theatre as metaphor.* Bloomington: Indiana University Press.

Zaner, R. M. (1970). *The way of phenomenology.* New York: Pegasus.

Critical Rhetoric and the Possibility of the Subject

RAYMIE E. MCKERROW

It is not enough to say that the subject is constituted
in a symbolic system. It is not just in the play of symbols that the subject is constituted. It is constituted in
real practices—historically analyzable practices. There
is a technology of the constitution of the self which
cuts across symbolic systems while using them.
    —Michel Foucault, "On the Genealogy of Ethics"

ONE VIEW OF THE SUBJECT IS AS THE PRODUCT OF THE
effects of social practices. From this perspective, subjects are
neither solely creatures of language nor agents independent
of the historical practices in which they engage. Rather, they
are constituted by both language and social practices. While
this analysis displaces the subject as the central actor or agent
of social change, it does not dismiss the subject in its entirety.
The question it raises is to what extent the subject is free from
the coercion of either language or social practice; that is, to
what extent can the subject recapture the center as the originator of thought or action? Corollary to this issue are several
other questions: To what extent is the subject self-constituted?
To what extent can the subject act as an agent? Is there a place
for the speaker as active agent seeking social change? What
role does the subject have in the guise of critic?

These are not idle questions. In the first place, Foucault's sense of the subject, as outlined above, is antithetical to the traditional conception of persuasion as grounded in the acts of rhetors. The study of public address assumes autonomous subjects acting on scenes—agents capable of discerning the requirements of a rhetorical situation (Bitzer, 1968) and responding in a fitting or appropriate manner. These questions also represent a challenge to the possibility of a critical rhetoric (McKerrow, 1989, 1991a, 1991b). Far from assuming "a stable, autonomous subject whose task is to achieve self-determination" (Hariman, 1991, p. 68), the critical rhetoric project as yet has not demarcated the senses in which a subject might exist as social actor. While outlining the conditions of a critique as a transformative practice, the project leaves one wondering about the "who" that is engaging in the performance as rhetor or critic.

An exploration of the "who" that acts in both these senses will include a brief discussion of the body as performer, the dismissal of the subject in recent accounts of the philosophy of the subject, and Foucault's shift from a purely historicized subject to one that actively incorporates an aesthetic of existence. With this discussion as a backdrop, the subject can be placed within a critical rhetoric as both agent of action and critic of social practices.

The Body as Performer

Before the subject is the body. That much is obvious. The question is whether the body is always subordinate to the subject in any discussion of action. Or, does the body act, in and of itself, as a political performer? If critique is performance, is the body alone sufficient as performer?

The objectification of the body has a long history. As Martin (1990) suggests, philosophers as diverse as Freud, Barthes, and Mead have interpreted the body's role in purely physical terms, thereby reducing it to a subservient role—the body acts only in concert with an acting mind. Language participates in objectifying the body as the medium for performance, but not as the sole source of political action, as the "physical agent of activity" (p. 40).

While contemporary theory resituates the body's role as coperformer, it does not situate the body as a physical agent. For example, the body's potentiality is given a place in ethnography's view of the engaged observer. Conquergood's (1991) discussion of the "return of the body" is a case in point. While noting the divergent opinions within the field of anthropology, his analysis constitutes a clear argument for ethnography as *"embodied practice"* (p. 180). The key term is *embodied*, as the focus shifts from passive observation with its corollary privileging of distance and presumed objectivity: "The return of the body . . . shifts the emphasis from space to time, from sight and vision to sound and voice, from text to performance, from authority to vulnerability" (p. 183). The body as present within anthropological space interacts with and intersects with others occupying that space. The observer is no longer detached from the event, no longer the disinterested notetaker. Instead, the body of the observer participates in the creation of meaning—the interpretation is no longer that of an 'outsider' looking in, but that of a person commenting from within.

Support for this sense of the body's rightful function is found in Schrag's (1986) repositioning of the subject: "The presence of the subject is a *bodily* presence" (p. 152). We can, from this perspective, invoke images of the body in metaphorical terms, as embodied presence: "Embodiment in its multiple metaphorical senses informs our descriptions of the subject in the spheres of art, politics, and religion" (p. 154). The point that is missing in this emphasis on the body as performer is precisely the point Martin (1990) wishes to address: the sense in which the body acts alone, without mind. While Conquergood's and Schrag's analyses do not admit the potentiality in direct terms, the sense of embodiment presented is compatible with such a perspective on performance.

In going beyond mind alone as sufficient for the explanation of political action, Martin explicates the role the body as performer can play in the enactment of politics. Drawing on Foucault's discussion of the discipline of the body (whereby regulation of body results in controls on its actions [Foucault, 1980a, p. 139]), Martin argues that "a place for the body in politics has been defined beyond the conscious subject" (1990,

p. 49). That place, in Martin's analysis, lies in dance as political performance. One can envision a mind-body "meld" in which the actions of the body take on a life of their own. In this scenario, a message of despair or exhilaration comes less from the sense of a commanding consciousness than from the activity of the body acting on its own. But, even then, is the mind very far removed from the body's disciplined action? I think not, and my sense is that Martin does not deny the possibility. What he does affirm, however, is that "the body's will to action, the concrete sense of possibility, subverts the passivity engendered by the dominance of the sign. The subject as performer confronts the culture of spectatorship" (p. 167). The potentiality is present for the body, as prior to the subject, to enact political change—to address or present for revision the social practices that constrain the subject's freedom.

What remains to be said, and will be postponed, is the sense in which body participates in the performance of a critical rhetoric. Suffice it to say, at this juncture, that if body can will its own act, can the possibility of a subject acting on its own be far away? That question turns us toward the subject as the next focus of analysis.

Displacement of the Subject

One distinction between modernity and postmodernity lies in the displacement of the subject. In the modern world, dominated by Cartesian rationality, the subject, both in its empirical, physical presence to the world and in its transcendental "I," occupies center stage. A subject, conscious of its own presence in the world, and actively engaged in thought about that world, operates as the originator of action.[1] Paradoxically, constituted in and through language, the subject is devoid of concrete substance: "The Cartesian subject is thus constituted in the order of representation as the symbol of a discursivity which cannot reflect upon its own practical reality. As an empty sign," the subject refers "both to the transcendental subject of philosophy and to the empirical autobiographical subject" (Judovitz, 1988, p. 84). Unable to think itself into existence without already preexisting, the subject reflects the capacity to know the world. That capacity responds to an ordered universe, in Cartesian terms, in an equally ordered or axiomatic manner. As empirical or epistemic subject, the "I" methodically reviews the evidence (systematic doubt) in assessing the world as object. What was "true" would be known by the individual conscious percipient, verified in terms of the methodology of systematic doubt.

This view of the subject was consistent with modern perceptions of rhetoric's proper role. Grounded in a thorough-going classicism, rhetoric was to give effective expression to truth. Individual speakers, acting as agents imposing their individuality on the world, could be held accountable for the manner in which they served truth. Public address criticism, particularly in the 1940s through the 1960s, held this as an axiomatic principle. As the protest era unfolded, critics began to broaden their vision, incorporating the insights of sociological accounts of movements. Even so, the focus remained in part on the leaders as forceful individuals whose actions were accessible and could be appraised as either facilitating or hindering the success of the broader social cause. The impulse to fragment the analysis, to focus on textuality or on forces outside the speaking subject, remained captive to the bonds of modernity—bonds set in motion by the Cartesian placement of the subject as the center of the knowing act.

From Heidegger to Rorty, philosophers and critical theorists have questioned the capacity of Cartesian rationality, and of the role of the subject in particular, to account for social actions in the world (Schrag, 1986, p. 7). My purpose in this brief review is not to recast their arguments or to provide a comprehensive history of the many and varied senses in which the philosophy of the subject has been attacked. Rather, I want to focus on *displacement* as the key term in the analysis of the subject. The subject is not dead (French Derrideans to the contrary) but decentered. The stranglehold of the subject on knowledge and rationality has been removed in a postmodern world. The subject, whether seen in Derridean or Foucaultian terms, is not the originator of meaning.

Granted, the death of the subject is one possible consequence of deconstruction. If the focus is on the text and the author disappears from the scene, it would seem that there is little value in recovering the subject. As Schrag (1986) clearly illustrates, both Derrida and Foucault do not abandon the subject as much as remove it from the center—its role as originator is replaced by an analysis of its functionality. Consider the following observations on the subject:

> It is a question of knowing where it comes from and how it functions. (Derrida, 1970, p. 271; cited in Schrag, 1986, p. 129)

> The subject should not be entirely abandoned. It should be reconsidered, not to restore the theme of the originating subject, but to seize its functions, its intervention in discourse and its system of dependencies. (Foucault, 1977, p. 137)

> One has to dispense with the constituent subject, to get rid of the subject itself, that's to say, to arrive at an analysis which can account for the constitution of the subject within a historical framework. (Foucault, 1980b, p. 117)

Derrida's point is clear—the subject's potentiality to assume center stage, as the originator of action, is removed. Its function is redescribed in its emergence in difference (Derrida, 1991, p. 100; Desilet, 1991). While Foucault does not prescribe the same function, the same displacement of the subject occurs with respect to its constitutive role. In this sense, the two statements cited above are not in opposition. When Foucault advises us to "get rid of the subject itself," the sense implied is that of an originator of action and meaning. In both perspectives, the subject emerges as an effect, as something constructed rather than constructing. The subject, in Foucault's view, is that agent formed via contingent historical circumstances. Thoroughly historicized, the subject that acts does so as a being already interpellated within a set of social practices.

Dallmayr (1981) was right to be concerned about the demise of the subject, Foucault and Derrida notwithstanding. In a series of essays responding to the question "Who comes after the subject?" (Cadeva, Connor, & Nancy, 1991) a group of French Derridians pose answers that, as a set, presume the death of the originary subject. Badiou (1991), for example, argues that "the subject is *woven* out of a truth, it is what exists of truth in limited fragments" (p. 25). In delineating his conception further, he proceeds by negation: a subject is not "a substance," "an empty point," "the organizing of a meaning of experience," "an invariant of presentation," "a result nor an origin" (pp. 26–27). There is nothing left of the subject of modernity in this conception. The subject, as the locus of a truth, is not simultaneously a knower of the truth of which it is the existent. Rather, it functions as one that believes: "Belief here is the yet-to-come that goes by the *name* of truth" (p. 30). The subject is intimately involved, though, in the naming process, as it generates the names by which events will come into truth. Clearly, we have moved the subject firmly into a postmodern condition and have shorn the shackles of Cartesian certainty:

> It is entirely impossible to anticipate or to represent a
> truth, as it comes to be only in the course of evaluations
> or connections that are incalculable, their succession be-
> ing solely ruled by encounters with the terms of the situ-
> ation. It follows that, from the subject's point of view,
> the referentiality of the names remains forever suspended
> upon the uncompletable condition of a truth. (p. 31)

Badiou's analysis places the subject on intimate terms with truth but denies that truth its former hallmarks of modernity: completeness and certainty.

The break with modernity does not trace its effects only to the displacement of a metaphysical, epistemic subject. One also can discuss the subject in terms of a being's subjection to rules of order. Balibar (1991) responds to the question "Who comes after the subject?" by noting that "*after the subject comes the citizen*. The citizen (defined by his rights and duties) is that 'nonsubject' who comes after the subject, and whose constitution and recognition put an end (in principle) to the subjection of the subject" (pp. 38–39).

Balibar turns our attention to political subjection in an argument that equates the dissolution of absolutism with the displacement of the subject by the citizen. He is arguing not that the dissolution is complete but that the process is irrevers-ible, dating from the publication in 1789 of the *The Declaration of the Rights of Man and of the Citizen* (1991, p. 44). This is not an idealistic paean to the stability of citizens enacting their rights in a utopian universe, though there are elements of the latter in the conception of the subject turned citizen. Balibar is not immune to the necessity for citizens to be constantly in a state of revolt with respect to the State, lest their rights be abridged and they be reconstituted as subjects. In fact, he encourages such a state of constant criticism. Until the State acts properly with respect to the control of excess or inequality, the citizen is both a part of that unequal condition and an "actor of a *permanent* revolution" (p. 54). The citizen-subject lives in a state of dialectical tension wherein the possibilities of being either solely subject or solely citizen are constants.

The Recovery of the Subject

Thus far, the analysis has focused on a decentered or displaced subject. Whether the perspective is that of Derrida, Foucault, or Badiou, the possibility of a centered agent becomes remote. Moreover, the subject that does exist as displaced appears passive, as the result of forces not of its own making. To recast the subject requires, in part, granting more "will" to the subject as actor—as agent who has some say in the conditions that will provide for, in Foucault's (1986) terms, "the care of the self."

That the recovery of the subject returns us to Foucault is not surprising, since the senses in which the subject is constituted were central to his own project. As he writes in *The Use of Pleasure: Volume 2 of the History of Sexuality* (1985):

> A history of the way in which individuals are urged to constitute themselves as subjects of moral conduct would be concerned with the models proposed for setting up and developing relationships with the self, for self-reflection, self-knowledge, self-examination, for the decipherment of the self by oneself, for the transformations that one seeks to accomplish with oneself as object. (p. 29)

Foucault provides just this kind of analysis in *The Care of the Self: Volume 3 of the History of Sexuality* (1986).

One could argue whether this view of the subject as active agent contrasts significantly with that presumed to be the product of effects (Dews, 1989; Poster, 1989; Siegel, 1990). As that issue is considered, however, one needs to keep in mind that, for Foucault, subjects do not possess characteristics. Rather, they are the characteristics they display (Langsdorf, 1988, p. 5). In the recovery of the subject, the attributes that constitute the self in a social scene are not given back to the subject. Rather, they are focused on more explicitly and precisely, to determine the "technologies of the self" that allow for their presence as part of the subject. Thus, on this analysis, Foucault has shifted the focus of study, but not the interpretation of the object of study.

In one of his last interviews, Foucault observed:

> I would say that if now I am interested, in fact, in the way in which the subject constitutes himself in an active fashion, by the practices of self, these practices are not something that the individual invents by himself. They are the patterns he finds in his culture and which are proposed, suggested and imposed on him by his culture, his society and his social group. (1988, p. 11)

The subject has an independent existence apart from other subjects and from those social forces that constitute it; simultaneously, the subject is subjected by those social forces (Siegel, 1990, p. 276). Independence does not constitute removal from dependence; nor does it preclude other organizational influences from displacing those presented to the self:

> I would call subjectivation . . . the process by which one obtains the constitution of a subject, more precisely of a subjectivity, which is clearly only one of the given possibilities of the organization of consciousness. (Foucault, *Les Nouvelles*, 28 June–5 July 1984, p. 41; cited in Siegel, 1990, p. 298)

The subjectivation process is more complex than Siegel (1990) suggests, since Foucault relies on more than the "mode of subjection [*mode d'assujettissement*]" for the constitution of

RAYMIE E. MCKERROW

the subject (1984, p. 353). The first aspect in self-constitution is the "ethical substance" that the subject considers (p. 353). That substance is open to change by the subject with respect to the manner in which it is incorporated or instantiated in the subject. The second feature is the mode by which subjection occurs, that process by which "people are invited to recognize their moral obligations" (p. 353). The third aspect is determining what the self is to do with reference to the ethical issue. Does one give in to desire, constrain desire and act otherwise, or what? The answer to that question rests with the fourth feature of the process: one's telos, or "the kind of being" one aspires to be or become (p. 355). The constitution of the self as an active agent involves all four interdependent features. The actions are not taken in isolation, apart from others. Taking care of oneself is to engage in a "true social practice" (Foucault, 1986, p. 51). This is true not only in Greek times but in the present time as well.

Foucault's accomplishment in what has been styled the "recovery of the subject" is to reenter the subject in a matrix of social practices of which it is a product. In the process, the reentering has not recovered the subject of modernity. What has been constituted is not a substance but a form. The subject takes on the form of madness or rationality, or some other form; it presents a face to the world as active or passive, as political or thoroughly subjected. The subject, as actor, is not the center of all experience and change; rather, it is constituted as one facet of the possibilities of change within social relationships. Engaging in actions that properly "take care of oneself" is to have influence in one's reordering of social practices.

As noted at the outset of this chapter, the subject is not reducible to symbolic constructs. Rather, the subject is more than the symbols used to refer to its characteristics. The social patterns that preexist the subject are instrumental in forming the self; the subject's own telos also participates in the act of self-constitution.

The Subject in a Critical Rhetoric

Having set forth some of the contemporary parameters of the issues involving subject and subjectivity, the task now is to demarcate the senses in which the subject participates in a critical rhetoric. Foucault's constitution of the subject is a project for a critical rhetoric, since the aim and orientation of a critical rhetoric resonates well with the kinds of questions Foucault is asking about the modes of subjection and the formation of a telos for a subject. Further, both are contextually grounded in history rather than seen in any sense as universal themes across history. The subject enters into a scene while being a part of that scene and transforms the social practices within that context. The questions raised at the outset of this chapter can be addressed by considering three interrelated themes: rhetoric as embodied performance, subject as critic, and subject as social actor and object of a critical rhetoric.

One of the principles underlying a critical rhetoric is to see critique as performance. As McGee (1990) has noted, "rhetoric is what rhetoricians do" (p. 279). The "doing," as in the practice of ethnography, is an embodied performance. The image of the social critic at a remove from the object of inquiry is recast in the context of a critical rhetoric. The social critic is resituated as bodily presence engaged in critiquing social practices. Distance recedes as a criterion of action, since the body is not "positioned" to form a critique: "Bodily presence is an event rather than a position" (Schrag, 1986, p. 155).

This perspective on the body does not require that we embrace Martin's (1990) provocative thesis on the body as political actor. At the same time, Martin's claim forces the practitioner to pay attention to the body as message. The claim also urges the critic to attend to those arts in which the body is cast as premier performer (dance, theater, sports). Rather than focus merely on spoken symbols, the critic needs to attend to a broader panoply of events that convey social practices. The body is not rhetorical, but those messages that the body conveys (either eclipsed by mind or acting on its own) can be accessed. The conditions of subjectivation can be expressed via bodily action. Where the voice is silenced, the body may be the messenger. To totally subsume the body within the control of the mind is to potentially miss the message. Hence, even if one does not accept Martin's argument in its entirety, one can nonetheless conceive of the mind and body as coequal contributors to political acts.

Gaonkar (1990), commenting on McGee's textual fragmentation thesis, complains that McGee's project results in the dissolution of rhetoric: "With McGee the dissolution reaches a point where it is dialectically transformed into a 'felt quality' of social life" (p. 308). While Gaonkar overstates the case in terms of "felt quality," he is correct in noting that rhetoric is resituated as traces embedded in a contingent world. Texts exist not as unitary and whole objects but as traces or fragments. They exist in a dialectical relationship with the social matrices out of which they spring. Real persons still give real speeches. That is not the point. The speeches are not given by subjects acting as originary beings at the center of a universe of discourse. Their words do not move outward from the center in concentric circles. Speeches are not rocks dropped in quiescent pools; rather they are rocks skipped across turbulent waters, with each point of contact leaving its trace.

The critic engages in critique[2] not as a centered subject originating thought but as a contributor to the universe of discourse. As inventor of texts, the critic's role is to re-present texts from a collection of fragmentary episodes. As McGee (1990) puts it: "Our first job as professional consumers of discourse is inventing a text suitable for criticism" (p. 288).

The invented text is produced by a subject constituted in and through the same contingent social practices of those for whom the critique is performed. Hence, it exists as a fragment in its own right. The goal, in this process, is not to produce a master text encompassing all known and possible conditions of its making. Rather, the goal is to pull together those fragments whose intersection in real lives has meaning for social actors—meaning that confines them as either subjects empowered to become citizens or social actors with a potential to enact new relations of power. As such, the invented text functions to enable historicized subjects to alter the conditions of their lived experience.

The critic as inventor acts not out of a substance but, as Foucault observes, out of a form; the critic assumes a face that is projected toward the world in the act of critique. That form/face may be as social actor engaged in political action or as "specific intellectual" (see McKerrow, 1989, 1991b) engaged in commentary on a scene. In neither case is the critic's function that of a social prophet speaking with reference to universalized truths. Badiou's (1991) analysis of the subject is relevant in this sense—the truth is found in the intersection of the critic/fragment/social actor: "One must absolutely abandon every definition of the subject that would assume that it knows the truth or is adjusted to it" (p. 30). The performance of critique is not that of truth in some final objectified sense. Through the process of giving names to events, critics, as embodied subjects, also name themselves. Thus, they implicate their own being as citizen-subjects or social actors, in the very process of advancing interpretations about the role of discourse in the construction and deconstruction of social practices. This is simply to affirm that a subject is reflected in the present act of critique and is implicated in the future practices that may emanate from taking the critique seriously.

The self as subject cannot exist apart from the "policing powers" (modes of subjection) of the society that determines its normalization. The citizen who speaks (in Balibar's sense) out of context or over or against the societal dictates is "insane." As a historicized individual, the citizen is subjected in the act of expressing his or her rights as citizen. Raising the subjected individual or the "insane" rhetor to heroic status is not a final answer. As Bourdieu (1990) notes, to consecrate the language of the dominated over or against the language of the dominant is not a sign of freedom; the only way the dominated can contextualize its language is conditioned by the dominant. One has not escaped from the bonds of domination (p. 154).

The escape can come through the practice of a critical rhetoric that outlines for the subject the conditions of domination and freedom. While one could subsume domination under freedom as the umbrella term, there is a distinct directional focus to each when considered as the object of critical inquiry. As noted elsewhere (McKerrow, 1991b), these complementary areas of analysis reflect the difference between emancipation from domination (freedom from) and emancipation from social relations (freedom to). The dialectical tension Balibar intimates between subject and citizen is analyzable within a critique of domination. To the extent that citizens are controlled by various bureaucracies without the condition of equality being realized, the critique of domination will illuminate the tensions that exist and the possibilities of emancipation.

For social actors embedded in a set of social practices that define as they constrain, a critique of freedom illuminates the possibilities of a new existence. The social actor, in this latter sense, has influence over those considerations. To care for oneself includes the remaking of social practices within which one is inscribed.

Conclusion

If the subject is decentered and viewed as a form rather than a substance, as the intersection of truth rather than the being that finds truth, can there be a role for the speaker as agent of social change? I answer this question in the affirmative. Resituating the subject does not necessitate the destruction of the speaker. Consistent with the move from a modern to a postmodern subject, however, the resituated subject is not the speaker of an older time in rhetoric's history. Consistent with Schrag's (1986) treatment of the decentered subject as temporal, multiple, and embodied, the discussion above suggests that the subject, as citizen and social actor, is capable of acting—the "who" of discourse is the "I" who speaks (p. 143). While not wholly formed through discourse, it is through that discourse that the subject gives expression to its "I" and thereby enacts self. The "I" implicates itself in both its past and future history as a contingently derived self. When the subject enacts self in the form of critique, its commentary is but one more fragment that enters the here and now as it reflects the past and conditions the future.

If that is all we are capable of in a postmodern world, why should we bother? Why, as consumers of discourse, with a particular training to discern patterns and connections among fragments and traces, should we attempt social change? Courtine (1991) provides an answer, although possibly not one he would agree with, arguing that "at the origin of the subject is the voice" (p. 79). Without the voice, there is no origin; without the origin, there is no subject. By giving voice to critique, the subject renews self in each instantiation of subject immersed in a matrix of social practices. Silence ends the practice of a critical rhetoric, and with it the possibility of the subject.

Notes

1. For recent analyses of the subject or subjectivity, see Cadeva, Connor, and Nancy, 1991; Cahoone, 1988; Dallmayr, 1981; Judowitz, 1988; Schrag, 1986.
2. Critique is differentiated from criticism in McKerrow, 1991a; the practice of a critical rhetoric presumes that critique is the aim of the critic.

References

Badiou, A. (1991). On a finally objectless subject (B. Fink, Trans.). In E. Cadeva, P. Connor, & J. Nancy (Eds.), *Who comes after the subject?* (p. 24–32). New York: Routledge. (Original work published 1988.)

Balibar, E. (1991). Citizen subject (J. Swenson, Trans.). In E. Cadeva, P. Connor, & J. Nancy (Eds.), *Who comes after the subject?* (pp. 33–57). New York: Routledge. (Original work published 1989.)

Bitzer, L. (1968). The rhetorical situation. *Philosophy and Rhetoric, 1,* 1–14.

Bourdieu, P. (1990). *In other words: Essays towards a reflexive sociology* (M. Adamson, Trans.). Stanford: Stanford University Press.

Cadeva, E., Connor, P., & Nancy J., (Eds.). (1991). *Who comes after the subject?* New York: Routledge.

Cahoone, L. E. (1988). *The dilemma of modernity: Philosophy, culture, and anti-culture.* Albany: State University of New York Press.

Conquergood, D. (1991). Rethinking ethnography: Towards a critical cultural politics. *Communication Monographs, 58,* 179–194.

Courtine, J. F. (1991). Voice of conscience and call of being (E. Haar, Trans.). In E. Cadeva, P. Connor, & J. Nancy (Eds.), *Who comes after the subject?* (pp. 79–93). New York: Routledge. (Original work published 1988.)

Dallmayr, F. R. (1981). *Twilight of subjectivity: Contributions to a post-individualist theory of politics.* Amherst: University of Massachusetts Press.

Derrida, J. (1970). Structure, sign, and play in the discourse of the human sciences. In R. Macksey & E. Donato (Eds.), *Languages of criticism and the sciences of man: The structuralist controversy* (pp. 247–72). Baltimore: Johns Hopkins University Press.

RAYMIE E. MCKERROW

Derrida, J. (1991). "Eating well," or the calculation of the subject: An interview with Jacques Derrida (P. Connor & A. Ronnell, Trans.). In E. Cadeva, P. Connor, & J. Nancy (Eds.), *Who comes after the subject?* (pp. 96–119). New York: Routledge.

Desilet, G. (1991). Heidegger and Derrida: The conflict between hermeneutics and deconstruction in the context of rhetorical and communication theory. *Quarterly Journal of Speech, 77,* 152–175.

Dews, P. (1989). The return of the subject in late Foucault. *Radical Philosophy, 51,* 37–41.

Foucault, M. (1977). *Language, counter-memory, practice: Selected essays and interviews.* (D. F. Bouchard, Ed.; D. F. Bouchard & S. Simon, Trans.). Ithaca: Cornell University Press. (Original publication 1969.)

Foucault, M. (1980a). *The history of sexuality: Vol. 1. An introduction* (R. Hurley, Trans.). New York: Vintage.

Foucault, M. (1980b). *Power/knowledge: Selected interviews & other writings, 1972–1977.* (C. Gordon, Ed.; T. Gordon, L. Marshall, J. Mepham, K. Soper, Trans.). New York: Pantheon.

Foucault, M. (1984). On the genealogy of ethics: An overview of work in progress. In P. Rabinow (Ed.), *Foucault reader* (pp. 340–372). New York: Pantheon.

Foucault, M. (1985). *The history of sexuality: Vol. 2. The use of pleasure* (R. Hurley, Trans.). New York: Pantheon. (Original work published 1984.)

Foucault, M. (1986). *The history of sexuality: Vol. 3. The care of the self* (R. Hurley, Trans.). New York: Vintage. (Original work published 1984.)

Foucault, M. (1988). The ethic of the care of the self as a practice of freedom (J. D. Gauthier, Trans.). In J. Bernauer & D. Rasmussen (Eds.), *The final Foucault* (pp. 1–20). Cambridge: MIT Press.

Gaonkar, D. P. (1990). Object and method in rhetorical criticism: From Wichelns to Leff and McGee. *Western Journal of Speech Communication, 54,* 290–316.

Hariman, R. (1991). Critical rhetoric and postmodern theory. *Quarterly Journal of Speech, 77,* 67–70.

Judovitz, D. (1988). *Subjectivity and representation in Descartes: The origins of modernity.* Cambridge: Cambridge University Press.

Langsdorf, L. (1988, December). Epistemic man and emergent self: A reconceptualization through Locke and Foucault. Paper presented at the annual meeting of the American Philosophical Association/Eastern Division, Washington, DC.

Martin, R. (1990). *Performance as a political act: The embodied self.* New York: Bergin & Garvey.

McGee, M. C. (1990). Text, context, and the fragmentation of contemporary culture. *Western Journal of Speech Communication, 54,* 274–289.

McKerrow, R. E. (1989). Critical rhetoric: Theory and praxis. *Communication Monographs, 56,* 91–111.

McKerrow, R. E. (1991a). Critical rhetoric and propaganda studies. In J. A. Anderson (Ed.), *Communication yearbook 14* (pp. 249–255). Newbury Park, CA: Sage.

McKerrow, R. E. (1991b). Critical rhetoric in a postmodern world. *Quarterly Journal of Speech, 77,* 75–78.

Poster, M. (1989). *Critical theory and poststructuralism.* Ithaca: Cornell University Press.

Schrag, C. O. (1986). *Communicative praxis and the space of subjectivity.* Bloomington: Indiana University Press.

Siegel, J. (1990). Avoiding the subject: A Foucaultian itinerary. *Journal of the History of Ideas, 51,* 273–299.

Aristotle and Heidegger on Emotion and Rhetoric

Questions of Time and Space

MICHAEL J. HYDE AND CRAIG R. SMITH

DURING ITS INFANCY, PHILOSOPHY WAS TAUGHT A LESSON by Socrates, Plato, and Aristotle. The lesson was this: Those individuals are noble and worthy of praise who can understand and communicate the truth such that others can live in accordance with it. Dialectic was the theoretical art (*technē*) given to philosophy by its mentors to help it acquire such understanding. And when philosophy then inquired about how it could express this understanding to others in a meaningful way, it was handed yet another art: rhetoric.

But how could this be? Had not Plato argued in his *Gorgias* and *Phaedrus* that rhetoric catered to its audience's emotional impulses, that it inhibited people from developing an intelligence (*noēsis*) based on a rational knowledge (*epistēmē*) of reality, and that it thereby encouraged the members of the polis to become the greatest of all sophists? Yes, but this question acknowledges only one side of Plato's dialectical assessment of the topic. On the other side lay the admission that the practice of rhetoric may indeed serve the truth. Socrates' personification of rhetoric speaks to this point:

> Why do you extraordinary people talk such nonsense? I never insist on ignorance of the truth on the part of one

who would learn to speak; on the contrary, if my advice goes for anything, it is that he should only resort to me after he has come into possession of truth; what I do however pride myself on is that without my aid knowledge of what is true will get a man no nearer to mastering the art of persuasion. (Plato, *Phaedrus*, 260d–e)

With Aristotle this point received further emphasis. After Aristotle answered Plato's call for an intellectual assessment of emotion and its relationship to truth and rhetoric, philosophy was presented with the following insights: (1) The emotional character of human beings plays an important role in their development; it constitutes a person's spirited potential for coming to judge what is true, just, and virtuous. (2) A moving of the passions is the sine qua non of persuasion; truth alone is not sufficient to guide the thoughtful actions of human beings. (3) Rhetoric, conceived as the art of persuasion, is a faculty or power (*dynamis*) in its nascent state, a potential for acting and doing; when actualized in discourse, this potential not only excites (*emovēre*) people to take an interest in the truth but encourages them to act in accordance with this truth (Hyde, 1984; see also Smith, 1970). "Rhetoric," in other words, "is the counterpart of Dialectic" (Aristotle, *Rhetoric*, 1354a1).

Was the lesson now clear? Would philosophy make peace with its sophistic heritage and allow itself to recognize and accept the good intentions and practical wisdom of a reformed discipline? The Latin tradition of philosophy (beginning with Cicero and Quintilian and extending at least to Vico) provides affirmative answers to these questions. Here are found serious efforts to join theory with practice, truth with emotion, dialectic with rhetoric. Owing to the influence of those like Descartes, Locke, Kant, and Hegel, however, philosophy was taught to demean such efforts and to see rhetoric not as a form of rational speech productive of truth but only as the form of "popular" and emotional speech that exhibits eloquence and that encourages people to form "wrong ideas" (Grassi, 1980).

The lesson, it seems, was not clear. Philosophy marches into the twentieth century under the banners of rationalism and empiricism, searching for a paradigm that could serve as the foundation for "true" knowledge, and avoiding any serious consideration of the relevance of rhetoric in human affairs. Instead it listened to the doctrine of logical positivism and was praised for its avoidance of the subjective in man. The reasoning here was quite simple: to acknowledge rhetoric is to concern oneself with emotive utterances. Such utterances, however, are not "factually significant"; they bespeak evaluative judgments that are nonverifiable. Hence, the study of emotive utterances must be dismissed by philosophy and relegated to those who want to struggle with the social, psychological, and ethical problems associated with such utterances.

The force of such reasoning is still with philosophy today, and rhetoric suffers because of it. But not all twentieth-century philosophy has allowed itself to be persuaded by the modernist discourse of positivism. Alternative instructions and passionate pleas for appreciating the legitimate scope and function of philosophy can certainly be heard in those discourses that go by the names of, for example, existentialism, existential phenomenology, hermeneutic ontology, critical theory, pragmatism, and poststructuralism. All of these discourses have a bone to pick with the means and ends of positivism; all, to a greater or lesser extent, have a stake in justifying the importance of a matter that positivism all too easily places on the margins of its interests. This matter—the contingency of human existence—stares us in the face everyday: "Because of the uncertainty of temporal existence life is always an experiment" (Jaspers, 1970, p. 125). When philosophy concerns itself with this contingency, this experiment, this "objective uncertainty" of our lives and times, its perception is of a place where rhetoric makes its living. As Aristotle reminds us, the business of rhetoric is to "deal with what is in the main contingent" (*Rhetoric*, 1357a15). Moreover, when philosophy writes to us about how we might best deal with the contingency of human existence, it affirms through its actions the importance and necessity of humankind's rhetorical enterprise. Or as the philosopher and argumentation theorist, Chaim Perelman (1982), would have it: "As soon as a communication tries to influence one or more persons, to orient their thinking, to excite or calm their emotions, to guide their actions, it belongs to the realm of rhetoric" (p. 162).

How rhetorically minded is philosophy today? It depends on who you read. For example, in their respective projects of philosophical hermeneutics, both Gadamer (1976, pp. 21–26) and Ricoeur (1977) have certainly made clear their appreciation of the theory and practice of rhetoric. Rhetorical agendas also motivate the competing projects of Habermas (1984–1988), Foucault (e.g., 1988), and Rorty (1979, 1989), although an explicit admission and discussion of the relevancy of this fact is unfortunately absent in these intellectuals' writings. With his project of deconstruction, Derrida (e.g., 1977, 1988) cannot write enough about the "presence" of rhetoric in philosophy; tropes and figures are everywhere. Schrag (1986), on the other hand, would have us avoid the deconstructionist's literary and reductionistic treatment of rhetoric (as tropology), to respect as much as possible the life-giving role played by rhetoricians sustaining what he terms "the hermeneutical space of communicative praxis." Philosophy has returned to the realm of rhetoric. But it presently dwells there in many different ways.

Importantly, rhetorical theorists and critics have not been reticent about pointing out philosophy's ways of dwelling rhetorically. Their response during the past thirty years has in fact been quite extensive; they have both appropriated the rhetorical findings of philosophers and criticized their interlocutors (including philosophically minded rhetoricians) for not saying enough or the "proper" things about rhetoric's scope and function (e.g, see Farrell, 1983). In returning to that realm where it now seeks to dwell, philosophy has been greeted by a gracious, but not totally forgiving, host.

How well philosophy and rhetoric will work out their similarities and differences in coming years is very much open to debate. Elsewhere we have made various attempts to supplement and counsel this debate (e.g., Hyde & Smith, 1979; Hyde, 1983, 1990; Smith, 1972, 1985). Our purpose here is to center the debate around a topic that, as suggested above, has been a thorn in rhetoric's side for quite some time. The topic, of course, is human emotion—that phenomenon that gives power to rhetoric's ability to influence thought and action. The debate between and among philosophers and rhetoricians over the scope and function of rhetoric must remain incomplete as long as the topic of emotion is not fully integrated into the conversation. As far as we can tell, attempts at performing this integration have been minimal at best.[1]

Our way of dealing with this problem is to offer a certain reading of Aristotle's treatment of the *pathē* in book 2 of his *Rhetoric*—a reading made possible by Martin Heidegger's hermeneutic phenomenology of emotion in his *Being and Time*. Heidegger (1962) credits Aristotle's treatment as the "first systematic hermeneutic of the everydayness of Being with one another" (p. 178). In light of what Heidegger tells us about this emotionally inspired way of human being, Aristotle's discussion of the emotions can be read as an interpretation of how these phenomena are related to the existential temporality and spatiality of our being-in-the-world. Rhetorical scholars have yet to explore this particular accomplishment in their literature; they thus have yet to acknowledge what we take to be a very important philosophical contribution to their field of inquiry (e.g., see Rowell, 1934; Solmsen, 1938; Black, 1965; Grimaldi, 1972; Fortenbaugh, 1975).

But the present essay is not intended to open only a one-way street in the debate. Although Heidegger is instructive for remedying a blindness in rhetorical scholarship, he ends up severely depleting the importance of rhetoric by describing our "everydayness of Being with one another" as constituting a realm of "inauthenticity" (1962, p. 178). With a Heideggerian reading of Aristotle's *Rhetoric* in hand, we will show how Heidegger's unfortunate characterization of the realm of rhetoric is misinformed. We will suggest, then, how rhetoric can return a favor by helping philosophy to rid itself further of a prejudice that is lodged in one of its most influential twentieth-century texts. If the debate between philosophy and rhetoric is to continue in an authentic manner, both parties must be willing to take the good with the bad. It is a two-way street.

Heidegger on Emotion, Time, and Space

Given the reading of Aristotle's *Rhetoric* that we wish to make, it is first necessary to see how Heidegger's understanding of emotion directs us toward the questions of time and space. In *Being and Time*, Heidegger offers an existential analytic of *Dasein* (human being) in an attempt to address the question, What is the meaning of Being? Of the reasons that Heidegger gives for why Dasein should be granted priority in his project of developing a "fundamental ontology," the one most important for our purpose is this: "Dasein is an entity which does not just occur among other entities. Rather it is ontically distinguished by the fact that, in its very Being, that Being is an *issue* for it" (1962, p. 32). Put another way, the "special distinctiveness" of Dasein that differentiates it from other entities is that this entity is *concerned with* its existence, its being, its way of becoming what it is (Heidegger, 1962, p. 32; also Macomber, 1967, p. 317). This concern for being is constantly demonstrated in Dasein's everyday involvements with things and with others. Reflecting on the meaningfulness of what is being demonstrated, Dasein can, and often does, raise the question of what it means to be. The question makes explicit Dasein's concern for being. Only Dasein is concerned enough to do this. And because it is also capable of under-standing to various degrees what it is doing out of concern for its being, Dasein can provide an answer to the question; hence, Heidegger decided to turn to an investigation of Dasein as a way to set forth his project of fundamental ontology.

Macomber (1967) notes that "Heidegger wishes to make a concerned attitude fundamental to all human activities in-cluding the most detached and disinterested speculative in-quiry." This position, Macomber perceptively points out, "has a peculiar status: it is not incontestable, but in contesting it we exhibit the concern which we wish to deny" (p. 31). Indeed, Dasein *is* that entity that is concerned with its being. But how is this manner of human existence made possible? For Heidegger, the answer to this question requires that we form an authentic appreciation of the scope and function of human emotion—an appreciation that he advances in his analysis of what he terms Dasein's "state-of-mind" (*Befindlichkeit*). He writes, "What we indicate *ontologically* by the term 'state-of-mind' is *ontically* the most familiar and everyday sort of thing; our mood, our Being-attuned" to the world by way of our emotional dispositions (1962, p. 172). With Heidegger, we are encouraged to see that these dispositions make it possible for Dasein to become open to the world and to enact its concern for being. "Dasein's openness to the world," writes Heidegger, "is constituted existentially by the attunement of a state-of-mind" (p. 176).

Heidegger (1962) recognizes that emotions function primordially as vehicles for the active sensibility of human beings; that is, they provide the perspectives for seeing the world as interesting, as something that matters and that warrants interpretation (pp. 172–182). Emotions are not primarily psychical phenomena originating purely from one's inner condition; rather, they take form in the interaction between a person and the world, as the world is perceived by the person through an act of consciousness. In this way, an emotion orients a person toward the world in a "concernful" manner (p. 176).

When any mode of emotional consciousness (for example, joy) is prolonged through time so that it continually influences how a person perceives and thinks about the world, a person's emotion becomes moodlike in nature. Moods are generalized emotions permeating a person's existence. Even one's passive indifference to the world wherein thought appears to vanish into the "pallid, evenly balanced lack of mood" still warrants recognition as being an emotional orientation between a person and the world; it is still a mood. Moods are therefore an ever-present quality of human existence. "The fact that moods can deteriorate . . . and change over means simply that in every case Dasein always has some mood," some mode of emotional consciousness that enables it to "disclose" and understand the world in a specific and meaningful way (Heidegger, 1962, p. 173).

In performing this interpretive or hermeneutical function, whereby Dasein demonstrates its concern for being, emotions are able to serve a "truthful" purpose. From an existential-phenomenological perspective, truth *happens* as a disclosure of the world, as a revealing or uncovering of something that is perceived to be (Heidegger, 1962, pp. 256–273). It may thus be said, for example, that the emotionally intense visions of suffering that Picasso was able to disclose in his 1937 paintings *Guernica* and *Head of a Horse* are displays of truth—displays that, in their own concerned way, are as reasonable and rational as the assertion "Two times two makes four." Unlike this "objective" assertion, which need only function on an intellectual level for its content to be apprehended, Picasso's displays are subjective and function first and foremost on an existential level. His paintings project a protest against the brutality of fascism in particular and modern war in general; at the same time, they project the *real* suffering that he was experiencing and living as he visualized the pain of creatures under attack and being destroyed. The paintings are not what Picasso thinks but what he *is* as an emotionally concerned being. They express an existential truth: "something which one *is* rather than *has*, something which one *lives* rather than *possesses*" (Schrag, 1961, p. 7).

Heidegger insists that any form of cognitive determining owes at least something to the disclosive capabilities of emotion. Reason itself poses no exception here. Even when reason is couched in the most positivistic language (such that it can be "objective" in its registration of "facts") its announcements will always be rooted in what emotion makes possible—that is, an interpretation of some matter of interest, a concern for being. Hence, the so-called dispassionate claims of reason—as made by science, for example—can never escape the emotion that begets their existence. By adhering (passionately?) to the belief that "man *is* a rational animal," Western philosophy devotes much of its twenty-five-hundred-year history to teaching us that this escape is not only possible but necessary if the thing called "truth" is to be discovered. Heidegger teaches otherwise.

In our discussion of Heidegger's understanding of human emotion, we have emphasized how Dasein's fundamental concern for being, a concern that distinguishes this entity from other entities, presupposes Dasein's emotionally inspired and disclosive ability to see the world as interesting, as something that matters and that warrants interpretation. Heidegger points to this fact in his earlier noted observation that "Dasein's openness to the world is constituted existentially by the attunement of a state-of-mind." But this observation speaks to us not just of the relationship that exists between emotion and concern but of how this relationship is itself associated with the temporality and spatiality of Dasein's existence.

As that which orients and directs Dasein's concern for

being, emotion also functions to structure what Heidegger describes as the essential meaning of this human phenomenon: "temporality." For Heidegger (1962), "*The 'essence' of Dasein lies in its existence,*" in its constant "projective" involvement with the temporal process of becoming and understanding what it is: its possibilities (pp. 67–68). This "potentiality-for-Being," a potentiality that constitutes the "not yet" of Dasein's future development, is what Heidegger refers to when he writes of the temporality of human concern, or what he also terms the "*primordial time*" of Dasein's "*authentic temporality,*" which "lies in advance" of our common everyday understanding of time (pp. 377–378). The distinction here is crucial if one is to appreciate fully how emotion functions to structure the temporality of human concern.

The terms *future*, *past*, and *present*, for example, are those of common, everyday time. They suggest what time is in a language of measurement and standardization; a language that separates time into a linear progression of discrete units; a language of seconds, minutes, hours, days, years, and so on; a language that spatializes time by representing it as an infinite succession of instants or "nows"; a language that makes its appearance in clocks, calendars, and maps. Such a language, however, does not account for the actual nature of the temporality of human concern, for the way this phenomenon happens before it is transformed, segmented, and reified by expressions that compose common parlance.

The way of temporality is that of a unity where future, past, and present are interpenetrating and inseparable *ekstases* rather than juxtaposed dimensions defined within an objectified spatiotemporal coordinate (Heidegger, 1962, p. 377). Dasein is not a "thing" that merely lives "in" time; it does not exist just "now" and "then" as does a coin in a pocket. No, Dasein *exists as time*, as a being who is presently living its "having been" that once was its future, and who, at the same time, is presently living-out the possibilities that are yet to come. The temporality of human concern is a "unitary phenomenon." The future, past, and present presuppose the ecstatic character of this phenomenon's existence. Hence, Heidegger writes:

> The character of "having been" arises from the future,
> and in such a way that the future which "has been" (or
> better, which "is in the process of having been") releases
> from itself the Present. This phenomenon has the unity
> of a future which makes present in the process of having
> been; we designate it as *"temporality."* (p. 374)

Notice here how the future becomes the pivotal *ekstasis*
in Heidegger's definition of the temporality of human concern. This way of putting the matter bespeaks Heidegger's
(1962) claim that *"The primary phenomenon of primordial and
authentic temporality is the future"* (p. 378). Heidegger makes
this claim in light of the fact that, as noted above, Dasein's
fundamental way of being-in-the-world shows itself as a constant "projective" involvement with the temporal process of
becoming what Dasein is: its possibilities. This "potentiality-
for-Being" names how it is that Dasein's existence is always
"on the way" (*unterwegs*) toward understanding what can or
will be in its life but is "not yet." Heidegger tells us that along
with the emotional dispositions that constitute its state-of-
mind, this potentiality-for-Being makes possible "Dasein's
openness to the world" (pp. 176, 182–188). Without this potentiality-for-Being, Dasein could not be open to the world because, as should be quite obvious, Dasein would not exist; its
time on earth would be over. However, without some state-
of-mind to orient and direct its concern for being, Dasein could
not actualize its potential for being open to the world by seeing
it as interesting, as something that matters and that warrants
interpretation. With this in mind, we are now in a position
to discuss not only how emotion functions to structure the
temporality of human concern but how this structuring gives
rise to Dasein's way of living a spatial existence.

Emotion structures Dasein's temporality by spatializing
it. The primordial occurrence of this phenomenon takes place
by way of Dasein's emotionally disclosive ability to see the
world as a matter of interest. Here, according to Heidegger,
Dasein becomes involved in an "encounter" with "what *has
presence* environmentally," with what can *now* be made into
an object of concern. This immediate making-present function

of emotion is ever present throughout Dasein's existence. As long as it is conscious of what is going on in the world, Dasein is never without some mood or emotion to direct its attention toward those objects with which it must deal circumspectively on a daily basis to live a meaningful life. Following Heidegger (1962), it can thus be said that the making-present function of emotion has the effect of situating Dasein's concern for being in the here and now, in the immediacy of its everyday existence, in that time and place called "the Present" (p. 374).

Earlier we alluded to this structuring of the temporality of human concern when we mentioned how time is commonly conceived as a spatialized succession of measurable units. When structured this way, time becomes a tool, an instrument, a piece of equipment—something that is "ready-to-hand" and thus can now be used for the practical purpose of managing moment by moment the "everydayness" of one's present existence (Heidegger, 1962, pp. 381–382). Is it not the case that in everyday existence "time is of the essence" because here and now there is so much to do and so little time to do it in that he or she who hesitates is lost? Yes, there are only twenty-four hours in a day, yet still the clock ticks—everyday. We created this ticking to help orchestrate the tempo of our lives. The ticking is there, however, because we first used our emotional capacity to see time as interesting, as something that matters and that warrants interpretation. The interpretation gives a certain structure to time. In everyday existence, time is spaced, and space is timed.

But, as Heidegger points out, emotion has a more primordial relationship with time and space than this. With its making-present function, emotion first and foremost situates Dasein's concern for being in a lived and attuned space, where distance is experienced not as metrical measurement but as existential remoteness and closeness. Heidegger (1962) illustrates this primordial spatiality of Dasein when he notes, for example, that while walking down the street

> one feels the touch of it at every step as one walks; it is seemingly the closest and Realest of all that is ready-to-hand, and it slides itself, as it were, along certain portions of one's body—the soles of one's feet. And yet it is

farther remote than the [friend] whom one encounters
"on the street" at a "remoteness" . . . of twenty paces
when one is taking such a walk. (pp. 141–142)

In the situation of this lived space, the presence of the street
is of little concern compared to the presence of the friend. The
street is a matter of indifference; the friend is a matter of joy.
Indifference makes what is close become remote; joy makes
what is remote become close.

Again, the spatiality of such an existential configuration
is not initially apprehended as one would measure the distance between two points in space. Rather, Dasein's primordial spatiality (which makes possible any such measurement)
is always there with it, immediately and constantly, by way
of its being open to the world through its emotional dispositions and its potentiality-for-Being. The making-present, or
disclosive, function of emotion allows for what Heidegger
(1962) describes as "Dasein's making room for itself" in its
everyday involvements with things and with others (p. 419).
The space of this room will vary in accordance with the different emotions at work defining the situation at hand. As Ellenberger (1958) notes, "Love, for instance, is 'space-binding':
the lover feels himself close to the beloved in spite of distance,
because in the spatial modality of love, distance is tran-
scended. Happiness expands the attuned space; things are
felt as 'aggrandized.' . . . Sorrow constricts attuned space,
and despair makes it empty" (pp. 110–111). Be it large or
small, empty or full, the presence of Dasein's lived space owes
much to the ways of emotion.

We must not forget, however, that there is something
else to which Dasein's emotionally directed spatiality is in-
debted, something that its existence presupposes. Heidegger
(1962) emphasizes this fact when he writes, *"Only on the basis
of its ecstatico-horizonal temporality is it possible for Dasein to break
into space"* (p. 421). In other words, the basis of Dasein's spatiality is its "potentiality-for-Being," its "primordial and authentic temporality," its essential way of living a "future which
makes present in the process of having been." Heidegger
makes much of this fact in stressing the importance of another
one: how the present and future status of our lived and at-

tuned space is always being modified by the past, by our constant involvement in the process of having been (p. 390). Although this second fact may appear to be something less than profound, its development by Heidegger is essential to the purpose of this discussion.

According to Heidegger, the modification of our lived and attuned space is rooted in our repeatedly being influenced to use our emotions for the purpose of seeing, interpreting, and becoming involved with the world in specific and meaningful ways. This influence shows itself as soon as we are "thrown" into the world through birth; we are subjected from then on to the manners in which the members of our culture employ its emotional dispositions to create and sustain a world of common sense and common praxis, a world of publicness, a world of "the everydayness of Being with one another." Throughout our having been and continuing to be a subject of, and in, this world, we come to understand the "appropriate" ways for structuring our temporality into a lived and attuned space that puts us in touch with others.

Instructed by his reading of Aristotle's *Rhetoric*, Heidegger cites the "orator" as one whose business it is to modify our lived and attuned space. No specific discussion of this rhetorical matter is offered by Heidegger (1962, p. 178); he leaves that to Aristotle. In turning now to a discussion of what this ancient Greek had to say about the matter, we will pay particular attention to how his "systematic hermeneutic of the everydayness of Being with one another" complements and extends Heidegger's understanding of the primordial relationship that exists between emotion, time, and space.

Aristotle on Emotion, Time, and Space

Like Heidegger, Aristotle recognizes that emotions (the *pathē*) function primordially as vehicles for the active sensibility of human beings: an emotion is an act of consciousness that serves to orient a person toward the world in a certain way. In book 2 of the *Rhetoric*, Aristotle employs this understanding of emotion to help the orator determine how to "put his hearers . . . into the right frame of mind" (1377b24) so that their orientation toward the world is advantageous to the speaker's persuasive intent. This advice is intended to promote the effective and just use of emotion and rhetoric in the polis. For Aristotle, knowing how to stir the soul rhetorically is essential because existential questions concerning the livelihood of society are not usually decided with the equations of demonstration or the syllogisms of dialectic. Existence is a gamble based on probabilities, and the emotional outlook of the *hoî polôî* influences their judgment at the time the bet is placed. If rhetoric is to perform its most worthy function of trying to move people toward "the good," it must cast a concerned and knowing eye on the emotional character of those whom it wishes to move. Thus, a moving of the passions is a sine qua non of persuasion; truth alone is not sufficient to guide the thoughtful actions of human beings.

Heidegger is correct on this point: The business of the orator is to modify the lived and attuned space of others by making present to them what the orator has reason to believe is true, just, and virtuous. The practice of rhetoric operates in the immediacy of the present; it seeks thought and action in the pragmatic world of the here and now. Rhetoric calls upon emotion in order to facilitate this pragmatic endeavor—an endeavor that makes possible a perceptual restructuring of a person's existential temporality and spatiality.

Aristotle's analysis of the existential relationship that exists between human emotion, time, and space takes form as he sets out a threefold process for examining the *pathē*. He specifies this process using anger as his model:

> Take, for example, the emotion of anger: here we must discover (1) what the state of mind of angry people is, (2) who the people are with whom they usually get angry, and (3) on what grounds they get angry with them. It is not enough to know one or even two of these points; unless we know all three, we shall be unable to arouse anger in any one. (*Rhetoric*, 1378a22–28)

This method of examining the *pathē* enables Aristotle to conduct a systematic investigation of individual emotions and to show not only how they are interrelated but how each emotion forms a continuum with its opposite. In his discussion of these matters, Aristotle addresses the issue of emotion's relationship to time and space and, in so doing, allows us to extend Heidegger's analysis of the topic. An exhaustive examination of all Aristotle says on the pathē and their interrelationships is beyond the limits of this chapter; however, the scope and depth of his analysis can be appreciated by following his specific investigation of anger.

Aristotle describes the emotion anger in personal terms. He does not mention the possibility of anger at an object, often the result of frustration. He implies that personal anger is more forceful in rhetoric than anger at an object, when he notes that the impulse is to "a conspicuous revenge for a conspicuous slight" received from someone close to us in some way (*Rhetoric*, 1378a32–34). Such a slight causes anger and its attending "pain." The pain involved remains as a privation in one's everyday existence until the slight is forgotten or redressed when one begins to envision and plot some form of revenge. According to Aristotle, revenge adds pleasure to the pain of anger, for "the angry man is aiming at what he can attain, and the belief that you will attain your aim is pleasant" (1378b3–5).

This expectation of revenge, wherein one's anger is now attended by pleasure, reveals an important temporal dimension associated with the experience of anger. The pleasure of anger emerges as people project themselves into the future— into another place in time and into another role—to visualize how their anger can be appeased. While imagining the act of revenge, the future becomes the present in an existential way; it becomes immediate, a place to be here and now. But as the presence of the future recedes into the past, and as one's expectations are fulfilled, relaxed, or forgotten, anger loses its intensity and its ability to move the listener. The object of anger becomes remote. Aristotle notes, "When time has passed . . . anger is no longer fresh, for time puts an end to anger" and converts it to calm (1380b5). Because orators seek to transform anger into calm as often as they seek to transform calm into anger, they need to understand how to move their hearers away from the circumstances that are now provoking the anger and thus away from the present pleasures of future revenge. Clearly, for the orator who is dealing with anger in order to excite or calm it, time is of the essence.

Anger modifies time by making present the "not yet" of some imagined future. At the same time, however, anger also modifies the lived space of our everyday being-with-others. Aristotle begins to develop this point when he continues his threefold analysis of anger and specifies why people become angry with others who slight them before their kin, their friends, or five other classes of people: "(1) our rivals, (2) those whom we admire, (3) those whom we wish to admire us, (4) those for whom we feel reverence, (5) those who feel reverence for us" (*Rhetoric*, 1379b24–26). But in order to form a more complete picture of how Aristotle appreciates anger's modification of the interpersonal dynamics of a person's lived space, one must understand with him how anger and fear are interrelated.

Aristotle maintains that those who make up the seven classes of people noted above have a certain potential power over a person who acknowledges their designated status. This power lies in their ability to affect the person's survival and/or self-respect, for they can be a source of physiological and psychological pain. When a person is slighted before these people, this pain can take effect. According to Aristotle, the pain involved is a "terrible thing"; it poses an immediate "danger" to the person's well-being. There can no longer be an imagined "safe distance" between the person and those who stand before the person in a vividly powerful way. The person's fear of these circumstances forces the realization that what was heretofore perceived to be remote (a potential threat) is actually close at hand (*Rhetoric*, 1382a30, 1382b20, 1383a15–20). Thus, the person would become not only angry with those who created such a situation through their slighting behavior but fearful of the threat that can accompany this behavior. In its interrelationship with fear, anger modifies the lived space of our everyday being-with-others.

Aristotle's discussion of this phenomenon within the context of anger's relationship to fear is elucidated further when he discusses pity. He notes, "Speaking generally, anything causes us to feel fear that when it happens to, or threatens, others causes us to feel pity" (*Rhetoric*, 1382b26). From this statement one can conclude (although Aristotle does not do so explicitly) that anger also can be directly related to pity. For example, if individual A perceives individual B to be slighting individual C, and if A can identify with C's circumstances, then A not only would pity C due to A's own fear of such circumstances happening to him/her but would be incited to experience anger toward B. The key to understanding this interrelationship between anger, fear, and pity lies in A's identification with C's circumstances (Aristotle alludes the importance of identification at 1386a1–3). This identification, this lack of remoteness between A and C, marks a modification in the interpersonal dynamics of A's lived space—a modification that brings C's threatening circumstances close to A. What is now brought close to A's personal existence gains a dimension of immediacy, a presence that is not without a past and future. "We feel pity," writes Aristotle, "whenever we are in the condition of remembering that similar misfortunes have happened to us or ours, or expecting them to happen in the future" (1386a1–3). Like the fear that can incite it, and like the anger that can then come about, pity is evoked in terms of time and space (1385b15–34).

The reader familiar with Aristotle's analysis of the *pathē* in the *Rhetoric* undoubtedly is aware that our discussion of this analysis so far has not adhered strictly to Aristotle's three-step procedure for investigating each emotion. Rather we have been reading Aristotle with a Heideggerian mind-set in order to illustrate how book 2 of the *Rhetoric* offers a "systematic hermeneutic of the everydayness of Being with one another." To see Aristotle's analysis of the pathē in this way credits his ability not only to appreciate how emotion is related to a human being's existential temporality and spatiality but to uncover some of the complexity of this relationship by suggesting how emotions enter into an interrelationship with one another. Aristotle deserves even more credit when his additional analysis of how an emotion forms a continuum with its opposite is explored.

According to Aristotle, the continuums defined by the *pathē* include anger-calm, friendship-enmity, fear-confidence, shame-shamelessness, kindness-cruelty, pity-indignation, and envy-emulation. These continuums serve a critical function in Aristotle's explanation of the workings of rhetoric, for they provide existential measures of the emotional movement that takes place whenever an orator is attempting to persuade an audience about some matter of interest. To be moved emotionally and rhetorically is to experience a modification of one's presently existing lived space—a modification that, for Aristotle, ought to end up situating us in a truthful and just relationship with others.

Aristotle defines the movement in terms of the "pleasure" and "pain" that are a part of any continuum because of the *pathē* they attend. He writes, "We may lay it down that Pleasure is a movement, a movement by which the soul as a whole is consciously brought into its normal state of being; and that Pain is the opposite. . . . It must therefore be pleasant as a rule to move towards a natural state of being." (*Rhetoric*, 1369b33–1370a4). For example, when the pain of anger is felt because of some slight, it is "natural" for a person to want to move from this state of being, this lived space, and toward another one wherein a modicum of "calmness" can prevail (1380a31). The effective orator not only must recognize this but must possess the necessary practical wisdom (*phronesis*) that will enable the orator to set an audience on a course whereby this collection of "souls" can experience the pleasure of such movement.

We have all been witness to the speaker who is so inept that no emotional movement takes place or, worse, the movement that takes place is inimical to the speaker's purpose. Aristotle would explain this failure by suggesting that the soul of the listener had not been moved along some continuum to a proper range or mean that was compatible with the aim of the speaker. In one case, the movement would fall short of the mean and would not achieve the desired effect. In the other and more rare case, the soul would be moved beyond the proper mean. For example, if the soul is moved to too much fear, the hearer might be incapacitated or overreact.

The noted Puritan preacher Jonathan Edwards provides a case in point.[2] He was so frightening from the pulpit during a sermon in Northampton, Massachusetts that he evidently drove his uncle by marriage, Mr. Hawley, to suicide. Undoubtedly, Edwards was seeking to put the fear of God in the assembled congregation. But in the case of his uncle, the emotional restructuring of this listener's lived space went beyond the intended mean and resulted in the old man slitting his throat. The causes of fear were brought too close to the listener. If a speaker uses unfitting appeals, the audience members are moved either too far beyond the range compatible with the rhetor's aim, as in Edwards' case, or not close enough to the range, as in the case of a speech that fails to touch the audience.

In Aristotle's terms, the ways in which a person relates to others in and through her/his lived space has much to do with the present location of the person's soul along any of the continuums. He makes this point when he notes, for example,

> It is shameless to deny what is obvious, and those who are shameless towards us slight us and show contempt for us: anyhow, we do not feel shame before those of whom we are thoroughly contemptuous. Also we feel calm towards those who humble themselves before us and do not gainsay us; we feel that they thus admit themselves our inferiors. (*Rhetoric*, 1380a18–13; see also 1382a32–34, 1383b6–7, 1386b20–25, 1387a13)

Importantly, the reader is also given here a further illustration of how the emotions enter into interrelationships with one another: shamelessness and humility interact with anger and calm. The emotionally oriented world of one's everyday lived space is a complex phenomenon. And the competent and just orator must know this. Since one emotion may incite another when brought into proximity with it, and since all the emotions exist along continuums, it is not enough for the orator to understand a single emotion in isolation or even its counterpart. Moving people toward the "good," "just," or "healthy" life is more involved than that.

Just how involved this task can be was recently captured in a newspaper headline: "MANDELA'S CHALLENGE: CALM WHITES' FEARS, BLACKS' FIRE." Part of the story contained under this headline speaks further to the point:

Nelson Mandela, the elder statesman of South Africa's black nationalist movement, spent much of his first week of freedom trying to reassure whites that they would have nothing to fear from a black majority government.

But a more ominous message came from Austin Kadiaka, a 23-year-old activist in the black township of Tembisa, near Johannesburg.

"All those whites who are panicking now are the ones who did something wrong to us," Kadiaka said. "Those who did a crime to our people will be dealt with after we take over."

Kadiaka is angry, hardened and embittered. His mother was killed when the family's home was fire-bombed in 1986 during a wave of black-on-black violence. The young man represents one of the toughest problems Mandela faces as he begins to preach reconciliation to blacks and whites more accustomed to generations of deadly conflict. (Witt, 1990, pp. 1, 12)

Though Aristotle's theory was based on empirical observation of what kinds of rhetorical discourse worked in the assembly, it was not designed with such an emotionally complex rhetorical situation as Mandela's in mind. The "civilized" *hoî polôî* of his culture marked the human boundaries of his theoretical formulations. Nevertheless, we would submit that if Nelson Mandela is to persuade those whom he wants to move toward the "good" life, he will have to know, at the minimum, something about the emotions: how they form continuums, how they are interrelated, and how they function to make present and modify the lived space of human beings. Heidegger credited Aristotle with possessing such knowledge. We have tried to show why Heidegger did this, why he saw Aristotle's analysis of the *pathē* as being "the first systematic hermeneutic of the everydayness of Being with one another." We now want to suggest how the relationship that exists between emotion, time, space, and rhetoric is more than what Heidegger, for the most part, says it is: a matter of inauthenticity.

Emotion, Time, Space, and Rhetoric

Heidegger (1962) agrees with Aristotle: the orator "must understand the possibilities of moods in order to rouse them

MICHAEL J. HYDE AND CRAIG R. SMITH

and guide them aright" (p. 178). Our Heideggerian reading of Aristotle's analysis of the *pathē* speaks to what is being agreed on here. But this agreement, unfortunately, is damning with faint praise on Heidegger's part. Although he does not state it explicitly, Heidegger encourages his readers to believe that rhetoric's necessary relationship with emotion constitutes an admission of inauthenticity on rhetoric's part. This point begins to unfold within the context of Heidegger's assessment of the making-present function of emotion.

As noted earlier, Heidegger appreciates this primordial function of emotion as that which orients and directs Dasein's attention toward those entities in the world with which it must deal circumspectively on a daily basis in order to live a meaningful life. The primary effect of this function of emotion is to situate Dasein's concern for being in the immediacy of its present existence, whereby arises Dasein's lived space and its involvement with "the everydayness of Being with one another." Heidegger (1962) acknowledges the importance of this common aspect of Dasein's existence when he notes, "So far as Dasein *is* at all, it has Being-with-one-another as its kind of Being" (p. 163). Heidegger also maintains that "when Dasein is [emotionally] absorbed in the world of its concern—that is, at the same time, in its Being-with towards Others—it is not itself" (p. 163). This is so because Dasein's everyday involvement with others—an involvement made possible by the making-present function of emotion—conditions Dasein to forsake and forget its own authenticity and thereby to live an existence that is typically inauthentic in nature. A closer examination of what Heidegger is maintaining here brings us to the point that we wish to advance concerning how he encourages us to think about rhetoric.

When Heidegger speaks of Dasein's authenticity, he is referring to what was described earlier as its constant "projective" involvement with the temporal process of becoming its possibilities. Heidegger equates this process with what he terms the "*constancy of the Self*": To be a self is to become a self, and to become a self is to be forever caught up in the temporal and historical process of acting out one's own existence for as long as one lives. The self of a human being is its existence, its temporality, its "potentiality-for-Being" its possibilities. A human being's "own Self" finds its existential origins here, in this ontological "ability to be" that makes possible, for example, one's becoming a teacher, a wife, a Christian, or whatever. For any human being, this "ability" is uniquely his or her "own" (*eigen*); it defines the "authenticity" (*eigenlichkeit*), the most primordial "truth," of human being. Hence, in the truest and most authentic sense of the term, this *self*-activity can be claimed by any person to be personally and properly "mine" (Heidegger, 1962, pp. 67–68, 163–168, 263, 369).

One hears this claim being made, for example, when patients assert their freedom and demand that they be treated as "persons," as unique individuals, and not only as diseased bodies whose treatment "only by the numbers" reduces their existence to the statistics of mortality and morbidity tables (Hyde, 1986). Speaking more generally, one hears the claim when oppressed people and their supporters decide to be true to their "selves" and thereby take on the task of calling for a more authentic use of power—one devoted to promoting humankind's freedom of choice and thus to what Nietzsche (1969) described as its "lofty *right* to its future" (p. 219).

For Heidegger, we have this "right" because of our authenticity; and if we are to make the best use of it, if we are to set forth the truth of our power to take charge of our own lives, then we must be courageous and committed enough to face our possibilities with anticipation and conscience, to assume the responsibility for affirming our freedom through resolute choice, and thus to become consciously/willingly/personally (that is, authentically) involved in the creation of meaningful existence. The option here is as simple as it is important: either we choose the way we want to live our respective lives (as selves) or allow others to do the choosing for us; either we achieve integrity through resolute choice or lose integrity through a retreat from choice. Such integrity would include for Heidegger the courage to admit at any time that one's chosen way of being a self is in need of revision (1962, p. 355). Integrity has its authentic requirements.

The challenge of living an authentic existence is always before us, always there to be met as we live out a future that "is in the process of having been" and try to make conscientious decisions about our future and past possibilities. According to Heidegger, however, this challenge is all too easily forsaken and forgotten in our emotionally directed and everyday way of being with others; for here we are subjected to, and come under, the control of those habits, customs, and conventions that make up what Heidegger terms the public world of the "they." In describing this world of "everydayness," he writes, for example,

> This Being-with-one-another dissolves one's own Dasein completely into the kind of Being of 'the others', in such a way, indeed, that the Others, as distinguishable and explicit, vanish more and more. In this inconspicuousness and unascertainability, the real dictatorship of the "they" is unfolded. We take pleasure and enjoy ourselves as *they* . . . take pleasure; we read, see and judge about literature and art as *they* see and judge; likewise we shrink back from the 'great mass' as *they* shrink back; we find 'shocking' what *they* find shocking. (Heidegger, 1962, p. 164)

The world of the "they" is one of standardized, ritualized, and institutionalized behavior; it breeds and demands conformity to secure amongst its inhabitants what Heidegger describes as an existence dominated by "averageness."

> The 'they' maintains itself factically in the averageness of that which belongs to it, of that which it regards as valid and that which it does not, and of that to which it grants success and that to which it denies. In this averageness with which it prescribes what can and may be ventured, it keeps watch over everything exceptional that thrusts itself to the fore. Every kind of priority gets noiselessly suppressed. (1962, p. 165)

Caught up in the warp and woof of this suppressed existence, Dasein "is not itself"; rather, it is who "they" command it to be. Hence, Heidegger (1962) argues that in the world of the "they," Dasein "turns *away from*" (p. 229) the challenge of living an authentic existence and toward those everyday ways of being that constrain Dasein to think and act like others. Here and now, and time and again, Dasein is situated in a lived space where "everyone is the other and no one is himself" (p. 165), and where assuming the responsibility for affirming one's freedom through resolute choice is uncalled for because others have already made the proper choices that are necessary for "leading and sustaining a full and genuine 'life'" (p. 222). Under the ever-present dictatorship of the "they," Dasein is not required to choose but only to be chosen; it is not required to be true to itself, to its own unique possibilities, but only to enjoy and sustain the "tranquility" that comes about from being one of the "they." In short, existing as a "they-self" in its "everydayness" of being with others, Dasein succumbs to a life of inauthenticity, a life where it "drifts along towards an alienation . . . in which its ownmost potentiality-for-Being is hidden from it" and easily forgotten (p. 222). As Heidegger sees it, forgetting one's "own Self" is a virtue for the "they"; but from the standpoint of Dasein's authenticity, it is also a "cowardly" way to live (pp. 298, 311).

With what he tells us about Dasein's authenticity and inauthenticity, Heidegger (1962) does not want to be understood as suggesting that the first of these two states of Being admits "a purer and higher 'primal status'" (p. 220). On the contrary, he emphasizes that *"Authentic Being-one's-Self"* is only an existential *"modification of the 'they',"* a modification that shows itself when Dasein takes charge of its own life by assuming the responsibility of affirming its freedom through resolute choice (p. 168). This qualification, however, does little to ease Heidegger's critical assessment of how communal existence conditions us to be average, to be self-forgetful, to avoid the responsibility for affirming our freedom through resolute choice, to live a tranquil but cowardly existence, while dwelling in the public time and space of the "they." All of this comes about by way of the making-present function of emotion; it is who we are in the inauthentic realm of our everyday being with others.

Rhetoric knows this realm well; it is where the art makes its home and its living twenty-four hours a day. Aristotle told how it does such things when he offered "the first systematic hermeneutic of the everydayness of Being with one another." Heidegger had precious little to say about rhetoric; he offers instead an assessment of that emotionally inspired realm of communal existence that sustains and is sustained by the workings of rhetoric. The community of the "they" and rhetoric go hand in hand. One need only make use of a tool of rhetoric, the enthymeme, to see what this implies about the art from a Heideggerian perspective: Rhetoric is inauthentic. Calling, as it must, upon the making-present function of emotion, rhetoric directs people to a temporal and spatial realm where their authenticity will be forsaken and forgotten.

Perhaps this assessment of how rhetoric enters into a relationship with emotion, time, and space contributed to Heidegger's lack of attention to the art. With this lack of attention, Heidegger fails to see not only how rhetoric can serve our authenticity in a way that is quite acceptable to him but how this authentic function of rhetoric invites a reconsideration of what Heidegger tells us about the making-present function of emotion and all that goes with it.

For Heidegger, among all of our emotions there is one that "is quite distinctive" because of the way in which it functions to move us out of the world of the "they" and into a direct relationship with our authenticity. This emotion is anxiety. The experience of anxiety signals a significant loss of meaning in our lives. It arises when our daily progress is impeded, if not shattered to its very core, by occurrences (e.g., illness) that disrupt our accustomed routines and relationships with others. Now, if only for the moment, we must confront the authenticity of our potentiality-for-Being; for now we are called upon to make a personal and conscientious decision about which of our past and future possibilities we care to employ in trying to restructure our lives in a meaningful way. According to Heidegger (1962), anxiety shows itself in this decisive confrontation with our possibilities; it

> makes manifest in Dasein its *Being towards* its ownmost potentiality-for-Being—that is, its *Being free for* the freedom of choosing itself and taking hold of itself. Anxiety brings Dasein face to face with its *Being-free for . . .* the authenticity of its Being, and for this authenticity as a possibility which it always is" (p. 232).

In short, anxiety "individualizes" Dasein by turning it away from its involvement with the world of the "they" and toward the primordial "truth" of its "own Self" (p. 233).

If anxiety can do this, so can rhetoric (Hyde, 1980). The abolitionist discourse of the nineteenth century and the anti-nuclear discourse of the twentieth century, to cite just two examples, incited anxiety in at least some of its hearers, so that they assumed the personal responsibility for affirming their freedom through resolute choice and thereby dissociated themselves from the tranquility of some everyday way of being with others. Abolitionist rhetoric so shook the foundations of society that President Jackson banned its distribution in the South. Antinuclear rhetoric brought many face-to-face with the possibility of immediate destruction and raised their anxiety to unprecedented levels. Rhetoric, in others words, can serve our authenticity in a manner that Heidegger could find genuine.

Aristotle omits any discussion of how rhetoric can employ anxiety to modify the lived space of those that it seeks to inform and persuade. He comes closest to offering such a discussion when he writes about fear. Heidegger (1962) admits that the two emotions are "similar"—so much so that "every understanding confuses [fear] with anxiety" (p. 394). But he also maintains that, unlike anxiety, fear is inauthentic, because its making-present, or disclosive, function is directed not toward the authentic temporality of Dasein's ownmost potentiality-for-Being-its-Self but toward an involvement with something or someone whose feared presence only enhances Dasein's preoccupation with its everydayness. "Fear [like all other "typical" emotions] is occasioned by entities with which we concern ourselves environmentally," writes Heidegger; "anxiety, however, springs from Dasein itself" (p. 395).[3]

Is all of this to say, then, that creating anxiety in others is rhetoric's only route to authenticity? With Heidegger, one is encouraged to offer an affirmative response to this question. But rhetoric has the capacity to call upon other emotions to have people take on the personal responsibility for affirming their freedom through resolute choice. Picasso's *Guernica* provides a case in point. With his "rhetorical" depiction of the

pain and suffering of creatures under attack and being destroyed—a depiction that simultaneously breeds pity for the
dead and dying, fear of this happening to us, and anger
toward the Fascist "they"—Picasso is certainly offering his
viewers an opportunity to make a personal and resolute decision about the horrors of war.

Consider the purer case of oratory provided by Martin
Luther King, Jr. when he spoke to the nation in August of
1963 about his "dream." This rhetorical effort used many of
the persuasive strategies explored by Aristotle in his *Rhetoric*,
especially those concerning emotion. The emotions evoked
included pity and shame for the past and present racist treatment of blacks in America, anger over this treatment, calm in
the nonviolent quest for civil rights legislation, pride for the
numbers produced for the march on Washington, D.C., and
hope for a future where we would be "free at last" of the
"they" (racism). Without these *pathē,* the speech would not
have stirred its hearers. They would not have felt fulfilled
about the march; they would not have adhered to Dr. King's
message with as much fervor or commitment; and surely, the
speech would not have become an enduring symbol of the
civil rights movement. Like Picasso's *Guernica*, this symbol
addresses the importance of assuming the responsibility for
affirming one's freedom through resolute choice; it stands
before us as a reminder of how rhetoric can make use of
various emotions to modify in an authentic way the everyday
lived space of others.

Thus, we have made a significant departure from Heidegger's path. With what he tells us about the making-present
function of emotion, and with what this implies about rhetoric, Heidegger encourages us to forget how rhetoric's relationship with emotion can serve authenticity. Such forgetfulness
turns us away from a phenomenon that admits a fascinating
complexity: when rhetoric calls upon our emotions, it involves
itself with acts of consciousness that are interrelated, that exist
along continuums, and that have the power to transform our
temporal and spatial existence. With his "systematic hermeneutic of the everydayness of Being with one another," Aristotle taught us how to appreciate this complex phenomenon;
he thus taught us about something that can be quite authentic

in scope and function. Heidegger, unfortunately, did not see it this way; he chose to "forget" how rhetoric can serve authenticity.

Conclusion

We began this chapter by briefly examining the historic bridges and schisms between rhetoric and philosophy. We believe that when bridges have been built philosophy and rhetoric have informed one another. We have tried to demonstrate how the process can work in the specific instance of emotion. Heidegger inspired this effort with his reference to Aristotle's hermeneutic of the *pathē*; we attempted to meet his challenge by reading in a new way Aristotle's passages on the emotions. The result was a more sophisticated understanding of how emotions change the temporality of our lived space, particularly our being-with-others.[4] Understanding how emotions interrelate and operate along continuums helps us establish a critical perspective useful in the analysis of rhetorical works and events.

At the same time, it is important to remember what Heidegger chose to forget. Rhetoric allows us to assert our power and our potential. It allows us to make time to go beyond association with the "they." We readily admit that not all rhetoric achieves this authentic level. Rhetoric can be inauthentic, as when Heidegger spoke for national socialism and associated himself with an inauthentic "they."

Clearly, what is needed is a more authentic use of rhetoric than Heidegger's. Had he acknowledged an authentic role for rhetoric, he might also have developed an authentic "they" that might have stood against the inauthenticity of national socialism. We hope we have laid a foundation for such a project by reexamining rhetoric's use of emotion. We hope we have demonstrated that such a use has the potential to call forth in the individual an authentic questioning of self, to call forth a move to separate one's self from the inauthentic "they," and to call forth an examination of one's potentiality-for-being. Like the philosophers Buber and Jaspers, we believe rhetoric has a role to play in what Heidegger calls the "authentic project." Like them, we believe there is an authentic "they" called into being by a Picasso, a Martin Luther King, Jr., or a Nelson Mandela. Furthermore, we hope that recognition, exploration, and development of such a "they" will be accorded its due by rhetors and philosophers operating jointly from a new critical perspective.

Our Heideggerian reading of Aristotle provides a corrective counterstatement to Heidegger's understanding of rhetoric and its uses. We have attempted to put his forgetfulness to better use; hopefully, we have built a bridge between what philosophy and rhetoric have to say about emotion and its impact on the temporality of lived space. As scholars attempt further research on emotion, time, space, and rhetoric, we are confident that they will open many more passageways between these two ancient disciplines.

Notes

1. In his *Communicative Praxis and the Space of Subjectivity* (1986, pp. 186–187), Calvin Schrag does attempt such an integration when discussing "Heidegger's explicit reference to Aristotle's *Rhetoric* as the first disciplined discussion of the hermeneutics of everyday life" (p. 186). As we hope to show, however, much more has to be said about this reference and its implications for rhetorical theory than Schrag would have us believe.

2. Edwards helped usher in the Great Awakening in colonial America. He was educated at Harvard, where his treatise on arachnids was used as a text in biology classes for years. Other treatises, particularly *A Treatise Concerning Religious Affections*, were widely circulated in the colonies and influenced many preachers and political orators. During the Great Awakening, Edwards' sermons often set off waves of weeping and hysteria. See Brock 1987, pp. 146–153.

3. Besides anxiety, there is only one other emotion that Heidegger specifically associates with authenticity: equanimity (p. 396). As best as we can tell, Heidegger would have us understand that this "mood" describes how a person experiences the world when this person takes control of his or her anxiety in preparation for making a resolute decision about some matter of interest.

> Anxiety can mount authentically only in a Dasein
> which is resolute. He who is resolute knows no fear;
> but he understands the possibility of anxiety as the

possibility of the very mood which neither inhibits nor bewilders him. Anxiety liberates him *from* possibilities which "count for nothing" . . . and lets him become free *for* those which are authentic. (p. 395)

4. After we finished writing this chapter, we turned to the task of deducing the implications for rhetorical criticism. Due to the arbitrary nature of publication schedules, that article was published first; see Smith & Hyde, 1991.

References

Aristotle. (1954). *Rhetoric.* (W. R. Roberts, Trans.). New York: Modern Library Series, Random House.

Black, E. (1965). *Rhetorical criticism: A study in method.* New York: MacMillan.

Brock, B. L. (1987). Jonathan Edwards. In B. K. Duffy and H. R. Ryan (Eds.), *American orators before 1900* (pp. 146–153). Westport, CN: Greenwood.

Derrida, J. (1976). *Of grammatology* (G. C. Spivak, Trans.) Baltimore: Johns Hopkins University Press. (Original work published 1967.)

Derrida, J. (1988). *Limited inc.* (S. Weber & J. Mehlman, Trans.) Evanston: Northwestern University Press.

Ellenberger, H. F. (1958). A clinical introduction to psychiatric phenomena and existential analysis. In R. May, E. Angel, & H. F. Ellenberger (Eds.), *Existence: A new dimension in psychiatry and psychology.* (pp. 92–124) New York: Basic.

Farrell, T. B. (1983). The tradition of rhetoric and the philosophy of rhetoric. *Communication, 7* (2), 151–180.

Fortenbaugh, W. W. (1975). *Aristotle on emotion.* New York: Harper & Row.

Foucault, M. (1988). *Politics, philosophy, culture: Interviews and other writings, 1977–1984,* (L. D. Kritzman, Ed.; A. Sheridan, J. Harding, D. Parent, A. Baudot, J. Couchman, A. Forster, T. Levin, I. Lorenz, J. O'Higgens, & J. Rhan, Trans.). New York: Routledge.

Gadamer, H-G. (1976). *Philosophical hermeneutics* (D. E. Linge, Trans.). Berkeley: University of California Press.

Grassi, E. (1980). *Rhetoric as philosophy: The humanistic tradition.* University Park: Pennsylvania State University Press.

Grimaldi, W. (1972). *Studies in the philosophy of Aristotle's* Rhetoric. Hermes, suppl. 25. Weisbaden: Fritz Steiner.

Habermas, J. (1984–1988). *The theory of communicative action,* 2 vols. (T. McCarthy, Trans.) Boston: Beacon. (Original work published 1981.)

Heidegger, M. (1962). *Being and time*. (J. Macquarrie & E. Robinson, Trans.) New York: Harper & Row. (Original work published 1927.)

Hyde, M. J. (1980). The experience of anxiety: A phenomenological investigation. *Quarterly Journal of Speech, 66*(1), 140–154.

Hyde, M. J. (1983). Rhetorically, man dwells: On the making-known function of discourse. *Communication, 7*(2), 201–220.

Hyde, M. J. (1984). Emotion and human communication: A rhetorical, scientific, and philosophical picture. *Communication Quarterly, 32*(2), 120–132.

Hyde, M. J. (1986). Treating the patient as a person. *Quarterly Journal of Speech, 72*(4), 456–469.

Hyde, M. J. (1990). Existentialism as a basis for the theory and practice of rhetoric. In R. Cherwitz (Ed.), *Rhetoric and philosophy* (pp. 213–251). Hillsdale, NJ: Lawrence Erlbaum Associates.

Hyde, M. J., & Smith, C. R. (1979). Hermeneutics and rhetoric: A seen but unobserved relationship. *Quarterly Journal of Speech, 65*(4), 347–363.

Jaspers, K. (1970). *Way to Wisdom* (R. Manheim, Trans.). New Haven: Yale University Press. (Original work published 1951.)

Macomber, W. B. (1967). *The anatomy of disillusion: Martin Heidegger's notion of truth*. Evanston: Northwestern University Press.

Nietzsche, F. (1969). *On the genealogy of morals* and *Ecce homo* (W. Kaufmann & R. J. Hollingdale, Trans.). New York: Vintage. (Original work published 1887.)

Perelman, C. (1982). *The realm of rhetoric* (W. Luback, Trans.) Notre Dame: University of Notre Dame Press. (Original work published 1977.)

Plato. (1973). Phaedrus. In E. Hamilton & H. Cairns (Eds.), *Plato: The collected dialogues* (R. Hackford, Trans.). Princeton: Princeton University Press.

Ricoeur, P. (1977). *The rule of metaphor: Multi-disciplinary studies of the creation of meaning in language* (R. Czerny, K. McLaughlin, & J. Costello, Trans.). Toronto: University of Toronto Press. (Original work published 1975.)

Rorty, R. (1979). *Philosophy and the mirror of nature*. Princeton: Princeton University Press.

Rorty, R. (1989). *Contingency, irony, and solidarity*. New York: Cambridge University Press.

Rowell, E. Z. (1934). The persuasion conviction duality. *Quarterly Journal of Speech, 20*(4), 469–478.

Schrag, C. O. (1961). *Existence and freedom: Towards an ontology of human finitude*. Evanston: Northwestern University Press.

Schrag, C. O. (1986). *Communicative praxis and the space of subjectivity.* Bloomington: Indiana University Press.

Smith, C. R. (1970). Actuality and potentiality: The essence of criticism. *Philosophy and Rhetoric, 3*(3), 133–140.

Smith, C. R. (1972). The medieval subjugation and the existential elevation of rhetoric. *Philosophy and Rhetoric, 5*(3), 159–174.

Smith, C. R. (1985). Martin Heidegger and the dialogue with being. *Central States Speech Journal, 36*(4), 256–269.

Smith, C. R., & Hyde, M. J. (1991). Rethinking "the public": The role of emotion in being-with-others. *Quarterly Journal of Speech, 77*(4), 446–466.

Solmsen, F. (1938). Aristotle and Cicero on the orator's playing upon the feelings. *Classical Philology, 33*(4), 390–404.

Witt, H. (1990, February 18). Mandela's challenge: Calm whites' fears, blacks' fire. *Chicago Tribune*, pp. 1, 12.

Rhetoric, Objectivism, and the Doctrine of Tolerance

James W. Hikins and Kenneth S. Zagacki

GERALD VISION'S (1988) RECENT OBSERVATION THAT, "from its inception to the present, philosophy may be viewed as a series of struggles between realisms and anti-realisms" is equally apropos of contemporary rhetorical theory (p. 1). Predominant postmodern theoretical trends in both English and communication studies have been robustly antirealist, yet realist strains in rhetoric are also present in some of this scholarly work (Cherwitz and Hikins, 1986; Hikins and Zagacki, 1988; Orr, 1978). Moreover, recent studies in philosophy suggest that the prevailing intellectual winds may be again changing direction, presaging not merely the revival of philosophical realism but what philosopher Thomas Russman (1987) calls the "triumph of realism" and the attenuation of currently dominant antirealist positions (see also Aronson, 1984; Grayling, 1985; Kelley, 1986; Harré, 1986). Combined with the collapse in numerous countries of the most significant antirealist political praxis of the postmodern era—late Marxism—more temerarious writers might be tempted to suggest that the age of postmodernism itself is waning, a scant half-century after its birth in the ashes of postbellum Europe. Given recent events in the Soviet Union, Czechoslovakia, Poland, Hungary, and China, Francis Fukuyama (1989) may well be right in his tart observation that the remnants of Marxism-

Lennism include only a few "isolated true-believers left in places like Managua, Pyongyang or Cambridge" (p. 18).

If these developments signal a return to realist philosophical influence, the principal tenets of postmodern rhetorical theory require reevaluation. Most in need of reassessment is what we believe to be a central tenet of late postmodern rhetoric, namely, skepticism. In this chapter, we argue for a realist rhetoric for the post-postmodern era.[1] We focus our remarks specifically on the claim, central to postmodern rhetoric, that realist rhetorics are inherently intolerant. This focus is not fortuitous, for we believe it vital not to reject postmodernism wholesale but to preserve its most valuable lessons and incorporate them into a realist rhetoric. One of the most valuable insights of postmodern thought is the requirement to maintain a constant vigilance against intolerance. Emerging from our analysis is a formulation of rhetorical realism that not only avoids intolerance but provides stronger guarantees of social toleration than rhetorics containing skeptical components.

Skepticism and the Doctrine of Tolerance

Tolerance has been defined by Maurice Cranston (1967) as "a policy of patient forbearance in the presence of something which is disliked or disapproved of" (p. 143). Philosophical arguments for toleration have been many; perhaps the most famous is John Locke's concern about the Christian arguments for suppression in the seventeenth century. In his *Epistola de tolerantia*, Locke argued that force of the kind applied by religious institutions to coerce nonbelievers into religious compliance was simply not an effective policy. It not only made one feign belief in the face of feared retaliation but was morally harmful since it encouraged hypocrisy. Locke also argued that religious institutions were different from civil ones, so that dissent in the former could not be expected to cause political upheavals in the latter. Indeed, the state existed precisely to protect one's rights. The state had no knowledge of what the true religion was. "Each man," writes Cranston of Locke's theory, "has his own faith, and every person's conscience is entitled to the same respect" (p. 144).

A more extended argument for toleration was later presented in the nineteenth century by John Stewart Mill, writing in *On Liberty*. Mill moved beyond Locke's concern for individual liberties in light of the interference of church and state to what Cranston (1967) calls "the limitations on human freedom that stemmed from unwritten law—the pressure of convention and public opinion. Mill wanted to see toleration extended from the realm of politics to that of morals and manners, to all self-regarding actions, as he called them" (p. 145).

Throughout the seventeenth and eighteenth centuries, skeptics like Pierre Bayle and David Hume presented more epistemologically-based arguments for tolerance. Bayle proposed that since all theories about the ultimate nature of reality were questionable, and since true beliefs could not be distinguished from false ones, the persecution of one's beliefs was not justified. In a similar manner, Hume professed neither a God nor any natural law to justify or ground the firmness of his beliefs. He thus located the source of all his convictions in human psychology, in the fact that we were conditioned to look for relationships in the world. Hence, our most powerful beliefs, in Hume's view, resulted from our strongest conditioning. In the world of political and moral conduct, Hume maintained that such conditioning took the form of customs, traditions, or conventions. The British tradition of the rights of the Englishmen had conditioned Hume to think he was, as Russman (1987) puts it, "a splendidly tolerant man" (p. 96). In addition, and also "because of his conditioning, [Hume] desired to promote toleration in a society as a whole and to make sure that the next generation would be conditioned to tolerance as well" (pp. 96–97).

In contemporary times, skeptical attacks against realist epistemologies on the grounds that they promote intolerance have continued. One of the more adamant skeptical voices is that of Richard Rorty (1979, 1982, 1987, 1988), who has offered a serious critique of realism, objectivism, and foundationalism. Rorty seeks to reject the claim that the philosophical enterprise has successfully provided us with standards of knowledge or that it may potentially sort out knowledge claims that are accurate reflections of objective reality from those that are not. Following Nietzsche and James, Dewey,

Wittgenstein, and Heidegger, Rorty (1982) notes that any claims about securing absolute truth or objective knowledge are misguided, "that even in science, not to mention philosophy, we simply cast around for a vocabulary which lets us get what we want" (p. 152). In Rorty's "pragmatic" view, philosophers should dismiss traditional epistemology as a search for truth and become "edifying philosophers." Edifying philosophers "refuse to present themselves as having found out any objective truth" (p. 370). Instead, philosophical discourse should be seen as merely expressing an attitude about a subject, as engaging in a conversation rather than contributing to an inquiry. The goal of edifying philosophy, claims Rorty (1979), is to keep "the conversation going rather than to find objective truth. Such truth . . . is the normal result of normal discourse" (p. 377). For Rorty (1979), "edifying philosophy is not only abnormal but reactive, having sense only as a protest against attempts to close off conversation by proposals for universal commensuration through the hypostatization of some privileged set of descriptions" (p. 377). Edifying discourse is important because it prevents advocates of normal discourse from deceiving others into believing that "from now on all discourse could be, or should be, normal discourse" (p. 377).

Rorty (1987) demonstrates that the implications of skepticism for political and social theory are critical: "To most thinkers of the Enlightenment, it seemed clear that the access to Nature which physical science had provided should now be followed by the establishment of social, political, and economic institutions which were 'in accordance with Nature'" (p. 43). In this objectivist account of culture,

> the criterial conception of rationality has suggested that every distinct culture comes equipped with certain unchallengeable axioms, "necessary truths," and that these form barriers to communication between cultures. So it has seemed as if there could be no conversation between cultures but only subjugation by force. (p. 44)

In Rorty's pragmatic and skeptical view of rationality and objective knowledge, these barriers simply do not exist, or so he claims.

For Rorty, differences between competing cultures (or competing value frameworks in general) are best decided through open and tolerant communication. Thus, Rorty (1987) argues that "pragmatists would like to replace the desire for objectivity—the desire to be in touch with a reality which is more than some community with which we identify ourselves—with the desire for solidarity with that community" (p. 45). Pragmatists promote the virtues "of relying on persuasion rather than force, of respect for the opinions of colleagues, of curiosity and eagerness for new data and ideas" (p. 45). Rorty (1988) suggests that these sorts of virtues are compromised when social institutions construct hierarchical orderings based on objective conceptions of human being. But pragmatists, Rorty (1988) insists, "envisage a society in which, no matter how discriminating we are in private, we do not let the institutions of society humiliate those whose tastes and habits we find contemptible" (p. 29).[2]

In general, then, Rorty is concerned about the impact of objectivism on social and political affairs, especially about objectivists claiming to have discovered a hierarchical ordering of human being. In view of his arguments about how cultures of differing value orientations attempt to subjugate one another and employ force, as well as his concerns about discriminating social institutions within particular cultures, Rorty's central problematic emerges as the practice of citizens imposing objective beliefs about religion, politics, or culture on those favoring dissenting positions. In the world of universal commensuration portrayed by Rorty, persuasion would break down, and coercion or force would take over.

The Rhetorical Progeny of Philosophical Skepticism

Philosophical skepticism and its views for tolerance have influenced two trends in contemporary rhetorical thought— rhetorical relativism (or intersubjectivism, as it is sometimes called) and the rhetoric of inquiry. Rhetorical relativists (sometimes identified as social contructivists or intersubjectivists) claim there simply is no objective knowledge. Knowledge or truth are relative to particular conceptual schemes, linguistic filters, or cultural ways of seeing. Truth, in this view, stems from the intersubjective agreement occurring through linguistic interaction among and between individuals. Reality, in essence, is something that is created in the rhetorical discourse that leads to intersubjective agreement. Expositors of this view include Robert L. Scott (1967, 1976), Barry Brummett (1976, 1981), and Walter Carleton (1978). Carleton makes the most definitive statement. For him, once the search for objective knowledge is abandoned and we understand that all knowledge arises out of human interaction, we can comfortably say that all knowledge and belief is "social" or "rhetorical." He wishes us to understand "that *no typically human knowledge is possible outside the framework such phrases denote.* That is, the genus term, 'knowledge,' is properly understood as 'social knowledge,' or knowledge made possible through 'the decision and action of an audience'" (p. 318).

This relativistic approach to rhetoric has important implications for the doctrine of tolerance. Like Rorty, rhetorical relativists fear that objectivist claims to "certainty" and "truth" lead to, or are allegedly only possessed by, tyrants and fanatics who would naturally impose their views of "truth" on others. Scott (1967) makes just this association between objectivism, tyranny, and intolerance in a relativistic account of human communication:

> By "truth" one may mean some set of generally accepted social norms, experience, or even matters of faith as reference points in working out the contingencies in which men find themselves. In such cases the word might be better avoided, for in it the breath of the fanatic hangs threatening to transmute the term to one of crushing certainty. If truth is somehow both prior and substantial, then problems need not be worked out but only classified and disposed of. Unwittingly, one may commit himself to a rhetoric which tolerates only equals, that is, those who understand his "truths" and consequently the conclusions drawn from them; such a rhetoric approaches those who are not able to take its "truths" at face value as inferiors to be treated as such. (p. 12)

Rhetorical relativists, however, assert that protection against intolerance is located in their relativistic notion of truth and communication itself. In Scott's (1967, 1976) terms, once we understand truth as situational, rhetors are ethically bound to the doctrine of tolerance where no view is seen as superior to any other, where all competing beliefs are discussed openly, and where one's own positions are given over to both self- and public scrutiny. Moreover, because knowledge is relative, disagreements, even those between differing cultures, must be resolved through what Brummett (1981) calls open communication or "negotiation" (pp. 293–297).

The second skeptical trend in contemporary rhetoric belongs to the rhetoric of inquiry, whose members include diverse thinkers like John Nelson, Allen Megill, and Calvin Schrag. The rhetoric of inquiry's views regarding toleration can be seen as a reaction against the philosophical quest for certainty. Nelson and Megill (1986), for example, declare that the quest for certainty has been "anti-rhetorical" and note that "after more than three centuries of" failed attempts by philosophical realists to discover objective truths, "not to mention the programs for their enforcement, we have every reason to resist their temptation and revise their anti-rhetorical premises" (p. 23). The rhetoric of inquiry movement has also been strongly influenced by what Nelson and Megill call "the philosophical attack on foundationalism" (p. 27), especially as this attack has been pushed by continental philosophers and American pragmatists, including Rorty. Nelson and Megill go on to employ the idea of "dictatorial rhetorics" to suggest that rhetorical objectivists have historically imposed tyrannical standards when setting forth their views. Nevertheless, these authors acknowledge the efforts of Foucault and Derrida to illustrate the flawed nature of these attempts to enforce objective, truth-oriented rhetorics: "Over and over, their writings portray our truths as reincarnations of old, partly repressed, but still dictatorial rhetorics and beliefs" (p. 27).

In a similar manner, Rorty's work has brought about a rapprochement between philosophical skepticism and the rhetoric of inquiry, particularly in the hermeneutical idea of rhetoric offered by Schrag. This hermeneutic argument begins from Rorty's skeptical assumption that traditional epistemology, so far as it makes claims to certify judgments as objectively true, is not a philosophically viable enterprise. Thus, since epistemology has lost its viability as an enterprise of truth seeking, it no longer provides a useful model on which to base theories of rhetoric. The task of rhetoric, then, should be one of hermeneutics, where hermeneutics is conceived in terms of communicative praxis. In other words, rhetoric seen as hermeneutic is similar to what Rorty called "abnormal discourse"; rhetoric viewed as epistemological is similar to Rorty's idea of "normal discourse."

That rhetoric grounded in epistemology is less likely to promote toleration than hermeneutic rhetoric is suggested in Schrag's (1985) claim that in the former "the telos of argumentation is reduced to the winning of points in a dispute, without regard to the contents of discourse that are made manifest or to the self-understanding of the rhetor and the interlocutor in their joint endeavors" (p. 172). For Schrag, rhetoric from this objectivist perspective is prejudiced, because it assumes grounding in a sort of "controlling knowledge which finds its center in an abstracted, rational, epistemological subject"; the move toward hermeneutics, however, requires a decentering of the epistemological subject and an understanding of rationality as "disseminated into the discursive practices that make up the republic of mankind" (pp. 172–173). In Rorty's terms, hermeneutic rhetoric presumably promotes toleration by seeking to maintain the conversation, to move beyond one's egocentric prejudices to achieve the goals of self-understanding and evocation through communicative praxis. By contrast, it is claimed that epistemological rhetoric advances intolerance by closing off discussion, by imposing objective standards external to the cultural conversation, and by constraining the very way in which the conversation itself is carried forth.

Contemporary rhetoric seems to have accepted both the skeptical attack on epistemology and suggestions for its replacement by hermeneutics. It has been sated by the postmodern feeding frenzy on the political excesses of the first half of the twentieth century, and there has been no pause in the headlong effort to abandon all forms of objectivism. The result of this haste has been the premature rejection of more tenable objectivist positions. These include a formulation of philosophical realism that has been developed as the framework for a theory of rhetorical realism—a rhetorical realism promoting many of the same goals espoused by postmodern skeptical thinkers, including tolerance.

On the Compatibility of Realism and Tolerance

The skeptical argument contends that realism is the enemy of tolerance—that one who claims to know will attempt to achieve rhetorical, if not political, hegemony over the beliefs of others. The skeptical argument has its devil terms: *objectivity*, *truth*, *positivism*, and *certainty*—all the concepts in some way linked to foundations of our beliefs. We are urged to abandon entirely all claims to knowledge, replacing them with such notions as "relative" or "situational" truth and "social" and "rhetorical" knowledge. We should, in the words of Rorty (1979), strive to "keep the conversation going rather than to find objective truth" (p. 377).

But is rhetoric's attack on truth-based philosophies cogent? We believe it is not. Our counterargument concerns the concept of rhetorical praxis. *Praxis* is a term that has been appropriated by a wide variety of postmodern movements, generally in an effort to distance the theorist from the complaint that he or she is *just* a theorist and will not, or cannot, make sense of practice. By and large, the complaints of skeptically motivated rhetoricians focus on the fact that philosophy (especially metaphysics and epistemology) has failed to provide us with any comfortable, veridical, grand (or, perhaps more to the point, grandiose) theories. Hence we are told that given rhetorics are incommensurable, just as the Ptolemaic and Copernican worldviews are incommensurable. We are asked to eschew notions of certainty in rhetoric because Heisenberg cannot determine both the speed and location of a subatomic particle at the same time. Scott (1990) recently invokes both Heisenberg's uncertainty principle and Godel's incompleteness theorems in support of the argument that we can know nothing with certainty. We are led by Johnstone (1973) to the not surprising conclusion that real philosophy must be essentially rhetorical and that rhetoric must be essentially alogical (where alogical refers to notions of formal validity grounding the rationality of a discipline). And Toulmin (1958) spends much time establishing the conclusion that formal philosophical analysis does not work very well when applied to actual real-world discourse. No wonder recent versions of antirealism are well satisfied merely to keep the conversation going—to limit useful discourse to the hermeneutical space of the conversational voice of humankind.

The paucity of focus on *real* pedestrian rhetoric has led to confusion concerning the nature of rhetorical praxis. Real-world rhetoric rarely, if ever, makes claims about grandiose theoretical schemes. In churches or synagogues, in union halls or on the political stump, and in newspaper editorials, the epistemic judgments being offered are more modest than most of our colleagues would have us believe. The farmer at the grange hall demands that the speaker discuss the maximum price supports likely in the fall; the advertiser wants you to know that Plax reduces plaque by 300 percent over brushing alone; Joe Isuzu wants you to know that the Isuzu pickup costs thousands of dollars less than its Toyota counterpart; a group of activists claims that the Galileo's nuclear generators are not sufficiently disaster-proof; an antiabortion activist wants to get the message across that a fetus reacts to poking stimuli, while a pro-choice activist counters with the fact that planaria react to poking stimuli too; and the president wants audiences to believe the deployment of troops to the Middle East is justified by the misdeeds of Saddam Hussein. These examples are pedestrian, and most theorists, significantly those with antirealist tendencies, disdain such pedestrian rhetoric—it is not the stuff of mathematical topology, relativity theory, cosmology, or higher-order predicate calculus. It is certainly awfully banal to be included in anything as prosaic as the hermeneutical space within which resonates the conversational voice of humankind. But pedestrian rhetoric is the stuff out of which the vast majority of rhetorical transactions in our culture emerge and throught which they are conducted.

Of course, it will not suffice simply to dismiss the antirealist position on the grounds that it fails to explore pedestrian rhetoric. In fact, a growing number of serious inquiries into the everyday practices of cultural groups—led by the likes of anthropologist Clifford Geertz, and many buttressed by the philosophical views of antirealists like Rorty—have challenged traditional notions about knowledge and truth. The argument advanced in these works is similar to those made by Thomas Kuhn and his followers—that because different cultural groups (or scientific paradigms) are incommensurate, these groups essentially live in different worlds, with different standards of rationality relative to the cultural practices and traditions of those groups (or paradigms). If claims in favor of incommensurability are borne out, there is no way of discovering a neutral, objective, or rational way in which to explain, compare, and evaluate differing cultural (scientific) perspectives.

But we dispute the antirealist claims that emerge from these studies. While different cultural groups or scientific theories may employ divergent theoretical assumptions, perhaps wholly different vocabularies, it does not follow that we cannot talk about these differences with some degree of objectivity. Precisely this point has been made by Donald Davidson (1980, 1982), echoing views that can be found three decades earlier in the work of Max Black (1952). Davidson points out that, though individuals from various cultures speak different languages, it is always possible to translate one language into another to obtain a measured level of communication. Davidson (1980) concludes that "we cannot make good sense of the idea that there are seriously different total conceptual schemes, or frames of reference, or that there may be radically 'incommensurate' languages." (p. 243). One finds it difficult to imagine, then, that cultural anthropologists or other scholars working from the skeptical framework can consistently or coherently subscribe to the thoroughgoing skepticism advanced among their ranks or in the writings of thinkers like Rorty.

Taken to its logical extreme, the sort of skepticism advanced by the these antirealists would render their work or any discussion of it, in principle, theoretically and methodologically impossible. As Cherwitz and Keith (1989) remind us, scholarly or scientific disputation requires commitment to the necessity of some criterion of real circumstance or meaning in order to decide rhetorical or cultural differences.

Yet, as shown by Rorty and Nelson and Megill, antirealists persist in their claim that commitment to any objective, rational criteria necessarily entails rigid, dictatorial adherence when arguers enter public debate. Such adherence, in their view, leads directly to intolerance of divergent cultural perspectives. But advocating rhetorical realism and standards of rational deliberation does not commit one to this sort of dogmatism and intolerance, not least of all because rhetorical realists are their own worst critics. While making claims to know at least some things objectively, they recognize that any given item of knowledge (cultural or otherwise) may be cast aside tomorrow, as better theories and methods for approximating reality develop.

Still, antirealists might reply that we have not met their primary criticism from the vantage of scientific metatheory, which, in their view, makes the understanding of objective reality an impossible task for two reasons: first, the nature of the subatomic world is such that any observation of this world obscures our understanding of it; second, all observation is value-laden. The first argument seems to assume that there are many extant phenomena that—by their very nature—are not amenable to current scientific understanding; therefore, as Radner and Radner (1982) observe, this view implies that "because there are questions about the universe not answered by current scientific theories, there is a vast domain in which they can cavort unhindered by the restraints of reason" (p. 100). Our position is that, despite the many anomalous phenomena in our universe, there exist numerous truths in which we can reasonably place our confidence. Furthermore, our knowledge of these truths—and all others—must be the product of systematic critical inquiry. On this minimal realist account, Radner and Radner (1982) conclude, the universe may indeed "turn out to be queerer than hitherto imagined . . . but not so queer that arguments and evidence, the mainstays of science, cannot serve as reliable guides" (p. 102).

We pose another objection to the first antirealist argument: while we grant the apparently chaotic nature of subatomic phenomenon, does not this chaotic nature itself reflect a certain objective state of affairs—a reality so complex that its inner structure and workings might well never be elucidated? To admit to this unknowable character of microreality by no means implies that theories of physics are themselves socially, rhetorically constructed, or that our understandings of the objective world are in all cases circumscribed; it only acknowledges certain limitations to our current knowledge and to the present theoretical and methodological tools we employ to achieve an understanding of the physical world.

The second argument—the notion that all scientific arguments and observations are value-laden, filtered as they are through human-made cultural conventions and symbolic structures—can also be met. Admittedly, our knowledge of the world is gathered up through observations, themselves rhetorically influenced. Yet, as philosopher Sean Sayers (1985) notes, it cannot be maintained that value-ladenness necessarily and systematically distorts reality in every instance. To argue such would not only commit one to an inductive fallacy but deny the possibility that human symbolic systems may also *transmit* images. "The image that is transmitted may indeed be a distorted one, but it is nonetheless an image *of the object*, both transmitted and transformed. The object, that is to say, is *refracted* in the image, but not *created* in it" (p. 133).

Another problem with the idea of the value-ladenness of observation is that, as philosopher Roger Trigg (1980) puts it, the antirealists' constant reference to reality being filtered through human consciousness makes it appear as if sciences about people must undergird any understanding of "the world. Yet even these sciences will presumably depend on man's consciousness" (p. 150). A regress results as we move from one layer of consciousness to the next, rendering the most trivial perceptions problematic and cognition itself meaningless. The really important point, argues Trigg, is to remember that observation does not take place in an objectless vacuum. Scientists (and arguers) are constrained in their observations by reality working on us. Frequently, the world acts in ways that are intractable, in ways that cannot be ameliorated through rhetoric or other means. If scientific discovery were as human-centered as some antirealists claim, our scientific discoveries would be more systematically felicitous, that is, more in accord with how we want the world to be constructed, if indeed we could so construct the world.

Real-world rhetoric operates within the context of the pedestrian world, where realism has presumption. As Tipler (1976) notes, "Except for the interior of the atom and for motion at speeds near the speed of light, classical [Newtonian] physics correctly and precisely describes the behavior of the physical world" (p. 2). As rhetorical animals, we live in the macroworld, not the subatomic world. Just as the unfortunate soldier in the foxhole cares not a whit about Heisenberg or Quantum physics when the issue is the parabolic curve inscribed by the mortar shells falling all around, the farmer, the priest, the rabbi, the used-car salesperson, and the politician give not a whit about theoretical arguments attempting to wrench them from the real world of perfectly respectable knowledge-claims—knowledge-claims that frequently build to establish probability, and occasionally even certainty, so that, as Scott argues, we can *act* on our rhetoric.

Those who eschew all forms of truth, certainty, or objectivism have gerrymandered the case against realism, confusing "pedestrian realism" with higher-order/ontological/scientific realisms (Hikins, 1990). An examination of rhetorical praxis and the epistemic judgments that inhere in such praxis will confirm our observation. But what of the ensuing attack against *any* form of realism—the attack based on the grounds that to speak of realism, objectivism, truth, and the like is to invite intolerance? We believe this claim is flawed. Our counterargument relies heavily upon the work of Richard Rorty's former student, philosopher Thomas Russman.

Russman, Realism, and the Doctrine of Tolerance

Russman (1987) makes five main points concerning realism and tolerance. First, theories that deny truth-based epistemologies are subject to as much, if not more, co-optation by abusive ideologues as are truth-based ones. For example, one might argue, as the skeptics do, that if truth cannot be distinguished from falsity one can have no good reasons for persecuting anyone based on race or political or religious beliefs. But in this view, one can have no good reasons for *any* judgment or action, "including the opinion that persecution is wrong or should not be allowed and including any action taken to prevent it" (p. 93). By this reasoning, skepticism in the end favors neither oppression nor tolerance.

Second, simply because one holds to certain objective

convictions, one is not logically or emotionally compelled to impose those convictions on others. Russman (1987) articulates this point when he observes, "It is possible for someone to have strong convictions, religious or otherwise, and to claim to have knowledge that many others lack, without desiring to persecute them" (p. 95). Indeed, one may attack, from a skeptical position or any other, arguments in favor of intolerance. However, it is sufficient for the case against intolerance to merely assault pro-persecution arguments; "a general attack upon all conviction or knowledge is not necessary" (p. 95). We would add that history records instances supporting Russman's contention. For example, in Nazi Germany, where the Nazis held to oppressive and intolerant views, surely members of the German underground embraced truths that not only fostered tolerance but denied the tenets of naziism itself. Critics, then, fail to note that toleration may well be held as an overarching, objective ethical principle, that is, as *objectively true*. When it is, a generalized attack on truth-based epistemologies is an attack against toleration.

Third, one is not logically required to deny all conviction or knowledge as a sufficient condition for toleration. In fact, skepticism does not save one from imposing political oppression, since skeptics are just as likely to reason from the premise that, because there is no way of objectively adjudicating moral/ political/religious disputes, they might as well enforce their own views or even act on whim. Thus, as Russman (1987) concludes, "pro-persecution premises are as available to the skeptic as they are to the convinced [objectivists]. The skeptic too may believe that the unity of the state requires singleness of framework and may persecute to achieve it" (p. 95).

Fourth, Russman (1987) also denies that appeals to history serve to justify the skeptic's cause against objectivism. Though thinkers like Bertrand Russell and Karl Popper have tried to hang such atrocities as the Holocaust on German interpretations of Hegel's metaphysical, objectivist thought, Russman argues that "the interbellum period in Germany had been characterized, not by metaphysical faith, but by skeptical despair. It was the *lack* of conviction and knowledge that made Germany an unresisting vacuum into which Hitler's vision could be poured" (p. 96). George Orwell's hellish depiction of future totalitarian states provides an equally compelling example of the potential political oppression that extreme skepticism and the use of relativistic political language might encourage. We think Russman would agree that convictions concerning the truth of egalitarianism, human justice based on the principle of equal rights for all, and the firm conviction in the falsity of ideologies based on intolerance offer greater protection against persecution than does any general skepticism.

Fifth, Russman (1987) spends much time attacking something that has come to stand at the heart of rhetorical analyses of human knowledge acquisition, namely, convention. It is useful for a moment to recall the theories of intersubjectivity, and of social or rhetorical construction of reality, along with notions like Schrag's (1985) that

> rationality is disseminated into the discursive practices
> that make up the republic of mankind . . . [is seen as] an
> achievement of communicative praxis rather than as a
> preexistent logos that antedates and governs it . . . [and]
> is illustrated in the struggle for agreement and consensus
> on what it is that is made manifest in the hermeneutic of
> everyday life. (p. 172–73)

These references, so pervasive in the literature of rhetorical theory, seem to reflect an unmitigated acceptance of the view that decisions are rendered by appealing to communicative or other conventions. But is a convention-based epistemology a viable alternative to more objectivist views?

What if a society has, by convention, come to embrace intolerance? If there really are no transcultural or transhistorical truths, then every historical instance of intolerance since the dawn of humanity has been the product of convention, just the sort of convention upon which the skeptical champions of toleration urge us to rely. This raises the following question: How does a society choose between competing candidates for a conventionally-held belief? Through a democratic process of majority agreement? Such a choice is certainly democratic and guarantees that those who have agreed on the belief in question have ultimate moral responsibility for its consequences. But, given the premise of no objective grounds for knowledge, such a certification process for belief is still arbitrary, and any notion of individual moral responsibility must then be rendered vacuous. By definition, the decision was a good one because it was democratic. If democratic action becomes the sole criterion of ethical decision making, there simply is no individual moral responsibility.

When convention alone—in the absence of any foundational truths whatsoever—is the arbiter of right and wrong, the phrase "tyranny of the majority" acquires a chilling maleficence. Where does one draw the boundaries encompassing a legitimate consensus-creating culture? In 1939, greater Germany had clearly defined national boundaries and linguistic and cultural tradition as arguments in favor of a claim to autonomous culture. It is not unreasonable to assume, then, that the Holocaust was the issue of convention and consensus. Worse yet, it follows that, if the majority of Germans agreed with Hitler's "final solution," not only was the decision right on the theory that cultures are the arbiter of what is right, but it became more and more right in relation to the growing percentage of the Aryan majority as more and more of its victims perished! Consensus theory must embrace the repugnant consequence that, had Hitler succeeded, his actions would have reached the epitome of moral propriety when the last non-Aryan ceased to exist. Obviously, conviction can lead to intolerance. But, as we have seen, skepticism, even mitigated by democratic conventionalism, fares no better and likely much worse. It should be clear that, to avoid intolerance, tolerant convictions are required, for as Russman (1987) notes, "toleration is based on conviction" (p. 105).

Intellectual Versus Social Tolerance

For rhetorical relativists, truth and knowledge depend upon intersubjective agreement. Yet it is important to realize that, although communities may reach intersubjective agreements that correspond with reality, there are many instances where agreement is mistaken. Parents, for example, often intersubjectively agree to perpetuate beliefs about the existence of fantastical beings, such as Santa Claus. Members of the Flat Earth Society have achieved intersubjective, albeit mistaken, agreement on matters concerning the earth's shape. And we suspect that our skeptical colleagues would agree that the intersubjectively arrived at beliefs of members of the KKK regarding the inferiority of minority groups are incorrect as well. Astronomers and most "reasonable" citizens maintain different views, also arrived at through intersubjective processes.

Whether the product of intolerance or not, if there is really no difference in the epistemic or ontological outcomes of these various intersubjective communities, intersubjectivity must invariably collapse into subjectivism—for the Flat Earth Society's or the KKK's intersubjective agreement is no better or worse than the subjective views of its individual members. As Trigg (1980) observes, in the absence of objectivity, people, whether they operate individually (subjectively) or as whole societies (intersubjectively), effectively decide what will count as true and what will count as false: "Neither allows for the logical possibility that the beliefs of an individual . . . or of a society . . . can be judged by measuring them against anything external to the beliefs" (pp. 3–4).

Of course, it could be maintained that a long history of scientific research has relied upon intersubjective agreement on matters of scientific proof and method. But this agreement is not based upon convention as it is normally defined by antirealists. For this group, conventions are socially created and shared through rhetoric. Yet the conventions of science— its topoi—are agreed upon as standard, canonical criteria for measuring the physical world. This is both because these criteria have consistently provided better descriptions, explanations, and predictions of objective reality and because they buttress the confidence of scientists and laypersons alike, since through their employment we are better able to handle the objective world of which we are a part. Certainly, scientists employ rhetorical topoi and other rhetorical devices to promote their claims or to position their work within the larger scientific tradition; and intersubjective agreement is one result of their rhetorical manipulations. Yet to suggest that this is all scientists do, or that their intersubjective agreements are entirely rhetorical, seems to strain credulity. For example, are we to believe that our well-designed modern airliners remain aloft simply because of the consensual agreement among aeronautical engineers rather than as a result of a comprehension of Bernoulli's principle? Science and scientific agreements are measured against, and imposed on by, the objective state of nature. As J. E. McGuire and Trevor Melia (1989) have recently noted, we must be cautious when examining the social/rhetorical quality of scientific texts: "Science is the result not only of textual representation, but also of extra-textual interventions with nature. . . . Scientific texts, unlike other texts, are not only the product of libraries, but also and notably of laboratories" (p. 97).

Critics of the line of thought we have been pursuing might complain that we beg the question, engaging in specious logic when we argue that scientific convention is more objective than everyday convention because it is based on an objective account of reality. But our argument is not so blatantly circular. In the examples that frame support for our premises, we have contended that reality frequently forces data upon us or compels certain conclusions, and that it does so in a way not comfortably accounted for by any version of constructivism. Were this not so, nothing would stand in the way of our creating a more felicitous world through intersubjective agreement. But the world is not nearly so tractable.

Moreover, to claim that we overlook the subjective—or intersubjective—aspect of scientific inquiry is to suggest that we do not recognize the proper role of the subjective in scientific (or any other) inquiry.[3] It is obvious to us that Galileo's or Newton's conclusions about motion were indeed conclusions drawn from their subjective assessment of the world around them—perhaps in conjunction with the intersubjective contributions of their colleagues. We admit that these thinkers' individual perceptions and impressions gathered and evaluated the data at hand. Yet, as the apocryphal legend of the apple falling on Newton's head illustrates, the individual subjectivities of the researcher are often compelled to apprehend the world the way the world would have it. We take it to be one of the principle purposes of ever-improving scientific research methodologies to facilitate reality's impingement.

Such notions as statistical manipulation, replicability,

and predictability cannot be viewed as just so much more social creation, and the success of so many of our scientific endeavors cannot be viewed in terms of mere pragmatics, except at the risk of looking foolish. Does anyone seriously believe that an airplane crash occurs because the crew and passengers suddenly disagree about Bernouli's principle, or that the orbits of the planets around the sun maintain generally elliptical patterns because somewhere there are astronomers who are consciously entertaining Kepler's laws? On the contrary, the success of science in our century, despite the foibles, miscalculations, and occasional errors by fallible human scientists, can only be accounted for on the premise that our science is about a largely human-independent universe, one that is, to be sure, recalcitrant, but one that nevertheless has yielded itself to innumerable human efforts to come to know it objectively.

Skeptics would no doubt reply that our criticism illustrates one of the very problems skepticism is designed to avoid, namely, an intellectual intolerance—if not plain arrogance—entrenched in claims that some privileged group has attained certain knowledge. But such a reaction is unwarranted, for it fails to distinguish between intellectual tolerance and social tolerance. The Flat Earth Society, American Nazis, the KKK, and radical constructivists have an inalienable right to believe whatever they choose to believe, and so far as their beliefs are harmless, they also have a right to act in accordance with them. (KKK members may, for example, choose to protest peacefully against policies of integration they perceive as inconsistent with their own value system, but they have no right to use coercion or force to overthrow these policies.) Still, that does not preclude both the right and the responsibility of others to engage in debate and, in the case of groups like the KKK, rigorous disputation, in accordance with the accepted standards of scholarly or public argument.

Ultimately, we would argue that in a democratic society, if we are to prevent deleterious ideas like those of the KKK from winning out in "the conversation of mankind," we must also have intellectual confidence that certain of our beliefs, such as the rights of individuals, rest on firm foundations, including correspondence with objective reality. The criteria for the acceptance of scientific conclusions are no different. Our hope is that the objectively grounded beliefs of science—beliefs based on objective, not situational or relativistic, criteria—might translate into public policies that limit the intolerant social practices of groups like the KKK, while at the same time the doctrine of tolerance will prevent their persecution. If we cannot maintain these balances between realism and skepticism, and between tolerance and persecution, the consequences portend not what Rorty called "edification" but intellectual and social chaos, in which it becomes impossible to differentiate between well-founded social policy and arbitrary and capricious whim, between rationally illuminated scientific discovery and quack pseudoscience. In a word, we believe that skeptically sustained, unbridled toleration is indistinguishable from generalized ataxia.

Conclusion

Elsewhere (Hikins & Zagacki, 1988), we have defended a version of "minimal objectivism." On this view, many of our assertions about the world are maximally justified, and we have every reason to suppose they are true; we acknowledge, however, that many of our knowledge-claims are clearly mistaken. Our use of the term *minimal* is important, because it tempers dogmatism with fallibilism, invites critical inquiry, and thus defends against skeptical attacks that objectivist views are dictatorial and the enemies of toleration. More specifically, our argument is that adopting realism as a foundation for a theory of rhetoric will not authorize rhetoric with the power to determine ultimate, objective truth—though like Karl Popper (1962), we hope objectivist inquiries will move in this direction. Our position is measured against the susceptibility of human judgment to error and bias and is not inconsistent with contemporary fallibilist epistemologies. Like Popper, we adhere to another sense of the term *skepticism*, namely, the idea that every knowledge-claim must be subjected to continual testing, and that the only viable method of obtaining objective knowledge is to doubt propositions until something nearly indubitable is found.[4]

Thus, we advocate for rhetorical discourse the presence of particular structural correctives beyond the general fallibilist orientation that meliorates the dangerous movements toward authoritarianism and dogmatism so feared by skeptics. We have in mind what rhetorical scholars like Henry Johnstone (1973) and Douglas Ehninger (1970) refer to as "self-risk," "bilateralism," and "correction." These correctives force us to be cautious about elevating beliefs and opinions to the status of knowledge. They force us to recognize that, when such claims are lifted to the status of knowledge, we must always reflect upon them, continually test the bases, empirical or otherwise, on which they rest, and constantly reevaluate them. In short, in the spirit of Popper, Ehninger, and Johnstone, we must incessantly subject our knowledge-claims to our best rational critique. Hence, by realizing that individuals are privy to limited—though real—aspects of the world, and that rhetors can, and do, present false descriptions of reality, there always remains, for the minimal realist, the requirement to inspect critically the rhetoric of one's own rhetoric and that of others.

The view we have offered in this chapter suggests that tolerance is inherently connected to a theory of ideal argument. In ideal argument, interlocutors seeking to move away from erroneous beliefs and toward veridical beliefs must always maintain a delicately balanced tension between their own commitment to personal, institutional, religious, or otherwise ideological beliefs and the possibility that one or more tenets of these beliefs may be mistaken (see, e.g., Golden, 1987). This is the familiar concept of self-risk. Moreover, from a methodological standpoint, tension must be properly managed by the constraints of the argumentative situation (the freedom to express beliefs in debate without fear of retribution, equal initiative and control of arguments, and decision on issues of public policy by disinterested adjudicators).

Finally, it should not go unnoticed that, for reasons specified in the previous section of this chapter, the absence of these same or similar methodological requirements from the skeptic's or pragmatist's argumentative practice would likely result in the same intolerance these positions decry. This would seem to be another indication that intolerance is a product of certain social/rhetorical practices and is not necessarily or inherently tied to one's epistemology or ontology.

In sum, tolerance need not be sacrificed on any altar other than the altar of intolerance itself. To believe strongly that X is true does not require that one must also believe in intolerance, or that one must believe that everyone else must hold X. Conversely, believing in tolerance does not commit one to abandon all other objective beliefs.

Whether or not we stand at the brink of a new, post-postmodern intellectual era, where the reticence to assent is measured against the given of human achievement in the arts and sciences, is difficult to determine. Historical pronouncements of such breadth are perilous. But we have arrived at a point in history where the sweeping skepticism of the past requires reassessment. Whatever the outcome of this retrospective, the doctrine of tolerance will demand recension as well. Given the egregious misuse of science, technology, and knowledge-claims that has characterized our century, the precise nature of any such recension demands the most careful attention of rhetorical scholars.

Notes

1. By realism, we refer to the collection of theories that proclaim that much of the world does not depend on humans or human perceptual/symbolic capacities for its existence, and furthermore, that humans are capable of knowing at least some aspects of the real world as it is in itself. Here objectivism is used synonymously with realism to mean that many objects of reality exist independent of human beliefs, attitudes, and symbolic interaction. Foundationalism is the view that knowledge-claims can be grounded in one or more world-related judgments in which the knower has confidence, that is, confidence that such judgments correspond to veridical aspects of the world.
2. It should be clear from this explication of Rorty's skeptical position that he is troubled by philosophical realists who claim to have found "a privileged set of descriptions," or a "normal discourse." By seeking to limit "the conversation" by searching for (perhaps even advocating) "objective truth," these thinkers would presumably, in Rorty's view, "deceive" others into be-

lieving that "from now on all discourse could be, or should be, normal discourse" (1979, pp. 370, 377).

3. Zagacki and Keith (in press) and Keith and Zagacki (in press) apply a topical approach to scientific revolutionary rhetoric, demonstrating how scientists manipulate their discoveries for epideictic and personal reasons.

4. We take very seriously indeed the skeptic's charge that, as Popper (1962) puts it, "the theory that truth is manifest not only breeds fanatics—men possessed by the conviction that all those who do not see manifest truth must be possessed by the devil— but it may also lead, though perhaps less directly than does a pessimistic epistemology, to authoritarianism" (p. 8). We recognize, too, Popper's claim that our knowledge has certain limits, that the main source of our ignorance is "the fact that our knowledge can only be finite, while our ignorance must necessarily be infinite" (p. 28).

References

Aronson, J. L. (1984). *A realist philosophy of science.* London: Macmillan.

Black, M. (1952). Linguistic relativity: The views of Benjamin Lee Worth. In *Models and metaphors* (pp. 244–257). Ithaca: Cornell University Press.

Brummett, B. (1976). Some implications of "process" or "intersubjectivity": Postmodern rhetoric. *Philosophy and Rhetoric, 9,* 21–51.

Brummett, B. (1981). A defense of ethical relativism. *Western Journal of Speech Communication, 45,* 286–298.

Carleton, W. M. (1978). What is rhetorical knowledge? A reply to Farrell—and more. *Quarterly Journal of Speech, 64,* 325–335.

Cherwitz, R. A., & Hikins, J. W. (1986). *Communication and knowledge: An investigation in rhetorical epistemology.* Columbia: University of South Carolina Press.

Cherwitz, R. A., & Keith, W. (1989). Objectivity, disagreement, and the rhetoric of inquiry. In H. Simons (Ed.), *Rhetoric in the Human Sciences* (pp. 195–210). Newbury Park, CA.: Sage.

Cranston, M. (1967). Toleration. In P. Edwards (Ed.), *The Encyclopedia of Philosophy* (vols. 7 & 8, pp. 143–146). New York: MacMillan and the Free Press.

Davidson, D. (1980). Psychology as philosophy. In *Essays in actions and events* (pp. 229–239). Oxford: Clarendon Press.

Davidson, D. (1982). On the very idea of a conceptual scheme. In M. Krausz and J. Meiland (Eds.), *Relativism: Cognitive and Moral* (pp. 66–80). Notre Dame: University of Notre Dame Press.

Ehninger, D. (1970). Argument as method: Its nature, its limitations and its uses. *Speech Monographs*, *39*, 102–105.

Fukuyama, F. (1989). The End of History? *The National Interest*, *16*, 1–26.

Golden, J. L. (1987). Douglas Ehninger's philosophy of argument. *Argumentation*, *1*, 23–40.

Grayling, A. C. (1985). *The refutation of skepticism*. LaSalle, IL: Open Court.

Harré, R. (1986). *Varieties of realism: A rationale for the natural sciences*. Oxford: Basil Blackwell.

Hikins, J. W. (1990). Realism and its implications for rhetorical theory. In Richard A. Cherwitz (Ed.), *Rhetoric and Philosophy* (pp. 21–77). Hillsdale, N.J.: Lawrence Erlbaum Associates.

Hikins, J. W., & Zagacki, K. S. (1988). Rhetoric, philosophy, and objectivism: An attenuation of the claims of the rhetoric of inquiry. *Quarterly Journal of Speech*, *74*, 201–228.

Johnstone, H. L., Jr. (1973). Rationality and rhetoric in philosophy. *Quarterly Journal of Speech*, *59*, 381–389.

Keith, W., & Zagacki, K. S. (in press). Rhetoric and paradox in scientific revolutions. *Southern Journal of Speech Communication*.

Kelley, D. (1986). *The evidence of the senses: A realist theory of perception*. Baton Rouge: Louisiana State University Press.

McGuire, J. E., & Melia, T. (1989). Some cautionary strictures on the writing of the rhetoric of science. *Rhetorica*, *7*, 87–99.

Nelson, J. S., & Megill, A. (1986). Rhetoric of inquiry: Projects and prospects. *Quarterly Journal of Speech*, *72*, 23.

Orr, C. J. (1978). How shall we say: "Reality is socially constructed through communication?" *Central States Speech Journal*, *29*, 263–274.

Popper, K. R. (1962). *Conjectures and refutations*. New York: Basic.

Radner, D., & Radner, M. (1982). *Science and unreason*. Belont, CA: Wadsworth.

Rorty, R. (1979). *Philosophy and the mirror of nature*. Princeton: Princeton University Press.

Rorty, R. (1982). *Consequences of pragmatism: Essays 1972–1980*. Minneapolis: University of Minnesota Press.

Rorty, R. (1987). Science as solidarity. In J. Nelson and A. Megill (Eds.), *The rhetoric of the human sciences* (pp. 38–51). Madison: University of Wisconsin Press.

Rorty, R. (1988, April 4). That old-time philosophy. *New Republic*, pp. 28–33.

Russman, T. A. (1987). *A prospectus for the triumph of realism*. Macon: Mercer University Press.

Sayers, S. (1985). *Reality and reason: Dialectic and the theory of knowledge.* Oxford: Basil Blackwell.

Schrag, C. O. (1985). Rhetoric resituated at the end of philosophy. *Quarterly Journal of Speech, 71*(1), 164–174.

Scott, R. L. (1967). On viewing rhetoric as epistemic. *Central States Speech Journal, 18,* 9–17.

Scott, R. L. (1976). On viewing rhetoric as epistemic: Ten years later. *Central States Speech Journal, 27,* 258–266.

Scott, R. L. (1990). Epistemic rhetoric and criticism: Where Barry Brummett goes wrong. *Quarterly Journal of Speech, 76,* 300–303.

Tipler, P. (1976). *Physics.* New York: Worth.

Toulmin, S. E. (1958). *The uses of argument.* Cambridge: Cambridge University Press.

Trigg, R. (1980). *Reality at risk,* Brighton, England: The Harvester.

Vision, G. (1988). *Modern anti-realism and manufactured truth.* New York: Routledge.

Zagacki, K. S., & Keith, W. (1992). Rhetoric, topoi, and scientific revolutions. *Philosophy and Rhetoric, 25,* 59–78.

Communication Studies and Philosophy

Convergence Without Coincidence

CALVIN O. SCHRAG AND DAVID JAMES MILLER

CONVERGENCE IS THE COMING TOGETHER OF THAT which is in some sense different. This coming together—at least as we propose to articulate it—is not, however, a coincidence. Convergence presupposes something that makes a difference, something that comes between that which comes together. In the convergence of communication studies and philosophy, what comes between them? What is it that makes a difference?

As the title indicates, we adopt the standpoint that something comes between the disciplines, something that makes a difference; and further, given this, we propose that the relation established in, and by, the convergence of communication studies and philosophy should be one of convergence without coincidence. Our position is that communicative praxis comes between the disciplines, and that it is by means of the transversal rationality found within it that communicative praxis can make a difference (see Schrag, 1986; Miller, 1987).

In part, we will write of differences in the ongoing positioning and counterpositioning of the disciplines, differences established, maintained, and transformed by disciplinary

126

practices. We will deal with these practices in terms of their horizontal and vertical axes. As we see it, the horizontal is an axis of differentiation constituted through practices of indifference and exclusion. The vertical, by contrast, is an axis of differentiation established through hegemonic practices, practices of hierarchy and domination. These axes are articulated in such a way that they produce an ongoing nexus of coordinates that position and counterposition the disciplines, or better their representatives, in a "proper" and relative order.

We will also write of making a difference in these disciplinary differences. We will set the possibilities of communicative praxis against the ongoing resolution of these possibilities in disciplinary coordination. With respect to the convergence of communication studies and philosophy, we seek to free communicative praxis from its bondage to disciplinary practices. We seek an emergent relation between the disciplines, a relation articulated not in terms of the horizontal and vertical rationalities of disciplinary practices but according to the tranversal rationality of communicative praxis. In seeking to establish this relation, we seek to contest the privilege afforded the horizontal and vertical rationalities of disciplinary practices, in favor of affording a privilege to the transversal rationality of communicative praxis.

Much falls within the purview of differences between communication studies and philosophy. In the current social, political, and economic organization of our colleges and universities, communication studies and philosophy mark out the horizontal boundaries of particular institutional structures.

There are differences within these more encompassing fields as well as between them. Rhetoric and public communication, technical communication, interpersonal communication, organizational communication, mass communication, and cultural studies, for example, are different areas within communication studies. In philosophy, too, there are standard divisions of both philosophical content and skills—for example, logic (both formal and informal), epistemology, metaphysics, value theory (ethics and aesthetics), and the history of philosophy. The placement of these different areas within the two fields, or on their fringes, follows no clearly defined institutional rules. Rhetoric, for example, is sometimes taught in departments of English and other times installed as a separate department. It is not uncommon for formal logic to be taught in departments of mathematics. And various philosophies (of science, language, society, religion, politics, etc.) forge sundry alliances with their cognate disciplines.

The representatives of these various departments, fields, areas, and subareas coexist in our modern day colleges and universities in varying degrees of alliance and conflict or, more often than not, simply exist alongside one another. These varying degrees of difference and indifference mark out the horizontal boundaries of the disciplines—boundaries that, as we have learned from such thinkers as Philippe Aries and Michel Foucault, are at least in part a consequence of the broader emergence of disciplinary practices. These disciplinary practices both articulate and are articulated within sociohistorical regimes of knowledge, where knowledge is put in the service of power and where power is put in the service of knowledge.[1]

The struggles of dominance in, and through, these practices, and the contestations that attend them, mark out the vertical boundaries largely within, but at times across, the disciplines. We find the disciplinary specificities of communication studies and philosophy in the shifting hegemonies and counterhegemonies that constitute this verticality—in the struggles over the constitution of textual canons, over topoi and modes of discourse, over genres of analysis, and over objects of study.[2] There is a plethora of vertical differences constituted by the disciplinary practices in these regimes of knowledge.

An analysis of the constitution and effects of these vertical differences as well as of the horizontal differences and indifferences we mentioned above constitutes a special task. Though exceeding the constraints of the present discussion, this task will be unavoidable in the end, if we are to discern, articulate, and disclose the convergence of communication studies and philosophy.

Surely horizontal and vertical differences come between communication studies and philosophy, but do they constitute what lies between them, or have we, in directing our attention to the differences *of* communication studies and philosophy, left what lies *between* them unexamined? This seems to be the case in the current and proliferating discussions on the topic. It would seem to be particularly so when the genre problem provides the locus of the discussion, as in the much discussed philosophical dispute between Jürgen Habermas and Jacques Derrida.

In the Habermas-Derrida debate, the issue is focused somewhat more specifically on the logical capacities of philosophy versus the creative capacities of rhetoric. Habermas (1987) indicts Derrida for a "leveling of the genres" that distinguish philosophy from rhetoric and then mounts an argument for the integrity and autonomy of each. Derrida, says Habermas, "wants to expand the sovereignty of rhetoric over the realm of the logical in order to solve the problem confronting the totalizing critique of reason" (p. 181). However, in doing so, Habermas claims, Derrida fails to recognize the distinction between "problem-solving capacities" and "capacities for world-disclosure" (p. 207). It is only the latter, Habermas would have us believe, that supplies the resources for rhetoric. Rhetoric is able to disclose novel ways of using language, or indeed seeing the world, but it lacks the capacities for solving problems in the domain of prosaic, innerworldly communication, where we carry on the business of our everyday affairs.

Derrida, himself (1982, p. 246), appears ready to embrace the collapse of philosophy into rhetoric, in such a manner that the "flowers of rhetoric" are seen to bloom in every philosophical backyard. From Derrida's point of view, the main rhetorical ingredient in the husbandry of philosophy is metaphoricity. Metaphor invades the entire domain of philosophy and transforms every *philosopheme* into a metaphorical trope. Although distinctions between philosophy and rhetoric might indeed be offered, these distinctions, themselves, upon careful inspection, turn out to be rhetorical in the end. There is, thus, nothing outside the rhetorical text.

Although we do not wish to contextualize our standpoint and define our position against the backdrop of the recent Habermas-Derrida difference (principally because we think that the question of genre distinctions should not be granted a priority in dealing with the philosophy-rhetoric relationship), an issue that comes to the fore in this dispute—the role of rationality in philosophical and rhetorical enterprises—merits particular attention. It is not surprising that rationality should surface as the principle bugbear in the dispute. Derrida is concerned to undermine the logocentric claims of reason. Habermas sketches a relationship of polar tension between the two enterprises, allowing each a degree of autonomy regulated by the requirements of what he calls "communicative reason." The issue of rationality is thus brought to the foreground, as it eventually must be.

Another prominent contemporary philosopher preoccupied with the issue of rhetoric, Hans Blumenberg (1987), intensifies our awareness of the need to come to grips with the issue of rationality, when he invites us "to see in it (rhetoric) a form of rationality itself" (p. 452). The rationality that Blumenberg discerns as being at issue in the rhetorical enterprise is no longer determined by the logocentric principle of sufficient reason but is rather a rationality that suffers the contingencies of insufficient reason (*principium rationis insufficientis*). This doxastic principle of insufficient reason is a quite natural consequence of Blumenberg's anthropological doctrine of the self as "a creature deficient in essential respects" (p. 447). This recognition of a built-in insufficiency of reason issuing from the inescapable limitations and deficiencies that make up the human condition requires a refiguration of the claims of reason as they operate in the rhetorical situation.

Unfortunately, Blumenberg leaves suspended the issue of the workings of this finite and fractured rationality within the interface of rhetoric and philosophy. Indeed, the method for addressing this issue remains undecided; and Blumenberg's indicators or pointers are not all that helpful.[3] Yet, his redefinition of the texture and role of rationality in rhetoric is at once imaginative and promising, and it provides certain directions for our own efforts to situate rhetoric vis-à-vis its alliance with philosophy.[4]

We will address these issues by developing a position—a thought-experiment, if you will—that places rationality between philosophy and rhetoric and defines the relationship between the two as one of convergence without coincidence. This will entail certain refigurations in the traditional configurations of philosophy and rhetoric alike. Philosophy will no longer be facilely defined as the guardian of reason, and *mutatis mutandis* rhetoric will no longer be viewed as being in want of the resources of reason, needing to import rationality from the outside. The economy of philosophy exporting reason/truth and importing figures of speech, strategies of persuasion, and means of communication from rhetoric is ruptured, as is its inverse. Our position is that reason and truth, on the one hand, and tropes of discourse and communicative practices, on the other, come between, and lie across, philosophy and rhetoric. The question is, In what sense do they come between, and lie across, these disciplines? To address this question requires a topological shift—a move away from preoccupations with the horizontal and vertical differences that comprise the disciplinization and institutionalization of communication studies and philosophy toward the space of communicative praxis in which they are always already situated.

The disciplinization of communication studies and philosophy, which proceeds along horizontal and vertical axes, is itself an effect of communicative praxis. Communicative praxis is older than both the communication that determines the agenda of communication studies and the communication that informs the philosophical enterprise. Both have tended to congeal—however understandably—in *post festum* analysis (be it, for example, in a programmatic of information exchange or in that of the translation and exchange of propositions).

Within the space of communicative praxis is the between in which are found the resources of a transversal rationality that extends across horizontal and vertical differences. The peculiarity of this space between resides in its occasioning of tendencies toward horizontality and verticality. It is the locality for the play of sameness with otherness, of similarity with difference, whence horizontal and vertical determinations arise. However, the transversal rationality we are seeking to exhibit not only occasions these tendencies but, because it occasions these tendencies, has the resources to disrupt them as well. And it can do so by taking hold of this play of sameness with otherness, of similarity with difference, at the heart of communicative praxis. It is precisely the possibilities of transversal rationality that have been occluded in the horizontal and vertical rationalities at work in discipline formation. This rationality takes shape in communicative praxis as a matrice of three coefficients: involved discernment, engaged articulation, and encountered disclosure.

Involved discernment is the evaluative coefficient of communicative praxis, the valuation of difference and similarity in practice. Turning to involved discernment entails deconstructing classical and modern theories of judgment and critique. These theories, with their metaphysical or epistemological guarantees of certainty, revolve around the postulation of an isolated subject, the demand for situationally independent, rule-governed procedures, and the legislation of a priori criteria. In contrast to these theories, involved discernment is communal (its epistemology is social rather than individual), it proceeds situationally, and it involves the local determination of criteria in the situated play of possibilities for convergence and divergence.[5] As the evaluative coefficient of communicative praxis, involved discernment entails both the responsiveness of involvement and the distantiation of discernment. In the play of similarities and differences, this responsive distantiation is the ongoing determination of responsibility in practice.

Engaged articulation is the performative coefficient of communicative praxis, the enactment of difference and similarity in practice. Turning to engaged articulation entails deconstructing the classical doctrine of the Logos. The Logos doctrine of ancient and medieval thought placed the resources of reason on the hither side of history. Guided by a metaphysics of presence, the Logos was assigned an ahistorical position and became the foundation for a knowledge of universals untainted by historical becoming. The Word, alleged to be present from the beginning, was elevated to the status of a cosmological principle. By contrast, engaged articulation remains attentive to the historical conditioning of reason and refigures the Logos as a gathering of the performative accomplishments of mundane practices. The claims of reason are transversal rather than universal. The Logos as Word and Deed articulates and is articulated in the conjunctures and disjunctures of our sociohistorical practices.[6]

As the performative coefficient of communicative praxis,

engaged articulation entails both the relationality of engagement and the perspectivity of articulation. In the situated play
of possibilities, marking out similarities and differences, this
relational perspectivity is the ongoing specificity of interaction
in discursive and nondiscursive practice.[7] In its enactment,
this relational perspectivity may be conflictual, cooperative,
or consensual. If we abandon the reified notion of consensus
and its requirement of homogeneity, it becomes clear that not
only conflict but cooperation and consent are the accomplishment of a similarity-within-difference (or a difference-within-
similarity) that configures our discursive and nondiscursive
practices. Conflict, cooperation, and consent preclude neither
similarities nor differences; indeed, they presuppose them.

Encountered disclosure is the pathetic (in the Greek
sense of *pathos*) coefficient of communicative praxis, the accomplishment and discovery of difference and similarity in
practice. Turning to encountered disclosure entails deconstructing recent doctrines of semiological, textual, and narrato-
logical closure. It disrupts these totalizations, forcing us beyond the system of signs, outside the bonds of textuality, and
out of the difficulties of narrativity. It effects a return to our
quotidian experience, determining our discursive and nondiscursive practices as elicited by, and being about, something,
as solicited by, and being with, someone. Thus, encountered
disclosure functions as the counterthrust to the closure of our
discursive and nondiscursive practices. This coefficient links
up with, and reinforces, the coefficient of engaged articulation, fulfilling reference and dislodging meaning (or sense)
from its entrapment in a system of signs, solidified habits, and
congealed institutions. As the pathetic coefficient of communicative praxis, encountered disclosure entails both the predica-
tive and prepredicative intentionality of encounter and the
incursion of that which is disclosed. In the situated play of
similarities and differences, this incursion into intentionality
is the ongoing pathos of alterity in practice.

The concept, figure, or metaphor of transversality is particularly well suited to our interdisciplinary interests. Its usage
has been installed in a variety of disciplines. In mathematics,
specifically topology, transversality is defined as the intersecting of a system of lines or surfaces that do not achieve

coincidence. Physics employs the grammar of transversality in its determination of transversal mass as the ratio of accelerating forces. In physiology, the notion is utilized to explain the interweaving of a band of fibres. In anatomy, a vertebra is described as a transversal lateral arrangement.

The polysemy of transversality is also at play in philosophy and the human sciences. In his attack on the doctrine of the transcendental ego, Jean-Paul Sartre (1937, p. 39) writes of "a play of 'transversal' intentionalities which are concrete and real retentions of past consciousnesses." Felix Guatarri (1984, p. 18), in seeking to render an account of the dynamics of the decision-making process in administering a psychiatric hospital, writes of a "transversality in the group," in which the degree of transversality achieved depends upon the effectiveness of dialogue across institutional and social roles as well as the enclaves of authority that make up hospital governance. Gilles Deleuze (1972, pp. 149–150) writes of a "transversal dimension" in which a multiplicity of viewpoints communicate such that a unity without unification, a whole without totality, is effected. In specifying antiauthoritarian struggles in confrontations of the subject and power, Michel Foucault (1982, p. 211) writes of a "'transversal' struggle" that crosses political/economic lines and forms of government. At issue in this polysemic play of transversality is the recognition of the play of differences and similarities, of physical, psychological, and social lines of force—touching, meeting, intersecting, but not in such a manner as to congeal into coincidence.

Our position is that the coefficients of communicative praxis—involved discernment, engaged articulation, and encountered disclosure—are transversal to the horizontal and vertical differences that separate communication studies from philosophy. The transversal rationality of communicative praxis—the transversal Logos if you will—comes between, extends across, and intersects the two disciplines, allowing for and facilitating a convergence without coincidence.[8] The transversal rationality of communicative praxis extends across the disciplines but does not become sedimented and exhausted within either of them. Cutting across their boundaries, it does not achieve coincidence with any horizontal, institutional form or with any disciplinary configuration of vertical differences. This comprises, against the horizontal and vertical rationalities of disciplinary practices, the antihege-monic dynamics of transversal rationality. Communicative praxis comes between the disciplines; the transversal rational-ity of communicative praxis can make a difference.

Although unable to supply the guarantees of founda-tional criteria for decision-making and evaluation in the public forum, transversal rationality provides reasons for selecting certain beliefs and practices because they are preferable to others. Admittedly, criteria for such selection cannot be deter-mined in advance. Neither their source nor their sanction exists a priori. They emerge from a collaborative discernment of the linkages and contrasts of accepted beliefs and practices with competing beliefs that are attendant to similar states of affairs.

In the course of our discussion, it will have become evident to the reader that our use of the concept of transver-sality trades heavily on the continued use of horizontality and verticality. We have suggested that the transversal rationality that takes shape in communicative praxis is a way of refiguring the horizontal and vertical rationalities of our disciplinary practices.

Questions may arise as to the peculiar status of hori-zontal, vertical, and transversal rationalities, as well as to that of the coefficients by means of which we characterized the latter. Are they to be viewed in some manner as givens, quasi-ontological structures presupposed in every practice and ev-ery claim of reason, or are they themselves historically spe-cific—possibly peculiar to Western modes of thought? These are admittedly important and unavoidable questions that need to be addressed within the more encompassing inquiry into possible ontological constraints on the historical specificities of communicative praxis. Our current project, however, has taken a somewhat narrower path, interrogating the state of affairs in which communication studies and philosophy find themselves in our colleges and universities in the latter part of the twentieth century.[9]

In the situation of our time, tendencies toward horizontal multiplicity and heterogeneity, on the one hand, and vertical regimentation, on the other hand, are very much in evidence.

In response to this state of affairs, we have explored the dynamics of a rationality that plays across the disciplines of communication studies and philosophy, and that plays in such a manner that it cannot become solidified in either one of them. We have exhibited this rationality as the transversal rationality that takes shape in communicative praxis, a rationality that proceeds by dint of the coefficients of involved discernment, engaged articulation, and encountered disclosure. Our thesis has been that this transversal rationality makes possible the convergence of communication studies and philosophy without coincidence, that this possibility takes shape in communicative praxis, and that communicative praxis makes a difference.

Notes

1. Aries (1962) is concerned with describing the constitution of adolescence in the progressive institutionalization of surveillance and punishment in the education of children, institutionalization that began in the waning years of the middle ages (see especially his chapter on "The Progressive Discipline"). For Foucault this knowledge/power nexus has come to regulate the installation of disciplinary practices not only within the organizational structure of the academy but also within the wider economy of sociohistorical institutionalization. Foucault (1965, 1970, 1973, 1977, 1985, 1986) was concerned with explaining the play of power in the constitution of the discourse of the human sciences; he sought to illustrate the motivations and strategies for control, domination, surveillance, and correction in the history of the clinic, the asylum, the prison, and patterns of sexuality.

2. The grammar of *hegemony* requires some clarification at this juncture. In the original Greek usage, from which the lexeme derives, *hegemony* simply meant "leadership." This meaning of the term needs to be distinguished from subsequent and wholly negative determinations. Following Gramsci (1971; see also Mouffe, 1979, pp. 168–204), we understand hegemony, or better, the struggle for hegemony, as the struggle of a particular group or alliance to constitute an allied ensemble of groups—to articulate a collective will for the purposes of directing that ensemble, while at the same time dominating antagonistic or counterhegemonic

groups. It is a struggle for, and a struggle on, the terrain of "common sense."

3. For example, to say that "rhetoric teaches us to recognize rhetoric, but it does not teach us to legitimate it" (Blumenberg, 1987, p. 448) does little more than reintroduce the problem at another level.

4. Likewise, we find the explorations of Gary Madison on this issue suggestive. Madison (1988, p. 164), reflecting and writing in the spirit of Vico, who had already given notice of his dissatisfaction with the modernist bifurcation of reason and rhetoric, puts matters such that the proper approach is one that "does not simply seek to substitute 'rhetoric' for 'philosophy'; it seeks rather to emphasize the rhetorical nature of philosophy and the philosophical status of rhetoric."

5. One can provide an etymological clarification of criterion as discernment by tracing the notion back to the Greek concept, and use, of *krínō*. In its original Greek usage, *krínō* gathers the praxis-oriented senses of separating, putting asunder, distinguishing, picking out, choosing, deciding, judging, and assessing. From this derives the Latin *cerno* and eventually the English *discern*. *Cerno* fraternizes with the Latin *certo*, and *discern* finds its chief cognate in *certainty*, setting the stage to theoretically construe critique as legitimation by appealing to criteria that ensure certainty. See Miller, 1987, p. 109.

6. Perhaps Plato and Aristotle already gave notice of the performance of reason in the notions of "giving an account" (*lógon didōnai*) and of "pointing out or exhibiting something" (*deloūn*). These notions may indeed comprise efforts on the part of Plato and Aristotle to flesh out a sense of *logos* as reason linked to performance and accomplishment, a sense that would precede the hypostatization of *logos* to the Logos in Platonism and Aristotelianism.

7. This notion of articulation has already received some attention in the rhetorical literature. Michael Hyde and Craig Smith (1979, pp. 347–348), moving out from Heidegger, have mapped the terrain of rhetoric in such a manner that "the primordial function of rhetoric" is viewed as "making known" the patterns of intersubjectivity as they are articulated within the dynamics of a rhetor/interlocutor engagement.

8. However, the transversal Logos is not a preexistent Logos that supplies criteria, rules, and general epistemic principles in advance. Such is the case with the criteriological, theoretico-epistemological notion of rationality that transversal rationality pur-

ports to subvert. Transversal rationality is neither a preexisting, untrammeled essence nor an a priori condition for thought and action. While the practice of transversal rationality leaves its inscription on the disciplines, it is important to realize that the disciplines also leave their inscription on it. One cannot step outside the history of the two disciplines. Each discipline has its own knowledge regimes: textual cannons, topoi and modes of discourse, genres of analysis, and objects of study.

9. The strategies of transversal rationality are applicable to a variety of other configurations of social and institutional practices. Foremost among them would be situations of negotiation in organizational disputes, such as labor and management conflict; efforts toward the establishment of policy in managing religious-ecclesiastical diversity; initiatives for curriculum reform in the university; and procedures for decision making on the local, national, and international level. The utility of the transversal model/metaphor for addressing these regions of concern remains to be explored and will need to be done with attentiveness to the specificities within each of these regions. For a concentrated discussion of the transversal working of reason, see Schrag, 1989.

References

Aries, P. (1962). *Centuries of childhood: A social history of family life* (R. Baldick, Trans.). New York: Alfred A. Knopf. (Original work published 1960.)

Blumenberg, H. (1987). An anthropological approach to the contemporary significance of rhetoric (R. M. Wallace, Trans.). In K. Baynes, J. Bohman, & T. McCarthy (Eds.), *After philosophy: End or transformation?* (pp. 429–458). Cambridge: MIT Press. (Original work published 1971.)

Deleuze, G. (1972). *Proust and signs* (R. Howard, Trans.). New York: George Braziller. (Original work published 1964.)

Derrida, J. (1982). White mythology: Metaphor in the text of philosophy (A. Bass, Trans.). In *Margins of philosophy* (pp. 207–272). Chicago: University of Chicago Press. (Original work published 1972.)

Foucault, M. (1965). *Madness and civilization* (R. Howard, Trans.). New York: Random House. (Original work published 1961.)

Foucault, M. (1970). *The order of things: An archaeology of the human sciences*. New York: Random House. (Original work published 1966.)

Communication Studies and Philosophy

Foucault, M. (1973). *Birth of the clinic: An archaeology of medical perception* (A. M. Sheridan Smith, Trans.). New York: Random House. (Original work published 1963.)

Foucault, M. (1977). *Discipline and punish*. (A. Sheridan, Trans.). New York: Random House. (Original work published 1975.)

Foucault, M. (1982). The subject and power (L. Sawyer, Trans.). In H. Dreyfus & P. Rabinow (Eds.), *Michel Foucault: Beyond structuralism and hermeneutics* (pp. 216–226). Chicago: University of Chicago Press.

Foucault, M. (1985). *The history of sexuality: Vol. 2. The use of pleasure* (R. Hurley, Trans.). New York: Pantheon. (Original work published 1984.)

Foucault, M. (1986). *The history of sexuality: Vol. 3. The care of the self* (R. Hurley, Trans.). New York: Vintage. (Original work published 1984.)

Gramsci, A. (1971). *Selections from the prison notebooks* (Q. Hoare and G. N. Smith, Trans.). New York: International Publishers.

Guattari, F. (1984). *Molecular revolution: Psychiatry and politics* (R. Sheed, Trans.). New York: Farrar, Straus & Giroux.

Habermas, J. (1987). *The philosophical discourse of modernity* (F. Lawrence, Trans.). Cambridge: MIT Press. (Original work published 1985.)

Hyde, M., & Smith, C. R. (1979). Hermeneutics and rhetoric: A seen but unobserved relationship. *Quarterly Journal of Speech, 65,* 347–363.

Madison, G. (1988). *The hermeneutics of postmodernity: Figures and themes.* Bloomington: Indiana University Press.

Miller, D. J. (1987). Immodest interventions: A response to Michael J. Hyde concerning Calvin O. Schrag's *Communicative praxis and the space of subjectivity. Phenomenological Inquiry: A Review of Philosophical Ideas and Trends, 11,* 108–114.

Mouffe, C. (1979). Hegemony and ideology in Gramsci (D. Derime, Trans.). In C. Mouffe (Ed.), *Gramsci and Marxist theory.* (pp. 168–204). London: Routledge and Kegan Paul.

Sartre, J. P. (1937). *The transcendence of the ego* (F. Williams & R. Kirkpatrick, Trans.). New York: Farrar, Straus & Giroux. (Original work published 1936.)

Schrag, C. O. (1986). *Communicative praxis and the space of subjectivity.* Bloomington: Indiana University Press.

Schrag, C. O. (1989). Rationality between modernity and postmodernity. In S. K. White, (Ed.), *Life-world and politics: Between modernity and postmodernity.* Notre Dame: University of Notre Dame.

The Algebra of History
Merleau-Ponty and Foucault on the Rhetoric of the Person

RICHARD L. LANIGAN

"PHILOSOPHY IS NOT AN ILLUSION. IT IS THE ALGEBRA of history" (Merleau-Ponty, 1963, p. 52). With this epigrammatical rhetoric of the aphorism found in Maurice Merleau-Ponty's *Éloge de la Philosophie*, we encounter at once the ambiguity of philosophical rhetoric binding the discourse of a story with the narrative of history, expression with perception, structure with form, and semiology with phenomenology (Lanigan, 1991b). Or as Michel Foucault (1972, p. 224) remarks with his philosophical proposition in *L'Ordre du discours* (a title whose translation is surely "Rhetoric"), "Disciplines constitute a system of control in the production of discourse, fixing its limits through the action of identity taking the form of a permanent reactivation of the rules" (see Lanigan 1991a). In both cases, we are witness to the ontological rhetoric of the person. Rather than a mere literary genre of inscription in the rhetorical tradition of French Science (Paul, 1980), the inaugural lectures given by Maurice Merleau-Ponty and Michel Foucault constitute a reversible rhetoric of the signifying (Sr) and signified (Sd) discourse of orality. The discourse is, indeed, the phenomenology of the lived-world, a philosophy of signs we call existence (*ekstasis*).

I propose to illustrate this eidetic thesis by explicating,

on a close reading and textual viewing, the rhetorical structure and form of the inaugural lectures given at the Collège de France by Merleau-Ponty and Foucault. In this discursive analysis, the phenomenology of communication emerges as the dialectical voices of *l'histoire* and *discours*.[1] In each lecture, there is the living presence of an active oral voice in which the self tells an existential story of the subject; there is the ontology of speech speaking (*parole parlante*). Between each lecture, there is the lived absence constituting a passive voice in which the anonymous other narrates an essential history; there is the ontological alterity of speech spoken (*parole parlée*). As Merleau-Ponty (1963, pp. 57–58; see Lanigan 1977, 1991b) summarizes, "Philosophy turns toward the anonymous symbolic activity from which we emerge, and towards the personal discourse which develops in us, and which, indeed, we are."

Thus, in his inaugural discourse, Merleau-Ponty (1963, p. 53) gives the ontology of speech speaking a rhetorical form by naming it with a classical figure of speech: prosopopoeia.[2] But, Merleau-Ponty does not define this rhetorical trope for reuse in the future (the goal of Aristotle's deliberative, political rhetoric). It remains a pure signifying praxis where personae, the silent voices of the past (Aristotle's forensic or judicial rhetoric), intersect with the disciplines they represent in the present (Aristotle's epideictic, or evaluative, rhetoric). For Merleau-Ponty, the *l'histoire* of philosophy is the *story* of the philosopher: philosophy as existential is rhetoric as phenomenological (Lanigan, in press).

With the fidelity of a student to his teacher, Foucault, in his inaugural lecture, completes the dialectic of reversibility in the ongoing discourse of the two inaugurals. In his opening words, he characterizes his speaking as a nameless voice, thereby defining the trope of prosopopoeia by designation. Yet, he neither names nor judges it! In fact, prosopopoeia is an imaginary or absent persona represented as the present oral speaking voice of the person. An excellent example of prosopopoeia is the opening line of the novel *David Copperfield* by Charles Dickens, which reads, simply, "I am born." Prosopopoeia is a discourse that creates within the narrative per se a new narrative voice that unexpectedly judges the person by replacing the narrative function with his or her own voice as lived. The self of discourse replaces the subject of narrative and, thereby, *represents* the person. For Foucault, this trope of speech (not language!) becomes a pure rhetorical praxis of the signified, where the disciplines of the past (knowledge or *connaissance*) intersect with the discursive voice of consciousness, the voice that can speak in future (power or *savior*), and the voice of the subject in the present (person or *sujet*). For Foucault, who completes the dialectical reversibility of Merleau-Ponty's thematic, the *l'histoire* of the philosopher is the *story* of the philosophy: philosophy as phenomenological is rhetoric as existential.

Persona for Merleau-Ponty and person for Foucault, as the representations of prosopopoeia in discourse, become the essential reversibility, the *chiasm*, that is the humane lived-world of the human, where persona/person is subject/subjected.[3] Vincent Descombes (1980, p. 27; see 1986) makes the point explicit: "The 'end of history' [*l'histoire*] is none other than the translation into figural and narrative language [*langage*] of what in the language of philosophy is known as absolute knowledge." Let us listen to the *lector in fabula*, the ontological strategy of philosophy as a discourse emergent respectively in the two rhetorical lectures that inaugurate philosophy.[4]

Merleau-Ponty's Inaugural: Eulogy to Philosophy

Remembering the traditional characterization of Merleau-Ponty as the philosopher of ambiguity, we must abandon the usual translation of his inaugural lecture title. To formulate *Éloge de le Philosophie* as "In Praise of Philosophy" is to corrupt the "good ambiguity" of discourse, the prosopopoeia, that Merleau-Ponty (1963) intends. Within the context of classical literature and the trivium (grammar, logic, and rhetoric) that both Merleau-Ponty and Foucault studied as French lycée students, we must understand and take the practice of "*éloge*" in its classical meaning as a rhetorical "eulogy".[5]

The eulogy is a part of what Aristotle in his *Rhetoric* (1358b5) calls epideictic oratory, in which the goal of the speaker is respectively to praise (confirm) a persona or blame (condemn) a person. In the case of praise, the orator speaks positively of the persona, because the person is a subject absent to the discourse, either by death or exile (the discursive ontology of simile). By counterpoint, the negative speech of blame is directed to the person, who is present to the discourse, because the persona in its immorality must remain subjected to absence, either by death or exile (the discursive ontology of irony). Thus in Merleau-Ponty's lecture, we as listeners are confronted with a discourse that offers to both praise and blame, thereby confirming and condemning philosophy in itself and for itself (the discursive ontology of synecdoche). We are asked to do both through the discursive agent of the person, who is the philosopher, and the agency of the persona, who is the sophist. Merleau-Ponty is concerned with the ontological orality of the philosopher, just as Foucault is concerned with the oral ontology of the sophist. Both are a concern in the discourse of the agent provocateur.

It will be helpful at this point to make a brief relational connection with the work of one of Husserl's students, Roman Jakobson. In his model of communicology (human communication), Jakobson phenomenologically corrects Saussure's structural semiotics by making the signifying (Sr) and signified (Sd) elements of the sign function according to an analogue logic of combination as opposed to a digital logic of exclusion (Holenstein, 1976, p. 138). According to Holenstein (1976, p. 2), this empirical success is due largely to Jakobson's eidetic use of the theory of parts and wholes in Husserl's (1970) *Logical Investigations.* In Jakobson's model of discourse, language operates in a rhetorical or tropic modality (called "poetic function") of paradigmatic and syntagmatic axes that respectively are reversible.

In brief, paradigmatic items in a process called "selection" are *vertically* substitutable for one another in a given category; for example, any noun can take a noun's place in a sentence. Hence, these rhetorical items are (1) *in absentia*; the units are not actually present, but could be (2) part of a code, for example, any *langue* or speech community practice, and (3) related by synchrony, that is, a static or simultaneous placement in time (consciousness). My previous use of the concepts of persona and the philosopher represent Merleau-Ponty's use of the paradigmatic perspective in the poetic function, or what he calls "chiasm." In a rhetorical frame of tropic reference, we might say with Merleau-Ponty that philosophy allows for the reality of fiction in discourse since the relation of metaphor (together with simile or irony) displays or represents the conditions of (a) selection or specification, (b) substitution, and (c) similarity or elements in combination.

By contrast, syntagmatic items in a process called "association" have their categorical identity by *horizontal* contiguity to other items; for example, any noun is known by its comparison/contrast with verbs, adjectives, and so on. Thus, these items are (1) *in praesentia*; the units are actually present, and must be (2) part of a message, for example, any *parole* or act of speaking, and (3) related by diachrony, that is, a dynamic or sequential placement in time (consciousness; Holenstein, 1976, pp. 137–164). The prior use I made of the concepts of person and the sophist represent Foucault's syntagmatic perspective in the poetic function, or what he calls the "nameless voice," that is prosopopoeia. In a rhetorical sense, we might say with Foucault that philosophy allows the fiction of reality in discourse since the relation of metonymy (together with synecdoche) displays or attributes the conditions of (a) combination or derivation, (b) contexture or designation, and (c) contiguity or articulation.

Turning specifically to Merleau-Ponty's inaugural lecture, there is an explicit semiotic phenomenology in his discourse (see Figure 1). It is a rhetoric of signified perception and signifying expression. He first combines the paradigmatic category of persona/perception in the progressive discussion of the philosophers Lavelle, Bergson, and Socrates. Then, he progresses in his discussion to a syntagmatic category of person/expression in the analysis of the disciplines of religion, history, and philosophy.

Lavelle and the World

By structuring his inaugural address in the manner of a discourse on history, Merleau-Ponty constructs an "order of analysis" in classic Husserlian fashion; that is, there is a deliberate construction of the ontological problematic of philosophy as the encounter of ego and *noēma* in the thematic rhetori-

144

The Algebra of History

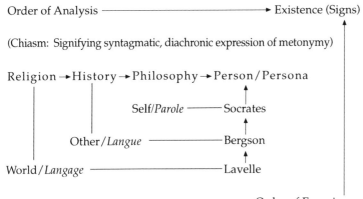

Order of Analysis ──────────────────────▶ Existence (Signs)

(Chiasm: Signifying syntagmatic, diachronic expression of metonymy)

Religion →History→Philosophy→Person/Persona

          Self/*Parole* ────── Socrates

          Other/*Langue* ────────── Bergson

World/*Langage* ────────────── Lavelle

Order of Experience

(Prosopopoeia: Signified paradigmatic, synchronic perception of metaphor)

Figure 1. Semiotic Phenomenology in Merleau-Ponty's Inaugural
Lecture. All relations are dialectically combinatory (metonymy)
and reversible (metaphor).

cal process of *noēsis* (Ihde, 1977, p. 50). The subject matter of
Lavelle's philosophy is for Merleau-Ponty a description of
phenomenology, a first step in critical method. The good and
bad ambiguity of the philosopher is the contest (Foucault's
"agon") between signified and signifying, world and self,
noema and ego, in which the problematic of equivocation
(Foucault's "catachresis") becomes the thematic of meaning.[6]
The agonistic rhetoric of Lavelle has its narrative function: "It
would be the function of philosophy, then, to record this
passage of meaning rather than to take it as an accomplished
fact" (Merleau-Ponty, 1963, p. 9). Lavelle is the signified voice
of the world that is a modality of rhetoric; Lavelle is the naming
voice of *langage*.

Bergson and the Other

Merleau-Ponty's discussion of Bergson is a phenomenological reduction; in this second step of critical method we
move from the description in Lavelle's differentiation of world
and self to Bergson's differentiation of self and other. With
Bergson's concern for alterity, "being itself is problematic"

145

RICHARD L. LANIGAN

(Merleau-Ponty, 1963, p. 14). "For an ego which is *durée* cannot grasp another being except in the the form of another *durée*," as Merleau-Ponty (1963, p. 15) argues. Because "the absolute knowledge of the philosopher is perception" (p. 16), a discourse of the other is not "a simple return to what is *given* [*data*]" (p. 18). The discourse of the other is an intuitive encounter with reality, where "it is necessary for me to appropriate to myself a meaning in which it is still captive [*capta*]" (p. 18). Just as living is reduced by speaking and speaking represented by writing, there is in reading an intuitive reduction of the other to a speaking subject who lives in the chiasm of discourse (a prosopopoeia as the inscribed discourse that thus presents an absent oral voice of self; recall the Dickens example, "I am born"). Philosophy "is, as Bergson happily said, a *reading*, the art of grasping a meaning in a style before it has been put into concepts" (pp. 19–20). With this probing rhetorical analysis of Bergson's philosophy, Merleau-Ponty does, indeed, locate a third methodological step (interpretation) in the phenomenological reduction of the self and other, ego and noema, as the noesis of discourse.

In this section of the inaugural lecture, Merleau-Ponty (1963) offers his famous hermeneutic definition of what we now call communicology (*communicologie*, to cite the *tout Paris* term), that is, the conjunction of philosophy and rhetoric: "Expression presupposes someone who expresses, a truth which he expresses, and the others before whom he expresses himself. The postulate of expression [rhetoric] and of philosophy is that it can simultaneously satisfy these three conditions" (p. 30). Indeed, Merleau-Ponty finds in the Bergsonian problematic a thematic that "shall have been" (to borrow the "in-order-to motive" from Alfred Schutz) the ground of Foucault's philosophy, that is, an agonistic rhetoric. This is to say that "the enigma of philosophy (and of expression) is that sometimes life is the same to oneself, to others, and to the true" (Merleau-Ponty, 1963, p. 32). Bergson is the signified voice of the other that is a modality of rhetoric; Bergson is the voice of *langue*. Foreshadowing Foucault's discussion of rhetoric, Merleau-Ponty (1963, pp. 22–23) quotes the voice of Jean Hyppolite in reference to Bergson's "*Matter and Memory*, a system of oppositions between the emptiness of the past,

146

The Algebra of History

the emptiness of the future, and the fullness of the present, like the oppositions between time and space."

Socrates and the Self

After reminding us that "the philosophy placed in books has ceased to challenge [persons]," Merleau-Ponty (1963) declares:

> In order to understand the total function of the philosopher, we must remember that even the philosophical writers whom we read and whom we are, have never ceased to recognize as their patron a man who never wrote, who never taught, at least in any official chair, who talked with anyone he met on the street, and who had certain difficulties with public opinion and the public powers. We must remember Socrates. (p. 34)

And so to the perceptual ambiguity of the perceived world and the expressive ambiguity of listening to, and reading about, the other, Merleau-Ponty adds a phenomenological interpretation.

The interpretation is the "good irony" of "double meaning" that we perceive not in reading the *Apology* inscribed by Plato but in the voice of Socrates that we can hear (Merleau-Ponty, 1963, p. 39). We can hear the "idea of philosophy" in the rhetoric of Socrates. The eidetic discourse of Socrates is not mere symbolism. "It exists rather in its living relevance to the Athenians, in its absent presence, in its obedience without respect" (p. 36). The noema of speech expresses the ontological ego through the noetic medium of speaking. Socrates is the signified voice of the self that is a modality of rhetoric; Socrates is the signifying voice of *parole*.

With existential fidelity and an incarnate phenomenology, Merleau-Ponty takes (*capta*) speech in Lavelle as signified meaning. He takes the spoken in Bergson. This equivocation of speech (*langage*) and the spoken (*langue*) becomes the "good ambiguity" and "good irony" of speaking. Speaking (*parole*) that is a problematic in the "speech spoken" (*parole parlée)* of rhetoric becomes thematic in the "speech speaking" (*parole*

147

parlante) of philosophy. In the dialectic of the chiasm, we are both the listening audience of Socrates as he speaks and the speaking voice that is Socrates (prosopopoeia). The signified story of Socrates is our signifying history. Rhetoric and philosophy are signs of expressing and perceiving discourse.

Religion and *Langage*

The conjunction of the world and *langage* is the problematic of religion and theology where philosophy speaks in silence. Language that speaks for the world hides the self. But, the world that is speaking expresses the self through *langage* and is the proper object of perception, "for to philosophize is to seek, and this is to imply that there are things to see and to say" (Merleau-Ponty, 1963, p. 41).

Merleau-Ponty (1963) remarks that the ontological problem of the existence of God no longer commands philosophical attention. Rather, the "abruptly disqualifying" (p. 42) voice of atheism or "human chauvinism" is heard (p. 44). Philosophy is not the rejection of theology; nor is it the voice of humanism. The concept of the human is neither a rejection of, nor a substitution for, the concept of God. Both atheism and humanism point to the grounding of theology, which is to remove "the contingency of human existence" (p. 44). But for Merleau-Ponty, "philosophy, on the other hand, arouses us to what is problematic in our own existence and in that of the world, to such a point that we shall never be cured of searching for a solution, as Bergson says, 'in the notebooks of the master' " (pp. 44–45). The ironic allusion to Nietzsche's (1984, p. 187) aphorism is clear: "What Socrates found out. If someone has mastered one subject, it usually has made him a complete amateur in most other subjects; but people judge just the reverse, as Socrates found out. This is the drawback that makes associating with masters disagreeable" (number 361). Thus for Merleau-Ponty, the signifying discourse of religion provides a phenomenological description of the world and, in its negation, is a consequent account of the self as a story (atheism) or an account of the other as a history (humanism).

Yet, Merleau-Ponty (1963) finds operative in this description the ontological rhetoric of negation, not the positive theology that would displace philosophy as a discourse: "A sensitive and open thought should not fail to guess that there is an affirmative meaning and even a presence of the spirit in this philosophical negativity" (pp. 46–47). The meaning described by the differentiation of world and language is not positively choosing one or the other as humane (i.e., as a persona), but indeed, choosing both as their combinatory negation of any posited ontology that is not the person. Philosophy in the world and rhetoric in language point to the dialectic of meaning in the binary analogue of both perception and expression, and "both consciousness and narrative [*l'histoire*] echo this" (p. 46).[7]

History and *Langue*

The ambiguity of *l'histoire* is the equivocation of history counterposed to philosophy (Merleau-Ponty, 1963), only to become thematic in the story of discourse (historical narrative as a rhetoric, a "human practice"; p. 48) and, dialectically in the chiasm, a thematic in the discourse of the story (philosophical narrative as a rhetoric, a "*praxis* in the meaning"; p. 50). The signifying discourse of history exemplifies a phenomenological reduction of *langue* in the other. Indeed, this is one reason that Foucault (1972) calls for the abolition of the "sovereignty of the signifier" (p. 229).[8]

The constitution of meaning (Merleau-Ponty's subject of "speech spoken"; Foucault's "subjection-subjected"; Kristeva's subject "on trial") and the person (Merleau-Ponty's subject of "speech speaking"; Foucault's "subject"; Kristeva's subject "in process") by prosopopoeia becomes explicit as the speech of history confronts philosophy. The problematic anonymous voice of history opposes things to consciousness, and that same voice as philosophy counterposes consciousness to things. But as a thematic voice, "historical meaning is immanent in the interhuman event, and is as fragile as this event. But precisely because of this, the event takes on the value of the genesis of reason" (Merleau-Ponty, 1963, p. 51).[9] Just because the world and *langage* are reversible with the event of the other and *langue*, the rhetorical structure of history (syntagmatic; Kristeva's "phenotext") becomes the semiotic

RICHARD L. LANIGAN

form of philosophy (paradigmatic; Kristeva's "genotext"). Indeed, "the theory of signs, as developed in linguistics, perhaps implies a conception of historical meaning which gets
beyond the opposition of *things* and *consciousness*" (Merleau-
Ponty, 1963, p. 54). The rhetorical conjunction of the speaking
subject and the institutions of meaning (subjects spoken; the
subjected) are a semiotic phenomenology of the world and
the other. They are a signifying practice of *langage* in the
story of history and a praxis of *langue* in the hi[gh]-story of
philosophy, that is, Foucault's "rarefaction" (1972, p. 229).
According to Merleau-Ponty, "an interconnection among
these phenomena is possible, since they are all symbolisms,
and perhaps even the translation of one symbolism into another is possible" (1963, p. 56; see Figure 4). History turns
philosophy "towards the personal discourse which develops
in us, and which, indeed, we are" (pp. 57–58).

Philosophy and *Parole*

Philosophy for Merleau-Ponty "is expression in act"; "it
comes to itself only by ceasing to coincide with what is expressed, and by taking its distance in order to see its meaning"
(1963, p. 58). Or as Foucault puts it, "To play on words yet
again, let us say that, if the critical style [archaeology] is one
of studied casualness, then the genealogical mood is one of
felicitous positivism" (1972, p. 234). By so characterizing the
rhetoric of philosophy, Merleau-Ponty and Foucault dialectically give us a philosophy of rhetoric. Here, the exacting
dialectic of person and persona is not a speech act, not the
subject spoken. It is not the voice of power "to realize" in
langue by "destroying" *parole*; nor is it the dialectic voice of
desire "to suppress" in *langage* and thereby "to conserve"
parole. In fact, "the philosopher of action is perhaps the far-
thest removed from action, for to speak of action with depth
and rigor is to say that one does not desire to act" (Merleau-
Ponty, 1963, p. 59). Rather the ambiguity, the dialectic signs
(chiasm) of *person* (private world) and *persona* (common
world), exists in the signifying mask (prosopopoeia) of religion, history, and philosophy that is removed in "speech

speaking" as we hear the signified mystery (prosopopoeia) of silence, the "speech spoken" by Lavelle, Bergson, and Socrates. For Merleau-Ponty (1963), as for ourselves, "the philosopher is the man who wakes up and speaks" (p. 63).

Foucault's Inaugural: The Order of Discourse

As a student of Merleau-Ponty, we may in fairness characterize Michel Foucault as a disciple of ambiguity in his own discourse as lived. As Foucault himself frequently points out, he is neither a structuralist nor a Husserlian phenomenologist. But then neither was Merleau-Ponty, even though, like Foucault, he wrote insightfully and critically about both. Rather, Foucault is a candidate for inclusion with the other "masters of suspicion" (Nietzsche, Freud, and Marx), as Descombes (1980, p. 3) designates them. The masters of suspicion are rhetoricians who know philosophy. Like philosophers, they are semiotic phenomenologists. Within the rhetorical movement of catachresis, they are the personae who are truly subject to discourse (*langue*; the subject spoken) and are no less than the persons who are the meaning of subjecting discourse (*parole*; the speaking subject), that is, they also are truly the subject of discourse. Like the chiasmatic voice of Socrates, Merleau-Ponty and Foucault are the disciples of ambiguity: they are phenomenologists of the signs of existence (prosopopoeia).

Thus, to proceed in the analysis of Foucault's inaugural by formulating the title translation of *L'ordre du discours* as "The Discourse on Language" is to corrupt the ambiguity of discourse, the enveloping catachresis, chiasm, and prosopopoeia that Foucault intends. In a retrospective comment on the *énoncé* of his inaugural lecture, Foucault (1982, p. 208) reminds us: "My work has dealt with the three modes of objectivation which transforms human beings into subjects." First, there is catachresis in "the objectivizing of the speaking subject in *grammaire générale*, philology, and linguistics." Second, there is chiasm by objectivizing the subject in "dividing practices." And third, there is prosopopoeia in "the way a human being turns him- or herself into a subject." In short, the title, *The Order of Discourse*, is an epigrammatical thesis about the speaking subject, the philosopher who knows rhetoric.

Are we to choose meaning in the discoursing order, the order imposed by the designating rhetoric of catachresis where the *sujet du* [of] *langage* is tied to his/her/its own identity in the world by a desire as "speech speaking"? Or will meaning choose us in the ordering discourse, which is controlled by the naming rhetoric of chiasm where one is *sujet a* [to] *la langue* as a dependence on the power of the "speech spoken" by the other? Shall we choose meaning in the order imagined as present in narrative form yet absent to the practice of discourse as structure? What order is manifest in the judging rhetoric of prosopopoeia where (in Merleau-Ponty's phrase) the subject of *parole* is "condemned to meaning" in speaking the spoken (*discours*), which is not the voice of what is said through speech (*langage; langue*)? Indeed, for Foucault (1982, p. 212), "there are two meanings of the word *subject* (*sujet*): subject to someone else by control and dependence, and tied to his own identity by a conscience or self-knowledge. Both meanings suggest a form of power which subjugates and makes subject to." Thus, Foucault (1982, pp. 211, 222; 1980b, p. 83; cf. Heyer, 1988) brings us quickly and forcefully to the "antagonism of strategies" in the rhetoric of "local memory" that is archaeology and to the "agonism" (or "reciprocal incitation and struggle") in philosophy as the "erudite knowledge" that is genealogy.

In Figure 2, the play of archaeology and genealogy is depicted with the same Jakobsonian poetic function (paradigmatic and syntagmatic axis; Husserl's orders of experience and analysis respectively) in mind that is used in Figure 1. Caution is warranted, however. White (1987, p. 120; cf. 1978) masterfully points out in his rhetorical analysis of Foucault's *The Order of Things* that "each period is studied 'vertically,' that is, archaeologically, rather than 'horizontally' or historically."[10] But in the inaugural lecture, Foucault critically responds to his own past work and changes his model. He counterposes the new genealogy to the old archaeology, now called the "critical perspective," which consists in those horizontal (syntagmatic) principles of "exclusion, limitation, and appropriation" or "rarefaction, consolidation, and unification" (respectively, Jakobson's "combination, contexture, and contiguity").

The genealogical perspective as now corrected forms the vertical (paradigmatic) principles of "appearance, growth, and variation" or "formation, at once scattered, discontinuous and regular" (in Jakobson's theory, "selection, substitution, and similarity"). Also, remember that the operation of Jakobson's poetic function is precisely the "reversal-principle" to which Foucault (1972, pp. 231–233) refers in making the critical or archaeological form of discourse (the rhetorical or tropic figure of metonymy) dialectical with the genealogical form (metaphor). To be sure, Foucault is adopting the same semiotic modification to Husserl's phenomenology that Jakobson and Merleau-Ponty established in their parallel, but separate, studies of human communication as semiotic phenomenology.

Translators have consistently rendered Foucault's use of the French *figura* into English as *form*, even in passages where the explicit phrase *les figures de la rhetorique* is used. In the play of memory, most of Foucault's commentators forget the rupture that occurs in his very first methodological work on discourse, *Death and the Labyrinth: The World of Raymond Roussel*. In this important work on the phenomenology of discourse, we find that "Roussel's experience is situated in what can be called the 'tropological space' of vocabulary" (Foucault, 1986, p. 16). The ontological procedures of a new rhetoric become quite clear in Foucault's approving quotation of Dumarsais:

> Thus by necessity and by choice, words are often turned
> away from their original meaning to take on a new one
> which is more or less removed but that still maintains a
> connection. This new meaning is called "tropological,"
> and this conversion, this turning away which produces it,
> is called a "trope." In the space created by this displace-
> ment, all the figures of rhetoric come to life. (p. 15)

As a matter of course in Foucault's work, this archaeological view (experience) of Roussel's surrealist literature in tropological space becomes a genealogical view (consciousness) in his later study of Rene Magritte's surrealist painting. The desire of tropic catachresis manifest in a *metagram* as the "law of discourse" in graphic terms (e.g., the sentential message that reads literally: "This is not a pipe.") becomes the figurative power of *calligram* in "the law of . . . communication," where the graphic figure is now a dialectic trope of the visual, as, for example, the following message (Foucault, 1983, pp. 161–162, 227):

This { [This is not a pipe!] } is not { a ⟨ ipe

To summarize and define the discursive algebra, "the metagram is both the truth and the mask, a duplicate, repeated and placed on the surface. At the same time, it is the opening through which it enters, experiences the doubling, and separates the mask from the face it is duplicating" (Foucault, 1986, p. 28). And yet by reversibility and poetic function (see Figures 3 and 4), "pursuing its quarry by two paths, the calligram sets the most perfect trap. By its double function, it guarantees capture [*capta*, "discovery"], as neither discourse alone nor a pure drawing could do" (Foucault, 1983, p. 22).

The Rhetoric of External Rules: Knowledge

Beginning the explication of Figure 2, we start as does Foucault in his inaugural lecture. He takes up the problematic of discourse formations as knowledge (*connaissance*) and power (*savior*). Within Merleau-Ponty's *prose du monde*, Foucault's (1972) initial concern is with the formations, or *figures*, of discourse that are manifest firstly in external rules, that is, the rules of exclusion: "We have three types of prohibition, covering objects, ritual with its surrounding circumstances, the privileged or exclusive right to speak of a particular subject . . . a complex web, continually subject to modification" (p. 216).[11] In this Socratic schema, discourse is first of all its own subject of intentionality as a pure catachresis (the idealism of Husserl's "object" is under critique). In this analytic move-

The Algebra of History

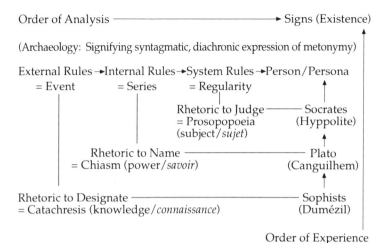

Order of Analysis ⟶ Signs (Existence)

(Archaeology: Signifying syntagmatic, diachronic expression of metonymy)

External Rules →Internal Rules →System Rules →Person/Persona
   = Event   = Series   = Regularity

                            Rhetoric to Judge ——— Socrates
                             = Prosopopoeia   (Hyppolite)
                             (subject/*sujet*)

             Rhetoric to Name ——————— Plato
        = Chiasm (power/*savoir*)   (Canguilhem)

Rhetoric to Designate ————————— Sophists
= Catachresis (knowledge/*connaissance*) (Dumézil)

                         Order of Experience
(Genealogy: Signified paradigmatic, synchronic perception of metaphor)

Figure 2. Semiotic Phenomenology in Foucault's Inaugural
Lecture. All relations are dialectically combinatory (metonymy)
and reversible (metaphor).

ment of regularity that traces out the phenomenology of semi-
osis, discourse becomes an event of experience, constituting
merely a part in the metynomic whole of a web (a series).
Ritual speech (sophistry) and the right to speak (philosophy)
are the remainders; they are yet to be figured as parts in the
eidetic web of meaning. Thus, speech is a subject of desire in
the sophistic period, where the voices of Hesiod and Plato
indicate the opposition of rhetoric and philosophy. There is
a desire to prohibit words, a tropic practice reminiscent for
Foucault of "psychoanalysis, with its strange logic of desire"
(pp. 216, 237). [12]
    This bifurcation of knowledge and power has its contin-
ued explication in a second opposition of "reason and folly,"
where there is both a division and a rejection—the division of
sanity and madness (ritual speech), where "we have even
come to notice these words of the madman in our own speech,
in those tiny pauses when we forget what we are talking
about" (Foucault, 1972, p. 216–217). At the level of the discourse as discipline, we are witness to the division made in the
sixteenth and seventeenth centuries between "observational

155

science" and "religious ideology." It is a division (event) based upon a differentiation (series) of rejection (regularity) and is reminiscent for Foucault of "mathematics and the formalization of discourse" (p. 237).[13]

Last, we experience the opposition of the "true and the false," in discourse, "the right to speak." But wait—are not the words of prohibition also the prohibition of words (censorship)? External rules are the designating rule of catachresis. The nineteenth century witnessed the opposition of "modern science and positivist ideology" that reminds Foucault of "information theory and its application to the analysis of life"(p. 237).[14]

To provide us with an aphorism that captures the intentionality of external rules, the catachresis, Foucault (1986) says of Roussel: "He does not want to duplicate the reality of another world, but, in the spontaneous duality of language, he wants to *discover* an unexpected space, and to *cover* it with things never said before" (p. 16).

The Rhetoric of Internal Rules: Power

Foucault next turns to "internal rules, where discourse exercises its own control; rules concerned with the principles of classification, ordering, and distribution." These tropes of discourse are the series dimension of "events and chance," that is, the rules of inclusion. Here, knowledge (*connaissance*) is contrasted with understanding, the special "know how" (*savior*), or power, to be the subject of and subjected to discourse as a practice. Foucault locates such figures and tropes as a "commentary" displaying a "gradation between different types of discourse within most societies." He is thinking of *l'histoire* as the story of society that is told by society, its "major narratives, told, retold and varied." These stories (events) are the internalized religious or juridical texts (regularity) that follow on the external rules (series) of reason and folly. They are the subject spoken in the space subject to discourse. Discourse as commentary becomes no more than "discourse which is spoken and remains spoken, indefinitely, beyond its formulation." Between speaking and what is spoken, there is a chiasm: "What is clear is that this gap is neither stable, nor constant, nor absolute." Discourse is in the world of "play," where there is only "a lyrical dream of talk reborn" (Foucault, 1972, p. 220).

In the discursive realm of commentary, a rarefaction of discourse creates the "author" who "is spoken" again and again as the subject of discourse in place of the person speaking (Foucault, 1972, p. 222): "Commentary limited the hazards of discourse through the action of an *identity* taking the form of *repetition* and *sameness*. The author principle limits this same chance element through the action of an *identity* whose form is that of *individuality* and the *I*." The "author" marks the chiasm in just the sense that Plato, absent as an author, is the present name we give to the absent voice of Socrates so clearly present in the dialogues. We think of the Platonic author of Socrates, now, as Foucault thinks of Roussel's "tropologial 'move' " in his authorship "that brings into play . . . [a] fundamental freedom . . . to form an inexorable circle which returns words to their point of origin by force of his constraining rules." Hence, Foucault's second aphorism on the subject of intentionality is complete: "This opens a chiasm in the identity of language, a void that has to be revealed and at the same time filled" (1986. 16–17; see n. 16). Thus disciplines are born in the regularity of the series of events in discourse.

The Rhetoric of Systems: Subject

"Disciplines constitute a system of control in the production of discourse, fixing its limits through the action of an identity taking the form of a permanent reactivation of the rules" (Foucault, 1972, p. 224). The figures of discourse that Foucault suggests to us as the disciplinary formations of "universal mediation" are exchange and communication, that is, the rules of ensemble (pp. 225, 228, 235). Here, the conjunction of knowledge (Merleau-Ponty's "world") and power ("other") produces subjects ("self"), persons who are subject to knowledge and yet the subject of power. These two figures of exchange (paradigmatic function; genealogy) and communication (syntagmatic function; archaeology) are the process of

RICHARD L. LANIGAN

discourse regularity in which complexity (series) becomes restrictive (event). Foucault's illustration is the concept and practice of "doctrinal adherence" (p. 226). Indeed, as Perelman and Olbrechts-Tyteca (1969, p. 1; cf. Genette, 1982, pp. 10–22) remark, "the study of the methods of proof used to secure adherence has been completely neglected by logicians and epistemologists for the last three centuries." Foucault's entire corpus is the radical introduction of the problematic and thematic of adherence in the contemporary human sciences.

"Doctrine effects a dual subjection, that of speaking subjects to discourse, and that of discourse to the group, at least virtually, of speakers," says Foucault (1972, p. 226). Doctrine is a discursive function that takes the "fellowship of discourse" (*sociétés de discours*) as relying on an "ambiguous interplay of secrecy and disclosure." Thus the religious, political, and philosophical doctrines come to constitute the "utterance of speakers" that are "permanently, the sign, the manifestation, and the instrument of a prior adherence—adherence to a class, to a social or racial status, to a nationality or an interest, to a struggle, a revolt, resistance or acceptance" (p. 226). System rules are a prosopopoeia in which the imagined voice of communication (event) is exchanged with every voice (series) that adheres to the utterance (regularity). The movements of ensemble from "fellowships" of discourse to doctrinal groups and then to social appropriation are the "main rules for the subject/subjection [*sujet*] of discourse" and constitute the "pastorship" of "the individualizing power" (1972, p. 227; see Foucault, 1981, p. 227).

Thus, to cite Foucault's (1986) third aphorism in his study of Roussel, the prosopopoeia is a rule of ensemble (exchange) discovered as the ensemble of the rule (communication): "The movement of repetitions and transformations, their constant imbalance, and the loss of substance experienced by words along the way are becoming, surreptitiously, marvelous mechanisms for creating beings; the ontological power of this submerged language" (pp. 26–27; see Wilden, 1987, pp. 245–279). In short, the rule of ensemble is that "a statement [*énoncé*] is always an event that neither the language [*langue*] nor the meaning can quite exhaust" (Foucault, 1972, p. 28).

158

The Sophists and Designation

Foucault (1972) reminds us that ever since "the exclusion of the activity and commerce of the sophists" philosophy has divided "thought and words." Philosophy as a discourse per se becomes no less than a rhetoric to designate, a critical form of exclusion (pp. 228, 231): "It would appear to have ensured that *to discourse* should appear merely as a certain interjection between speaking and thinking; that it should constitute thought, clad in its signs and rendered visible by words or, conversely, that the structures of language themselves should be brought into play, producing a certain effect of meaning" (p. 227). The definition of *catachresis* could not be more apparent than it is in this thematic quotation. Foucault subjects philosophy to a phenomenological reduction in which the metaphors of logic and grammar are seen to be the events of external rules. The events, by their own proper rule (!), are already committed to an axiology of the deontic. To adhere to what is proper is to do what one should.

The metaphor as a rhetorical figure, as the external rule of thinking (that in practice becomes the trope of metonymy), that opposes the literal (logic in the trivium) to the fictional (grammar in the trivium), is discovered to be a trope of speaking (rhetoric in the trivium). The trope is catachresis where the "ancient elision" is manifest as the distinction between the proper and the insipid or improper (White, 1987, p. 115). Thinking should be valued as fair and just in words (or if insipid, at least justifiable); thus, logic can elide rhetoric. Yet, meaning should be justifiable (or if insipid, at least just) in thinking; hence, grammar can elide rhetoric. "This very ancient elision of the reality of discourse in philosophical thought has taken many forms in the course of history" (Foucault, 1972, p. 227). In the case of the Sophists, the form is "the philosophy of a founding subject" that embodies a "complicity with the world . . . to designate." Writing is the rupture of thinking and speaking; it de-signs existence as alterity. The person as a speaking subject in orality is subjected to inscription as the invention of persona, the subject spoken (pp. 222, 228). The words of *langage* become the prohibited words of *langue*, and the voice of *parole* is silenced.

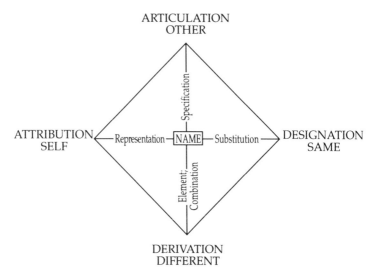

ARTICULATION
OTHER

ATTRIBUTION / Representation —[NAME]— Substitution \ DESIGNATION
SELF   SAME

Specification

Element;
Combination

DERIVATION
DIFFERENT

Figure 3. Lanigan Schema of Foucault's Quadrilateral Model of Discourse.

Dumézil is Foucault's (1972, p. 235) "model and prop," his persona, of the sophist: "It is he who taught me to analyze the internal economy of discourse quite differently from the traditional methods of exegesis or those of linguistic formalism." Dumézil is the founded subject (the subject spoken who is the proper, same self) of the founding subject (the speaking subject who is the insipid, different other, namely, Michel Foucault). Catachresis is one trope (the signs) in the rhetoric of *le même et l'autre*, the philosophical pair that designates the persona and the person in the tropic ratio self : same : : other : different (see Figures 3 and 4). *Existence* names, that is, designates, in rhetoric the dialectic and ambiguity of the persona (as self and same person) in opposition to the person (as other and different persona). "To *name* is at the same time to give the *verbal representation of a representation* "(Foucault, 1970, p. 116, emphasis added). We can now designate the tropic function of the name, in which the representation of self : same : : other : different also represents *l'histoire et le sujet* as the ratio discourse : history : : subject : subjection, which is to say story : narrative : : self : other. As Benveniste's basic research so insightfully leads us now to conclude, the signs of existence (*ekstasis*) are the narrating story (*discours; parole parlante*) discovered critically in genealogy that stands in opposition to the story of narration (*l'histoire; parole parlée*) discovered by comment in archaeology (Benveniste, 1971, p. 215). Thus, what we learn from Dumézil is a genealogical lesson: "to restore to discourse its character as an event" (Foucault, 1972, p. 229).[15] We must learn that lived discourse (the history of the story; 1972, p. 220) is play, or what the the American semiotic phenomenologist Charles Sanders Peirce called "abduction."[16]

Plato and Nomination

"A division emerged between Hesiod and Plato, separating true discourse from false. . . . And so the Sophists were routed," reflects Foucault (1972, p. 218). With this allusion to Hesiod, we recall that in oral verse the famed presocratic poet eulogizes the human anguish of the laboring poor in his farmer's almanac *Works and Days*, yet he also eulogizes the gods by his canonical work of Greek mythology, the *Theogony*. Indeed, the true discourse separates from the false. But where

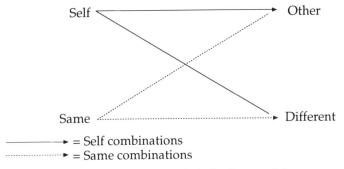

——————▶ = Self combinations
· · · · · · · · · · · ▶ = Same combinations

Self - Other = synecdoche: part/whole; Same - Other = metaphor: substance/whole; Same - Different = metonymy: substance/attribute; Self - Different = simile [positive]; irony [negative]: part/attribute.

Figure 4. The Quadrilateral Discourse Model of *Le Même et L'Autre*.

is the opposition and the exclusion? The rhetoric to name is the chiasm that Plato finds in the analytical combination of *logos* and *mythos* that requires a critical *logos* of *logos*. The human voice opposes the divine voice, and each excludes the other. What the humans can say, the gods cannot hear (the exclusion of reason made concrete in the enthymeme). The inventions of the gods cannot be understood as the human world (the exclusion of folly made concrete in the syllogism). The rupture of reversible exclusion in the confrontation of person and persona, the chiasm, names the discourse that precedes and succeeds itself. As such, the rupture of present and absent voices is locked in an endless series of internal rules. The site of these series is the "form of a cogito, prior significations, in some ways already spoken" (Foucault, 1972, p. 228). The site is what we read; it is the text of discourse that names experience. Catachresis joins by opposition to chiasm to foretell the "nameless voice" of prosopopoeia; that is, the story of history narrates the history of a story in which the speaking voice (*lector in fabula*) is "on the other side of discourse" (p. 215).

Having cited Hesiod's history of discourse, Foucault cites, and thereby sites, his own discourse of history. In the persona of Canguilhem,[17] Foucault (1972) voices what he has read:

> If I have wished to apply a similar method [referring to Dumézil] to discourse quite other than legendary or mythical narratives, it is because before me lay the works of the historians of science, above all, that of Monsieur Canguilhem. I owe it to him that I understood that . . . one could—that one should—treat the history of science as an ensemble, at once coherent, and transformable into theoretical models and conceptual instruments. (p. 235)

Reading is not just the invented opposition of self narration (the human, the person, the speaking subject) and the other's narration (the divine, the persona, the subject spoken). It is a discovery of alterity as a critical form of limitation. Here, we confront the problematic of "a philosophy of originating experience" (Foucault, 1972, p. 228). Reading exemplifies the auditing process in which we perceive "the form of a cogito, prior significations, in some ways already spoken." The text names that of which we have knowledge, because it cannot be experienced. The reader encounters the catachretic work of the founding subject of the speech community (*langue*), who has "signs, marks, tracks, letters at his disposal" (p. 228). To read, then, is to become the problematic and equivocal founding subject of an originary experience of consciousness, the spoken. External rules conflate internal rules, and events become series in the ontological process writing invents (p. 222). What we learn from Canguilhem is a second genealogical lesson according to Foucault: "to abolish the sovereignty of the signifier (signifiant)" (p. 229).[18] We learn that the power of discourse (the story of history) is its constitution of utopia (p. 220).

Socrates and Judgment

We come now to the third system of exclusions: the true versus the false. In the regularity of system rules, discourse becomes no less than the rhetoric to judge. As Foucault (1972, p. 232) says, "I will take first the age of the Sophists and its beginning with Socrates, or at least with Platonic philosophy, and I shall try to see how effective, ritual discourse, charged with power and peril, gradually arranged itself into a disjunction between true and false discourse." In this short aphorism on the Greek sophistic, Foucault both announces and summarizes what we have suspected all along about discourse as a "universal mediation." The dialectic and digital opposition of paradoxical discourse (the semiotic of death in rupture) for the Sophists and Plato is the analogic ambiguity of opposition by combinatory reversal of discourse (the semiotic of birth in rupture) for Aristotle and Socrates. We are concerned no longer with writing and reading (event and series, that is, death and birth) but with the endless regularity of ontology in sign exchange (rupture; p. 228; see n. 11). For Foucault, Aristotle's (*Rhetoric*, 1358b4–1359a29) genres of rhetoric are turned on their head in their very statement (*énoncé*), in order to become a "now" and "here" rupture of the Socratic maieutic of conscious experience.

RICHARD L. LANIGAN

For Foucault, the discourse of external rules and the trope of catachresis, as the rhetoric of designation, is no less than the reversal of Aristotle's genre of political (deliberative) oratory. The event of discourse in the persona of the Sophists points to the person, the existential subject, in the lived experience of a "speaking subject" who must both accept and reject consciousness as the lived future. Such a future is the terminus ad quem of Cicero or the "in-order-to" motive of Schutz, namely, the birth/death within "what shall have been." The exclusion of discourse as rupture is both expediency (person) and harmfulness (persona).

Second, the discourse of internal rules, the trope of chiasm, constituting the rhetoric of nomination is no more than the reversal of the Aristotelian category of judicial (forensic) oratory. The series of discourse in the persona of Plato existentially indexes the person in the consciousness of a "speaking subject" who must both attack and defend the experience of the lived past. This past is the terminus a quo of Cicero or the "because" motive of Schutz, namely, the death/birth within "what had been." The exclusion of discourse as rupture is both justice (reason) and injustice (folly).

Last, there is the discourse of system rules, the trope of prosopopoeia, establishing the rhetoric of judgment that entails both the political and the judicial oratories. The opposition of political and judicial is in turn, and in itself, opposed to the genre of evaluative (epideictic) oratory. The regularity of discourse in the persona of Socrates is an existential sign of the person who must both praise and blame the consciousness of the future and the experience of the past in the lived present (*ekstasis*). The exclusion of such discourse is both honor (truth) and disgrace (falsity). Indeed, the rhetoric of judgment is the epideictic rhetoric, the eulogy of inaugural, where Merleau-Ponty's lecture begins to *praise* Socrates, and with which Foucault's lecture ends by *blaming* Socrates. The naming voice of now and here (Merleau-Ponty's inaugural of present absence; rupture and birth) reverses to become the nameless voice of nowhere (Foucault's inaugural of absent presence; rupture and death). Rhetoric (event) is the counterpart of dialectic (series), yet maieutic inaugurates the reversal (eulogy) of both as a critical form (regularity) of appropriation (Foucault, 1972, p. 231).

For this argument, Foucault's (1972) illustrating persona is Jean Hyppolite, like Socrates for Plato, a "model and prop" of maieutic discourse—the reversal that is the adhering interrogative statement:

> For Hyppolite, philosophy, as the thought of the inaccessible totality, was that which could be rejected in the extreme irregularity of experience; it was that which presents and reveals itself as the continually recurring question in life, death, and in memory. Thus he transformed the Hegelian theme of the end of self-consciousness into one of repeated interrogation. (p. 236)

With this birth (a visible metaphor for "genealogy") of the rhetorical question as statement (a visible metonymy for archaeology), Foucault offers us his third genealogical lesson: "to question the will to truth." Thereby, we must learn that uttered (*énoncé*) discourse is anguish (Foucault, 1972, p. 220, 229).[19] The genealogy of this agonistic rhetoric initiates the practice of discourse as it struggles with the reciprocal strategy of rhetoric (antagonism) in the method of archaeology. The "critical . . . which sets the reversal-principle to work" is a poetic rupture, both a death (exclusion, limitation, appropriation) and birth (appearance, growth, variation) of rhetoric (pp. 231–232). As Merleau-Ponty (1963, p. 14) says, "Something of the nature of the question passes into the answer."

The Voice of Discourse

Foucault's inaugural lecture articulates the problematic of discourse, the sign that beckons the human being to existence. It is the problematic of existence found in the ontological alterity of the signifying and the signified. The equivocation of the articulated statement that makes the signifying or the signified stand apart, each as its own voice, becomes the phenomenological thematic in Foucault's rhetoric of archaeology. And yet, archaeology itself submits to the interrogation of genealogy. Merleau-Ponty's philosophical demand of Hus-

serl is also met by Foucault: existence is first of all a phenomenology of phenomenology, a genealogy of archaeology. Foucault's confession of mere commentary in his early
archaeological work is exposed for its equivocation and
thereby becomes the thematic of criticism, not unlike the semiotic confession of Umberto Eco (1983) in *The Name of the Rose*.
Critical method replaces archaeological methodology (history
as the death of words in the labyrinth) just as genealogical
method (discourse as a birth of signs) is announced in the
semiotic ruptures of linguistic practice. Precisely these ruptures have come to visibility as the examination of human
practice in the many discourses constituting the corpus of
Foucault's research.

In point of fact, "the difference between the critical and
the genealogical enterprise is not one of object or field, but
point of attack, perspective, and delimitation" (Foucault, 1972,
p. 233). The original vertical paradigmatic order of archaeology
is replaced by the horizontal syntagmatic order of criticism
(the sign as signified), so that genealogy (the sign as signifying) may properly become the new, correct vertical paradigm. Properly understood, Foucault's genealogy and archaeology constitute a semiotic phenomenology defined by
existence as signs (genealogy) in "poetic" combination (Jakobson's sense) with signs as existence (archaeology). The discourse of the signifying subject (speech speaking) ruptures
the history of the subject signified (speech spoken), so that "a
human being turns him- or herself into a subject" (1982, p.
208) in order to "at last . . . restore it to *speaking* (1972, p. 229).

> The subject should not be entirely abandoned. . . .
> Rather, we should ask: under what conditions and
> through what forms can an entity like the subject appear
> in the order of discourse; what position does it occupy;
> what functions does it exhibit; and what rules does it fol-
> low in each type of discourse? In short, the subject (and
> its substitutes) must be stripped of its creative role and
> analyzed as a complex and variable function of discourse.
> (Foucault, 1977, p. 137–138)

Foucault's phenomenology of genealogy and archaeology makes certain explicit, complex methodological demands

The Algebra of History

on the semiotics of discourse (illustrated in Figures 2, 3, and 4). However, Foucault's own systemic rhetoric provides us with four principles of interrogation and articulation that are his critical method for depicting the phenomenology of discourse. These principles provide us with a way to systematically express the tropic impact of Foucault's rhetoric of the person.

1. **Reversal (metonymy: same-different).** The events of signification (*langage*) function as external rules of discourse to designate meaning. These are the rules of exclusion in rhetoric that distinguish archaeology. Thus, appearance as the reversal of the events of signification is a catachresis where the genealogical goal of criticism is "to restore to discourse its character as an event" (Foucault, 1972, p. 229). In other words, we discover the genealogical "rule of the tactical polyvalence of discourses" (Foucault, 1980a, p. 100).

2. **Discontinuity (simile, irony: self-different).** The series of originality (*langue*) functions as internal rules of discourse to name meaning. These are the rules of limitation in rhetoric that distinguish archaeology. Thus, growth as the discontinuity of the series of originality is a chiasm where the genealogical goal of criticism is "to abolish the signifier." Thus, we encounter the genealogical "rule of double conditioning" (Foucault, 1980a, p. 99).

3. **Specificity (synecdoche: self-other).** The regularity of unity (*parole*) functions as system rules of discourse to judge meaning. These are the rules of appropriation in rhetoric that distinguish archaeology. Thus, variation as the specificity of the regularity of unity is a prosopopoeia where the genealogical goal of criticism is "to question our will to truth." Here, the "rules of continual variations" point to a genealogy (Foucault, 1980a, p. 99).

4. **Exteriority (metaphor: same-other).** The semiotic condition of creation (*discours*) functions as the reversal-principle to describe meaning (phenomenologically). These are the narrative rules (*l'histoire*) in rhetoric that distinguish archaeology. Thus, explication is figurative or tropic where the genealogical goal of criticism is "the possible conditions of existence" (Foucault, 1972, p. 230). In short, Foucault's genealogical "rule of immanence" is, indeed, named by Merleau-Ponty's "theme of the 'flesh' " (Foucault, 1980a, p. 98).

With this discursive evidence of semiotic phenomenology, let my voice close rhetorically with a eulogy of explication for Foucault's (1972) inaugural voice as it speaks (p. 215):

I would really like to have slipped imperceptibly into this lecture, as into all the others I shall be delivering, perhaps over the years ahead. [= the voice of catachresis, the name of metaphor]
I would have preferred to be enveloped in speech, borne way beyond all possible beginnings. [= the voice of chiasm, the name of irony and Simile]
At the moment of speaking, I would like to have perceived a nameless voice, long preceding me, leaving me merely to enmesh myself in it, taking up its cadence, and to lodge myself, when no one was looking, in its interstices as if it had paused an instant, in suspense, as a sign beckoning to me. [= the voice of prosopopoeia, the name of metonymy]
There would have been no beginnings: instead, the discourse would proceed from me, while I stood in its path—a slender gap—the point of its possible disappearance. [= the voice of persona, the name of synecdoche]

Through the inaugural discourse of Michel Foucault, the nameless voice of Maurice Merleau-Ponty in his critical genealogy warns us about the voiceless name in the algebra of discourse: "It is Socrates himself who teaches us to correct Socrates" (Merleau-Ponty, 1963, p. 39).

Notes

1. I am accounting for the signifying amibiguity of *l'histoire* by the double translation where *history* is *narrative* (figure of language; fiction) and *story* is equal to discourse (trope of speech; fable). Thus, I am following the communicological distinction in discourse practice established by Emile Benveniste (1971). See n. 4 below, where Foucault distinguishes fiction and fable. Peirce (1931–1963) makes a similar point about the algebra of discourse when he says:

   It will be necessary to use signs or symbols repeated in different places and in different juxtapositions, the signs being subject to certain 'rules,' that is, certain general relations associated with them by the mind. Such a method of forming a diagram is called *algebra*. All speech is but such an algebra, the repeated signs

The Algebra of History

being the words, which have relations by virtue of the meanings associated with them. (codex 3.418)

2. The trope *prosopopoeia* is a special case of metonymy in which there is a comparison by degree (binary analogue) of the real (substance) and the imaginary (attribute). Hence, prosopopoeia is a judgment of narrative (nameless) voice. In Aristotle's 'rhetoric' this trope is parallel to the proof called *ethos*, that is, a reason in argument derived from performance where embodiment is equal to "the forgetfulness of rationality" (Foucault, 1970, p. 352) or *magikos*. "It is this global sense of *ethos*, involving traditions, attitudes, and historicity of man's dwelling in the world, that was later degraded into the ethical as an autonomous branch of philosophy" (Schrag, 1986, p. 220). Thus, we understand Merleau-Ponty's (1981) provocative thesis on the existential phenomenology of embodiment as expression: "The relationship between my decision and my body are, in movement, magic ones" (p. 94). Note that a trope creates a change in signification (change of meaning) whereas a figure gives emphasis to a signification (change in words); see Thonssen & Baird 1948, pp. 420–423.

3. The trope *chiasm* (L. chiasmus; E. chasm) is a special case of irony (negative) or simile (positive) in which there is a comparison by degree (binary analogue) of presence (part) and absence (attribute). Hence, chiasm is a judgment of reversibility. In Aristotle's 'rhetoric' this trope is parallel to the proof called *pathos*, that is, a reason in argument derived from silence or *mystos*. The trope *persona* is a special case of synecdoche in which there is a comparison by degree (binary analogue) of the appearance (part) and the concrete (whole). Hence, persona is a judgment of perceived (named) voice. In Aristotle's rhetoric this trope is parallel to the proof called *enthymeme*, that is, a reason in argument derived from the form and matter of the syllogism. See Lanigan, 1975, and 1984, chap. 5.

4. Foucault (1988) explains:

> In every work of narrative form, we distinguish between *fable* and *fiction*. Fable is that which is told: episodes, characters, their functions in the narrative, events. Fiction is the realm of narrative [*l'histoire*; figure of language], or rather the various realms of the "narrating." . . . Fable consists of elements placed in a certain order. Fiction is the web of relationships that has been established, by means of the

speech [*discours*] itself, between the speaker and what is spoken. Fiction is an "aspect" of fable [*l'histoire*; trope of speech]. (p. 1)

For a detailed analysis, see Eco 1979, pp. 200–260, and Certeau, 1984, pp. 159–162.

5. The importance of rhetoric as a pedagogical influence on French intellectual thought is noted by Annie Cohen-Solal (1987, p. 62).
6. The trope *catachresis* is a special case of metaphor in which there is a comparison by degree (binary analogue) of the proper (substance) and the insipid (whole). Hence, catachresis is a judgment of propriety. In Aristotle's rhetoric this trope is parallel to the proof called *logos*, that is, a reason in argument derived from speech or *mythos*.
7. Note that an echo is an empirical example of prosopopoeia while a narrative consciousness is an eidetic example. And, the reversibility of these two examples is a chiasm. Another example might be a book title that reads (orally and visually) as a calligram: "Umberto Eco, *The Name of the Rose*." The point has been rendered blunt by a subsequent hermeneutic calligram: *Foucault's Pendulum*.
8. Kristeva (1984) announces her semiotic phenomenology by arguing that "we shall see that when the speaking subject is no longer considered a phenomenological transcendental ego nor the Cartesian ego but rather a *subject in process/on trial* [*sujet en procès*], as is the case in the practice of the *text*" (p. 37). And further,

> The object of a particular science, the material where the subject and his knowledge are made, language is above all a *practice*. A daily practice that fills every second of our lives, including the time of our dreams, speaking and writing, it is a social function that is manifested and known through its exercise. The practice of ordinary communication: conversation and information. Oratory practice: political, theoretical, or scientific discourse. Literary practice: oral folklore, written literature; prose, poetry, song, theater, etc. The list could be lengthened: language invades the entire field of human activity. (1989, p. 278)

9. As Kristeva explicates (1984): "If these two terms—genotext and

phenotext—could be translated into a metalanguage that would convey the difference between them, one might say that the genotext is a matter of topology, whereas the phenotext is one of algebra" (p. 87). The respective allusion to Foucault and Merleau-Ponty is clear.

10. The "quadrilateral of language" model is discussed in Foucault, 1970, p. 115. See Foucault, 1972, p. 158) for the quadrilateral as archaeology, and note that in later work the archaeological method is renamed "critical" method (1972, p. 233); for the quadrilateral as genealogy, see Foucault, 1980, pp. 92–102. A detailed examination of the model is the subject of Lanigan, 1991a.

11. A clear allusion to the semiotic order of experience and analysis offered in Plato's dialogue *Sophist*, which Foucault is following; see "Semiotic Phenomenology in Plato's *Sophist*" in Lanigan, 1988.

12. An allusion to the *Sophist*, in which the persona of the statesman represents political rhetoric (knowledge of the future).

13. An allusion to the *Sophist*, in which the persona of the philosopher represents judicial rhetoric (knowledge of the past).

14. An allusion to the *Sophist*, in which the persona of the Sophist represents evaluative rhetoric (knowledge of the present).

15. Cf. n. 12 above, the task of the statesman in the *Sophist*.

16. "Play" is a traditional human science metaphor for "communication theory" as "deutero-learning" or the logic of *abduction*; see Bateson & Bateson, 1987, 36–49 on abduction, and Peirce, 1931–1963, codex 2.619 on "Ampliative Reasoning."

17. For a discussion of Canguilhem, see Gutting, 1989.

18. Cf. n. 13 above, the task of the philosopher in the *Sophist*.

19. Cf. n. 14 above, the task of the Sophist in the *Sophist*.

References

Aristotle. (1963). Rhetorica. In D. Ross (Ed.), *The works of Aristotle* (12 vols.). Oxford: Clarendon.

Bateson, G., & Bateson, M. C. (1987). *Angels fear: Towards an epistemology of the sacred*. New York: Macmillan.

Benveniste, E. (1971). The correlations of tense in the French verb (M. E. Meek, Trans.). In *Problems in general linguistics* (pp. 205–216). Coral Gables: Miami University Press. (Original work published 1966.)

Certeau, M. de (1984). The science of fables (S. F. Rendall, Trans.). In *The Practice of everyday life* (pp. 159–162). Berkeley: University of California Press. (Original work published 1980.)

RICHARD L. LANIGAN

Cohen-Solal, A. (1987). *Sartre—A Life* (A. Cancogni, Trans.). New York: Pantheon. (Original work published 1985.)

Descombes, V. (1980). *Modern French philosophy* (L. Scott-Fox & J. M. Harding, Trans.). New York: Cambridge University Press. (Original work published as *Le Meme et L'Autre*, Paris: Les Editions de Minuit, 1979.)

Descombes, V. (1986). *Objects of all sorts: A philosophical grammar* (L. Scott-Fox & J. M. Harding, Trans.). Baltimore: Johns Hopkins University Press. (Original work published 1983.)

Eco, U. (1979). Lector in fabula: Pragmatic strategy in a metanarrative text. In *The role of the reader: Explorations in the semiotics of texts*. Bloomington: Indiana University Press.

Eco, U. (1983). *The name of the rose* (W. Weaver, Trans.). New York: Harcourt Brace Jovanovich. (Original work published 1980.)

Foucault, M. (1970). *The order of things: An archaeology of the human sciences* (Anon., Trans.). London: Tavistock Publications. (Original work published as *Les Mots et les choses*, Paris: Gallimard, 1966.)

Foucault, M. (1972). *The archaeology of knowledge* and *The discourse on language* (A. M. Sheridan Smith, Trans.). New York: Pantheon. (Citations of French and retranslations are from *L'ordre du discours*, Paris: Gallimard, 1971.)

Foucault, M. (1977). *Language, counter-memory, practice: Selected essays and interviews* (D. F. Bouchard, Ed.; D. F. Bouchard & S. Simon, Trans.). Ithaca: Cornell University Press.

Foucault, M. (1980a). *The history of sexuality: Vol. 1. An introduction* (R. Hurley, Trans.). New York: Vintage. (Original work published as *Volente de savior*, 1976.)

Foucault, M. (1980b). *Power/knowledge: Selected interviews and other writings 1972–1977* (C. Gordon, Ed.). New York: Pantheon.

Foucault, M. (1981). *Omnes et singulatim*: Towards a criticism of "political reason." In S. M. McMurrin (Ed.), *The Tanner lectures on human values 1981, Vol. 2*. Salt Lake City: Utah University Press; Cambridge: Cambridge University Press.

Foucault, M. (1982). The Subject and power (L. Sawyer, Trans.). In H. L. Dreyfus & P. Rabinow (Eds.), *Michel Foucault: Beyond structuralism and hermeneutics*. Chicago: University of Chicago Press.

Foucault, M. (1983). *This is not a pipe: With illustrations and letters by Rene Magritte* (J. Harkness, Ed. & Trans.). Berkeley: University of California Press.

Foucault, M. (1986). *Death and the labyrinth: The world of Raymond Roussel*. (C. Ruas, Trans.). New York: Doubleday. (Citations

The Algebra of History

of French and retranslations are from *Raymond Roussel*, Paris: Gallimard, 1963.)

Foucault, M. (1988). Behind the fable. *Critical Texts*, 5(2), 1–5 (Original published as L'Arriere-Fable, *L'Arc 29*, 1966.)

Genette, G. (1982). *Figures of literary discourse* (A. Sheridan, Trans.). New York: Columbia University Press. (Original work published 1966–1972.)

Gutting, G. (1989). *Michel Foucault's archaeology of scientific reason*. New York: Cambridge University Press.

Heyer, P. (1988). *Communications and history: Theories of media, knowledge, and civilization*. New York: Greenwood Press.

Holenstein, E. (1976). *Roman Jakobson's approach to language: Phenomenological structuralism*. (C. Schelbert & T. Schelbert, Trans.). Bloomington: Indiana University Press.

Husserl, E. (1970). *Logical investigations* (2 vols.). (J. N. Findlay, Trans.). New York: Humanities Press. (Original work published 1900, 1913.)

Ihde, D. (1977). *Experimental phenomenology: An introduction*. New York: Capricorn, Putnam.

Kristeva, J. (1984). *Revolution in poetic language* (M. Waller, Trans.). New York: Columbia University Press. (Original work published 1974.)

Kristeva, J. (1989). *Language: The unknown; an initiation into linguistics* (A. M. Menke, Trans.). New York: Columbia University Press. (Original work published 1981.)

Lanigan, R. L. (1975). Enthymeme: The rhetorical species of Aristotle's syllogism. *Southern Speech Communication Journal*, 40(2), 127–141.

Lanigan, R. L. (1977). *Speech act phenomenology*. The Hague: Martinus Nijhoff.

Lanigan, R. L. (1984). *Semiotic phenomenology of rhetoric*. Washington, DC: Center for Advanced Research in Phenomenology & University Press of America.

Lanigan, R. L. (1988). *Phenomenology of communication: Merleau-Ponty's thematics in communicology and semiology*. Pittsburgh: Duquesne University Press.

Lanigan, R. L. (1991a). *The human science of communicology: A phenomenology of discourse in Foucault and Merleau-Ponty*. Pittsburgh: Duquesne University Press.

Lanigan, R. L. (1991b). *Speaking and semiology: Maurice Merleau-Ponty's phenomenological theory of existential communication* (2nd ed.). Berlin: Mouton de Gruyter.

Lanigan, R. L. (in press). A good rhetoric is possible: Ricoeur's philosophy of language as a phenomenology of discourse in the human

173

sciences. In L. E. Hahn (Ed.), *Paul Ricouer: The library of living philosophers*. Peru, IL: Open Court.

Merleau-Ponty, M. (1963). *In praise of philosophy* (J. Wild & J. M. Edie, Trans.). Evanston: Northwestern University Press. (Original work published 1953.)

Merleau-Ponty, M. (1981). *Phenomenology of perception* (C. Smith, Trans.; corrections by F. Williams and D. Guerriere). Atlantic Highlands, NJ: Humanities. (Original work published 1945.)

Nietzsche, F. (1984). *Human, all too human: A book for free spirits* (M. Faber, Trans.). Lincoln: Nebraska University Press. (Original work published 1878.)

Paul, C. B. (1980). *Science and immortality: The éloges of the Paris Academy of Sciences (1699–1791)*. Berkeley: University of California Press.

Peirce, C. S. (1931–1963). *Collected papers of Charles Sanders Peirce* (C. Hartshorne & P. Weiss, Ed., vols. 1–6; A. W. Burks, Ed., vols. 7–8). Cambridge: Harvard University Press.

Perelman, C., & Olbrechts-Tyteca, L. (1969). *The new rhetoric: A treatise on argumentation* (J. Wilkinson & P. Weaver, Trans.). Notre Dame: Notre Dame University Press. (Original work published 1958.)

Schrag, C. O. (1986). *Communicative praxis and the space of subjectivity*. Bloomington: Indiana University Press.

Thonssen, L., & Baird, A. C. (1948). *Speech criticism: The development of standards for rhetorical appraisal*. New York: Ronald.

White, H. (1978). Foucault decoded: Notes from underground. In H. White (Ed.), *Tropics of discourse: Essays in cultural criticism* (pp. 230–260). Baltimore: Johns Hopkins University Press.

White, H. (1987). Foucault's discourse: The historiography of anti-humanism. In *The content of the form: Narrative discourse and historical representation*. Baltimore: Johns Hopkins University Press.

Wilden, A. (1987). *The rules are no game: The strategies of communication*. New York: Routledge & Kegan Paul.

Learning to Stop

A Critique of General Rhetoric

Ian Angus

> One starts things moving without a thought of how to
> stop them. In order to speak. One starts speaking as if
> it were possible to stop at will. It is better so. The
> search for the means to put an end to things, an end
> to speech, is what enables the discourse to continue.
> —Samuel Beckett, *The Unnamable*

PHILOSOPHY, *ESPECIALLY FOR THE LAST HUNDRED YEARS,*
has meditated on its own end and has perhaps even turned
this meditation into its constitutive feature. While it is in one
sense a specific genre, philosophy also initiated delimited
scientific domains and attempted to enclose science, art, and
ethics within a unity. This unity shaped a rational cultural
form opposed to mythic, religious, or irrational forms. Such
components, if not eradicable, were rigorously subordinated
to philosophical unity.

In this sense, philosophy is not simply a genre but a
universality encompassing, and giving form to, the plurality
of genres. In large part, this unity conferred a cultural unity
on European civilization, the West. It is by no means an acci-
dent that when Edmund Husserl rearticulated this cultural

unity in the face of fascist barbarism in Vienna in 1935 he pointed out that it did not include Papuans or Gypsies (Husserl, 1970, pp. 273, 290). Within the very formation of the idea of philosophy as the emergence to self-consciousness of essential human capacities is the tension between such universality and the particular cultural-historical formation within which it emerged. Though such universal capacities can, in principle, be awakened in anyone, such awakening involves a fundamental transformation of other cultural forms along lines first illuminated by the European one. Essential insight into the possibilities of humanity as such remains interwoven with a factual cultural unity that encounters other cultural forms, its "outside," with a certain privilege. This privilege is not that of a specific genre but is transferred from the universality of that genre to the cultural form as a whole. The end of philosophy is thereby an episode of the end of the West in the epoch of emergence of a planetary culture. But, more than an episode, the end of philosophy seems to plunge into an abyss the categories through which this emergence might be comprehended.

Philosophy may end in at least three ways. Through neglect, it may be forgotten or buried under the greater effectivity of other genres and traditions. Or it may announce itself as completed, as having finished its task. Hegel is the great figure of the reconciliation whereby the task of philosophy claimed to be completed in the synthesis of reason with world history: "That this 'idea' or 'reason' is the *true*, the *eternal*, the absolutely *powerful* essence; that it reveals itself in the world, and that in the world nothing else is revealed but this and its honor and glory—is the thesis which . . . has been proved in philosophy." (Hegel, 1956, p. 9–10). Philosophy, as both the completion of world history and the inner principle that directs it, announces its own end.

But further, the end of philosophy may be announced from outside. This must be distinguished from an announcement by the genres historically coexisting with philosophy— such as rhetoric, religion, hedonism, and so forth—that competed with philosophy for political or theoretical hegemony. Such competitions presuppose the ongoing vitality of the competitors in the assertion of their different tasks. The end of philosophy is genuinely announced from outside when it is argued that philosophy is inadequate to the task that philosophy set for itself. Thus philosophy is circumscribed as an unself-conscious task within world history that must be comprehended by a thinking that goes beyond philosophy.

This announcement was made in the nineteenth century by both Marx and Nietzsche. To select just one of many formulations, Nietzsche's diagnosis was

> that if a philosopher *had* been conscious of what he was, he would have been compelled to feel himself the embodiment of *nitimur in vetitum* [we strive for the forbidden]—and consequently *guarded* against "feeling himself," against becoming conscious of himself." (Nietzsche, 1969, pp. 112–113; cf. Seebohm, 1985, pp. 11–23; Schurmann, 1987, pp. 44–60)

The basis of this announcement was the experience of history, not simply of events within history but of history itself as the origin of the themes and horizons of an epoch, an epoch that could not be comprehended by philosophy, since it is the presupposed ground upon which the task of philosophy is articulated. Thus, philosophical thought is traversed by an "unthought" such that its own task is unfulfillable in principle.

Yet this announcement from outside is not simply outside, in which case it would be a competing genre, but is an outside made possible by philosophy itself. The experience of history as the origin of epochal determinations not only radicalizes the attempt of "first philosophy" to determine the fundamental principles upon which reason rests but depends upon the announcement of the end of philosophy in the second (Hegelian) sense: only after the reconciliation of reason with world history can the experience of history as origin encompass philosophy also. The entwinement of philosophy with historical events posits a unity of thought and being that can subsequently be determined as an epoch when combined with the radicalized experience of history as origin rather than events. Thus, this announcement from outside is also a reaching outside by philosophy. Subsequent thought has had to appeal to this outside but is unable to determine it since

determinations are formulated within the philosophy circumscribed by an epoch. The end of philosophy is caught in the
announcement of a certain closure and the inability definitively to step outside the closure. It confronts an other that it
cannot name.

Philosophy, then, comes to an end through a reconciliation of the relation between reason and the world that, subsequently, can be radicalized. One of the conditions for this
reconciliation is thus that philosophy is fundamentally concerned with knowledge and reason. It is characteristic of philosophy to treat the various modalities of human experience
as variations of theoretical positing of states of affairs that can
then be determined with respect to their adequacy. In a move
emblematic of the philosophical tradition, Edmund Husserl
asserted that it is possible to transform any experiential modality into a "doxic positing," and that, in consequence, logic
includes the modalities of emotion and volition (Husserl, 1969,
p. 136). This theoretical modification expresses the commitment of philosophy to reason and indicates that philosophy
operates within a presupposed gnoseological horizon.[1]

The circumscription of a gnoseological horizon constitutive of the philosophical tradition does not imply that the
striving for knowledge can be neatly separated from philosophy. Nevertheless, this horizon has not defined the whole of
philosophical practice, and at the present time, its circumscription is necessary to reveal marginalized dimensions of philosophy that are central to its renewal in the contemporary turning
point of the West, which may be defined through the end of
philosophy. Indeed, the possibility of such a circumscription
is both indicative and constitutive of the turning itself.

In contrast to the theoretical modification characteristic
of philosophical tradition, after the announcement of the end
of philosophy, a performative modification of experience has
appeared in various forms. Language, especially, can be considered primarily as an action, that is, as historically effective
rather than descriptive of anterior events. For this reason, the
theoretical situation after the end of philosophy is constitu-
tively opened toward rhetoric—since viewing language as action is characteristic of the rhetorical tradition. However,
because traditional rhetoric was a competing genre to

philosophy it was concerned with historical effectivity as distinct from, or opposed to, the philosophical concern with truth. In contrast, the present opening toward a performative modification of experience occurs after a breakdown of this separation into genres. Consequently, rhetoric is itself expanded in its range, function, and self-conception. This chapter captures this phenomenon by describing key characteristics of what may be called "general rhetoric." At issue now is the production of truth, or truth effects, by the historical effectivity of language. The new set of questions that this puts on the intellectual agenda is indicative of the end of the classical separation of philosophy and rhetoric. More widely, it is indicative of a practical historical situation that has been called the "postmodern condition."

To address the intellectual issues of this postmodern condition, it is necessary to follow through the performative modification thoroughly and consistently. The core of the philosophical tradition is summed up and given a radical formulation in Edmund Husserl's discovery of the transcendental reduction—the suspension of belief in a world subsisting independently of anyone's perception of it. Such belief is not denied but simply suspended in order that it may be held up for inspection and its pervasive influence described (Husserl, 1982, pp. 51–62). This is the contemporary, radicalized form of the Greek "wonder" that was taken to be the origin of philosophy and that motivated the inquiry into truth that came to be constitutive of the philosophical tradition. Thus, the explication and development of the theory of the transcendental reduction is a central theme for a contemporary defense of philosophy. In the present context, characterized, in part, by the development of a general rhetoric, the core philosophical experience must be reformulated and rediscovered in relation to the active productions of discourse.

This chapter suggests that the end of philosophy pertains specifically to its gnoseological dimension. Thus, while it develops the notion of a general rhetoric, it does so in order to circumscribe the limitations of even the widest conception of rhetoric and to rediscover the origin of philosophy. It charts a deeper terrain through discovery of a practical ascesis—one might say, a transcendental reduction in language—that is attuned to a transformation, rather than an abandonment, of philosophy. This transformation shifts the locus of the origin of philosophy from a universality required to unify particular discourses toward a practical ethics of translation situated at the moment of encounter between discourses. In order to accomplish this task, this chapter considers successively the conception of general rhetoric, the postmodern condition as a translation between discourses, and silence as a constitutive moment of philosophy.

As long as language is considered in relation to knowledge, its task appears to be reporting on states of affairs to which it corresponds and that it represents with greater or lesser accuracy. Every language use implies a dual task of clarification and critique, directed, in the first place, at the specific fusing of theoretical statement and state of affairs and, in the second place, at the general conditions under which representation can occur. Within this gnoseological horizon, philosophy is thus concerned with the representation of representation—that is, with the formulation of the general conditions of knowledge such that specific researches find their place and ongoing justification within this ground plan. Philosophy is both the prior laying out of the possibility of representation and the posterior ordering of representations within an actualized architectonic of forms of knowledge.

Language can also be considered, apart from its ability to represent events, as an event itself. Language events perform actions that intervene in worldly events. Commenting on someone's appearance, for example, is not only (or even primarily) a description of a state of affairs but the setting up of a certain relation between the speaker, that which is spoken about, and the one spoken to. An organized set, or system, of these language events is generally called a discourse. A discourse is a finite group of utterances that together constitute a set of social relations that are brought into play whenever the discourse is invoked. The positions that one may occupy in these social relations are thus not brought by preexisting subjects into the discourse but constituted within the discourse by the ongoing system of utterances. Thus, if these utterances shift in their systemic role, the relations between subject positions shift. Consequently, an important question for analysis of a discourse is the internal social relations that come into being, mutate, and pass away with it.

From this point of view, a science is itself a system of utterances. One is less concerned with the laws of physics, for example, than with the system of knowledge development and exchange, relations between physicists, the process of education that inducts a new scientist, relations between physicists and nonphysicists, and effects of the discourse of physical science—the nuclear bomb, for example. In this sense, the laws of physics are simply formalizations of discursive practice. The entire edifice of scientific representation that refers to states of affairs is a product of a more fundamental discursive formation that constitutes both social relations and states of affairs.

Therefore, such a discursive formation as this must have an outside. The world does not, and cannot, consist of one discursive formation. First of all, a discursive formation does not consist of all possible utterances, or even of all meaningful utterances, but of all actual utterances—though of course embedded in these utterances are conditions under which it is appropriate to make new utterances. Nevertheless, new utterances often are provoked by developments within other discourses—such as a different system of subject positions or a formalization that can be given an analogous role in a different discourse. The distinction of internal from external sources of innovation and especially the interaction between them are significant for analysis of continuity and change in a given discursive formation.

But, more fundamentally, a discourse cannot, in principle, extend to the totality of given discourses, because in order to do so self-referential statements would need to be entirely enclosed within the discourse. Such internal coherence can only be an attribute of a very simple system. Any system of at least the complexity of elementary arithmetic is necessarily incomplete, and its consistency cannot be proven within the system. The idea of a discursive formation without an outside is based upon the ideal of formalization within the gnoseological horizon of representation. But the formalization of a system through isolating a conceptual structure and exhaustively defining its properties through axiomatization and rules of trans-

IAN ANGUS

formation has come upon internal limitations (Godel, 1931; Findlay, 1942; Rosser, 1939). In the case of systems difficult to formalize, those pertaining to social life, historical events, emotions, and so forth—in short, the rhetorical subject matter of the human sciences—limitations to the project of isolation upon which the theoretical ideal of self-enclosure through coherence and completeness rests are even more central for the theoretical system. Thus, even within a representational model, the requisite enclosure of self-reference is impossible (Angus, 1984, pp. 19–40). It is even less justified within a discursive model of language, because the move to actual language events undermines the formalization required for axiomatization. Self-reference always overflows the boundaries of a given discursive formation.

The postmodern condition can be characterized as a shift from language as representation to discourse as action, which entails the loss of a unifying foundation and architectonic— or as Jean-François Lyotard says, "grand narrative"—for the plurality of discourses. Since the attempt to recuperate discursive plurality through grand narratives of knowledge or emancipation is characteristic of modernity, Lyotard has defined postmodernity as "incredulity toward metanarratives" (Lyotard, 1984, p. xxiv). Consequently, subjects and social relations cannot be guaranteed through a prior metanarrative, or recuperated within a subsequent totalization, but are positions constituted within discursive formations. This condition generalizes the critical task of rhetoric and undermines its subservience to philosophy. While the history of rhetoric has at many times contested this subservience, the contemporary shift to language as performance and the consequent expansion of rhetoric's terms of reference make such subservience even more difficult to maintain. A contemporary debate between rhetoric and philosophy cannot, therefore, rest on the terms established in the philosophical tradition by Plato and Aristotle. It is analogous to the debate engendered by the appearance of Socrates among the Sophists prior to the fixing of philosophy into representation. A postrepresentational debate encounters a new, open field, in which rhetoric and philosophy seem to merge.

Learning to Stop

The postmodern condition thus requires a transition from a restricted to a general rhetoric due to the key role that productive discourses take in defining the postmodern condition. Rather than being confined to the exterior transmission of a previously discovered truth, rhetoric penetrates to the center of all discursive formations. The generality of general rhetoric thus pertains to the key figural-persuasive dimension of all discursive formations, combined with their centrality to the social formation as a whole.[2]

As Aristotle defined it, rhetoric is "the faculty of observing in any given case the available means of persuasion." While special arts, such as medicine and geometry, instruct and persuade solely with respect to their own subject matter, rhetoric pertains to any subject matter. Moreover, rhetoric deals with judgments in which we deliberate without arts or systems to guide us: "Individual cases are so infinitely various that no systematic knowledge of them is possible" (Aristotle, *Rhetoric*, 1355b, 1356b–1357a). In this classic formulation, rhetoric undermines neither the expertise nor the independence of special arts or sciences. Rather, it is concerned simply with the means of persuasion independent of subject matter and the application to individual cases. This may be called a "restricted rhetoric" because, despite a certain universality of range and application, it is neatly distinguished from both delimited scientific truth and the universality of philosophy, or dialectic. In this classic formulation, rhetoric has the universality of ethico-political life. While any art, or *technē*, aims toward an end, the end is beyond the activity itself. Making shoes, for example, is not for the shoemaker but for the comfort of the one who wears the shoes. It is characteristic of politics and ethics, by contrast, that the end toward which they are oriented is the activity itself. The good life is its own goal (Aristotle, *Rhetoric*, 1356a; Aristotle, *Nichomachean Ethics*, 1094a).[3]

The shift from restricted to general rhetoric occurs with the postmodern plurality of discourses, due to the inability to stabilize a grand narrative that could perform the integrative, theoretical, universal, and rational role that philosophy assumed within the representational tradition. The most spontaneous move of philosophical criticism is to ask the reflexive question "Within what discourse is this plurality of discourses comprehended?"—in other words, to try to totalize the open field through a discourse of knowledge and then to justify and explicate the rules of this discourse as epistemology. This reflexive move doubles, or repeats, the performative dimension of discourse with a claim to knowledge that is embedded in performance. It reinscribes the turn to language as performance within language as representation and will consequently have little difficulty in restricting rhetoric and subordinating it to philosophy, as action to truth, in quite classical fashion. This spontaneous philosophical move expresses the deep-rooted commitment of philosophy to reason, to a way of life centered on knowing. But this is, at bottom, simply a refusal to complete the intellectual transition toward language considered as action that transforms rhetoric from restricted to general. Such a reflexive move is not wrong, but it is a failure of philosophy to enter the debate with rhetoric on the grounds constitutive of the postmodern condition.

The new, open field revealed in the postmodern condition is populated by a plurality of discourses and the absence of a grand narrative that could unify them. Within this field, the distinction between philosophy as representational truth and rhetoric as situational enactment is replaced by a convergence on the utterance. The contemporary debate between rhetoric and philosophy centers on their respective ability to produce utterances in the new, open field and the type and role of criticism of discourse that is possible and desirable within it. This chapter develops the idea of an expanded general rhetoric in order to argue that, despite this convergence, philosophy cannot be collapsed into rhetoric. It finds in the production of a specific type of utterance—those that prepare for the silence initiated by their own ending—the philosophical nodal point that cannot be inscribed within rhetoric. By being synthesized with the philosophical moment of silence, general rhetoric can perform its discursive criticism without succumbing to the endless proliferation of discourses that it produces.

The postmodern situation is characterized by the recognition of a plurality of discourses, the internality of considerations of legitimation or justification (in the epistemological,

ethical, and aesthetic senses) to a given discourse, and therefore, the confrontation of a new, open field that cannot be
subsumed under any definitive organization. This new, open
field has been characterized from several different angles.
Indeed, it is a central feature of the postmodern situation that
any attempt to characterize this open field will begin from
specific discourses but will encounter different discourses in
the very description of the postmodern situation itself.

Richard Rorty uses the term *hermeneutics* to describe his
response to the new, open field revealed by the critique of
representation:

> Hermeneutics is an expression of hope that the cultural
> space left by the demise of epistemology will not be
> filled—that our culture should become one in which the
> demand for constraint and confrontation is no longer felt.
> The notion that there is a permanent neutral framework
> whose 'structure' philosophy can display is the notion
> that the objects to be confronted by the mind, or the
> rules which constrain inquiry, are common to all dis-
> course, or at least to every discourse on a given topic.
> Thus epistemology proceeds on the assumption that all
> contributions to a given discourse are commensurable.
> Hermeneutics is largely a struggle against this assump-
> tion. (Rorty, 1979, pp. 315–316)

This hermeneutic hope wants to continue "the conversation
of the West" in which philosophy becomes "useful kibitzing,"
without its traditional ambition to become the regulator, syn-
thesizer, and provider of foundations for the various contributions to culture. Philosophy is reduced to professional inhab-
itors of university philosophy departments, who have read a
certain canon of received texts and, it is hoped, can say something useful in various cultural discourses as a result (Rorty,
1979, pp. 393–394).

The positivist reduction of this view of philosophy is an
emblematic, though ideological, response to the new, open,
discursive field: once one cannot claim to totalize and provide
foundations for the plurality of discourses, it may seem that
the only option is to keep existing discourses going. Legitimation of discursive practice tends toward the criterion of contin-

uing the conversation. This discursive legitimation converges with the technocratic legitimation "If we can do it, it should be done," so far as the claim to provide an evaluation of a discourse (tied to a representational idea of knowledge) shrinks into an evaluation, or legitimation, of utterances solely within a given discourse. The tendency toward purely internal discursive legitimation by performance replaces the grand narratives, such as knowledge or emancipation, developed within the philosophical tradition, and seems to throw out the idea of critical reflexion upon practices central to philosophy (except so far as local critical reflexion is already part of an ongoing conversation). Thus, the tendency to internal legitimation within existing discourses is characteristic of the postmodern condition, though if it were the whole story, it would make impossible the characterization of this condition as a plurality of discourses.

In order to clarify the emergence of a moment of universality within postmodernity, we may return to a significant turning in the tradition of Frankfurt Critical Theory expressed in the introduction to *Dialectic of Enlightenment*:

> We had set ourselves nothing less than the discovery of why mankind, instead of entering into a truly human condition, is sinking into a new kind of barbarism. We underestimated the difficulties of interpretation, because we still trusted too much in the modern consciousness. Even though we had known for years that the great discoveries of applied science are paid for with an increasing diminution of theoretical awareness, we still thought that in regard to scientific activity our contribution could be restricted to the criticism or extension of specialist axioms. (Horkheimer & Adorno, 1972, p. xi)

Previously, the critical task was limited to extending or criticizing the specialized scientific results that emerged from ongoing scientific discourses in regard to their impact on the possibilities for enlightenment or domination. At this point, however, Horkheimer and Adorno were concerned to diagnose the contribution to increased domination by exactly those scientific and technical potentials that were previously expected to contribute to enlightenment. In so doing, their perspective took leave of the assumptions of modernity and became a critique of civilization as a whole. Thus, the framework within which the possibilities of enlightenment or domination could be articulated could no longer be left uninvestigated. The key assumption of modernity—that there was a universal metadiscourse (philosophy) that was both internal and external to specialized discourses and could thereby encompass and harmonize them—was dropped.

The most characteristic modern philosophy, from this perspective, is that of Hegel. Hegel defined the movement of speculative philosophy as follows:

> The self-moving concrete shape makes itself into a simple determinateness; in so doing it raises itself to logical form, and exists in its essentiality; its concrete existence is just this movement, and is directly a logical existence. It is for this reason unnecessary to clothe the content in an external [logical] formalism; the content is in its very nature the transition into such formalism, but a formalism which ceases to be external, since the form is the innate development of the concrete content itself. (Hegel, 1979, pp. 34–35)

Speculative philosophy is thus a complete speech, encompassing all other discourses, which may then be called specialized because their limits have been determined. Such complete speech is equivalent to silence in the sense that any articulation, properly understood, represents and leads to the totality and is therefore not distinct "in truth," but only "accidently," from any other articulation (Dauenhauer, 1980, pp. 86–92). Modernity thus consists in a recognition of the plurality of discourses integrated with a simultaneous grand narrative of totalization. The turning in critical theory emerges from the realization that such a grand narrative both permeating and transcending specific discourses in such a manner that it can decide whether utterances within specific discourses are contributions to enlightenment or mystification is unsustainable. The development of the plurality of discourses undermines the claim to totality. The tensions of modernity have

IAN ANGUS

ushered in the postmodern condition, which appears, at least initially, to be a condition of pure plurality.

Thus, the tendency to purely internal legitimation of discourses must be reckoned a key component of postmodernity. Nonetheless, there is another tendency that is no less key: the postmodern condition also involves the attempt to universalize legitimation by performativity into an attempted steering of the whole social system. This nightmare of the "totally administered society," in Adorno's phrase, haunts all attempts to respond to the new, open field that characterizes the postmodern condition. This is not to say that such a possibility can become an actual state of society, but by articulating itself as a principle for society as a whole, performative legitimation encounters a contradiction that can be unmasked as ideological.

As John Keane puts it:

> Corporate organizations seeking to administer their environments by means of scientific-technical rules are obliged continually to solicit the active participation of their members and clients, whose initiative and autonomy these organizations must nevertheless forbid. . . . The end of ideology thesis is evidently contradicted by the intense controversies over the limits of state action and the future of state-administered socialism. These controversies indicate a *renewal* of ideological forms of discourse. They signal the return of types of vindicative discourse within social conditions which have become problematic for the dominant power groups, who defend themselves through justificatory arguments. (Keane, 1988, pp. 227–228)

Such a contradiction emerges only to the extent that the criterion of performativity is articulated as a principle for the social system as a whole, that is, to the extent that it is proposed as a metanarrative spanning discourses. By making such a universalizing claim, it becomes subject to a critique that reveals its functioning as furthering specific particular interests, or as ideological. It is not the reduction of legitimation to performativity alone that is at issue here but the combination of this reduction with its articulation as a system principle.

Learning to Stop

While ideology critique of the reduction to performativity within a discourse, and a technocracy of cybernetic system-engineers, is both possible and important, if it remains satisfied with unmasking their nonuniversality, one is thrown back into the plurality of discourses.[4] The particularity of the performance criterion may well be matched by the particularity of the critical standpoint that is doing the unmasking. In order to oppose the reduction to performance and to provide a justification for critical reflexion, Habermas argues that every discourse incorporates the counterfactual assumption that discursive practice is oriented to the reduction of systematically distorted communication: "Communicative action has nothing to do with propositional truth; but it has everything to do with the truthfulness of intentional expressions and with the rightness of norms" (Habermas, 1979, p. 119).[5] Thus, a given case of systematically distorted communication motivates reflection on the truthfulness of utterances considered as actions in a language game—Do the utterances obscure the goals that they tend to bring about?—and on the validity of the intersubjective norms to which the participants in the discourse accede—Are the subject positions produced by coercion? These counterfactual assumptions enable a reflexive critique of communicative distortions that seeks to reorient discourse toward consensus.

There are three possibilities here: the resources that enable reflexion may stand outside, and above, the given discourse (such as the metanarrative of modernity); they may be within it (as in hermeneutic continuation of the conversation); or they may emerge in the process of translation between discourses. In the first case, the discursive resources enabling binding reflexion are rooted in the metanarrative of knowledge or emancipation that has become incredible in the postmodern condition. Such an approach fundamentally disputes the description of the postmodern condition as a plurality of discourses and seeks to reinvigorate the analysis of modernity as a conflict between specialized systems and the sociohistorical totality.[6] In Habermas' words, "it is a question of building up restraining barriers for the exchanges between system and lifeworld and of building in sensors for the exchanges between lifeworld and system" (1987, p. 364).

In the second case, the discourse is assumed to possess exactly the universal characteristics of reflexion that the theory is designed to establish. There is a hermeneutic circle implied between the characterization of a specific communicative interaction as distorted, the appeal to universal norms with which to criticize the distortion as systemic, and the enactment of critical intersubjective reflexion in a reorientation of discursive practice toward consensus. The circle of interpretation requires the context of tradition in order to proceed. That is, the subjects engaging in a given discourse must all have access to common discursive resources that enable the reflexive move and imply its universal bindingness. If not, the hermeneutic alternative of continuing the conversation amounts simply to conventionalism or, worse, to a positivist elevation of what exists into a norm. Thus, in the case of this alternative, one must either place critique hermeneutically within an existing tradition or appeal to the first alternative of a metanarrative of emancipation above a given discourse.

The third possibility is not explored by Habermas. In his review of Hans-Georg Gadamer's *Truth and Method*, he follows Gadamer's emphasis on translation in order to overcome the Wittgensteinian view of self-enclosed language games as modes of life—which leads to a view of purely internal legitimation that we have seen in Rorty's notion of continuing the conversation—and to legitimate hermeneutic interpretation as a "fusing of horizons" in which the "unity of language, submerged in the plurality of language games, is reestablished dialectically in the context of tradition" (Habermas, 1977, p. 340). However, when Habermas argues against Gadamer that tradition is interwoven with domination, he does not employ or develop the notion of translation to legitimate critical reflexion, but argues that language is an incomplete model for social theory because of the legacy of nonnormative, noncommunicative components, "not of deceptions within a language but of deception with language as such" (Habermas, 1977, p. 360). From this, Habermas develops his own synthesis of interpretive and explanatory sociology, which are held together by a higher legitimation of critical reason. Here, the same problem reemerges: either the context of tradition supercedes the unmasking of domination, in which case language is assumed to possess sufficient resources to enable the possibility of critique—which is Gadamer's hermeneutic alternative—or the inability of tradition to legitimate a sufficiently independent concept of critique leads to a standpoint outside language. In short, when the question of translation did arise in the context of a confrontation between critical theory and hermeneutics, it was relegated to subsidiary status, and consequently, the earlier alternative of situating critical reason either in a metanarrative or as presupposed within language games was reasserted. However, this interchange did have the merit of establishing that the relationship of discourse and critical reason must be approached through the notion of a plurality of discourses that are not external to each other.

In contrast, Lyotard, by virtue of his diagnosis of the postmodern condition, must definitively avoid the recourse to metanarrative legitimation of critical reflexion. But the difficulty is that, since not all existing discourses provide sufficient resources for binding critical reflexion, in the postmodern condition the utilization of these resources outside of their legitimation within specific language games appears to be as arbitrary as existing practices (which may well incorporate forms of domination). In response to this situation, in which he can appeal to neither of the two alternatives, Lyotard (1984) proposes a local form of criticism that he terms "paralogy" (p. 22), which he claims is characteristic of contemporary science. Whereas innovation is a move within the language game as constituted—or a continuing of the conversation in Rorty's sense—paralogy is the proposal of new norms for understanding, an utterance that shifts the rules whereby new utterances are produced. The production of paralogy is always in response to a local situation and disturbs the existing consensus. Paralogical interventions may call forth from the existing consensus a response that seeks to remove one of the players from the game—a countermove that Lyotard calls "terrorist" (p. 22). From this point of view, the consensus on binding reflexion on norms embedded in language games, to which Habermas appeals, appears as coercive rather than emancipatory, as enforcing the rules of a given discursive formation rather than disturbing them. In short, if reflexive resources exist, they are too local to address the postmodern condition as a whole, and in many discursive formations, they do not exist at all.

This paralogical strategy for addressing the new, post-modern, open field suggests that recognizing the plurality of heteromorphous language games requires recognizing any consensus as local, a temporary contract that can be criticized by a multiplicity of finite meta-arguments limited in space and time. Moreover, Lyotard suggests that, despite the tendency to universalization of the criterion of performativity, the present postmodern condition also contains a tendency to such locally oriented metacritiques, and we may add that it is to the extension of this tendency that criticism should aim (Lyotard, 1984, pp. 60–67).

Paralogy is the local disruption of consensus. One may immediately ask whether Lyotard's justification of paralogy is itself a local intervention in a discourse. When he identifies paralogy with contemporary science, he seems to imply a general legitimation of the strategy (Lyotard, 1984, pp. 53–60). This would be simply a new form of scientism—the normative imposition of the rules of one discourse that is unaccountably elevated to metanarrative legitimation. But his diagnosis of the postmodern condition rules out this implication. Also, in order not to fall into the classic skeptical or relativist self-contradiction of proposing a universal theory that denies the validity of universal theories, one must interpret paralogy as locally justified. The justification of paralogy is itself paralogi-cal. In this sense Lyotard's logic is akin to the Sophistic logic that would negate the applicability of a universal logic only in this case and remain agnostic about its universality as such.

But, in this case, what entitles us to distinguish paralogi-cal interventions from terrorist countermoves? Either intervention will simply modify the positions of the subjects—which is simply continuing the conversation and does not need paralogical justification—or, by disturbing consensus, paralogy will disrupt, reverse, and perhaps eliminate them. If terrorist and paralogical interventions are indistinguishable in principle, does not all of this amount to saying that one can always overturn the board if the game does not come out well? This seems a rather thin justification of critical reason.[7]

In response to this concern, Keane suggests that "democracy cannot be interpreted as merely one language game among others," and that institutional procedures to prevent a hegemony of one discourse over others and safeguard a plurality of public spheres are a necessary component of a postmodern recognition of plurality of discourses (Keane, 1988, pp. 239–240).[8] Here we come back to the alternative we found in Habermas: we either must resurrect a metanarrative to justify the emancipatory component of reflexion or, because every language game does not distribute the possibility of reflexion throughout its subject positions, must appeal to the special privilege of those factual discourses within our tradition that do so to get the hermeneutic process going.

The legitimation of critical reflexion in the postmodern condition thus seems to be forced toward one of two alternatives: the existing discourses that contain resources allowing subjects within the discourse to appeal to binding norms of reflexion, or the (attempted) metanarratives of reflexion and emancipation. But the logic of this appeal to hermeneutic and/ or metanarrative resources must be to deny that the new, open field of discursivity presents an unprecedented problem—in short, to argue that the postmodern condition is, in principle, similar to that of modernity. Critical reflexion seems to be hung on a dilemma: its universality can only be guaranteed by denying the loss of metanarrative that constitutes the postmodern condition, whereas its practical effectivity relies on existing discourses that harbor reflexive resources but whose universality is denied. But there was another logical possibility—that the activity of translation itself is the locus of critical reflexion.

There is a reflexive component in the activity of characterizing the postmodern condition. The response to the situation is also a characterization of the situation, and this reflexivity invokes a universality that can be considered as an action apart from claims to truth or representation. The characterization of a plurality of discourses as a plurality requires a conception of a field, or space, within which these discourses encounter one another. Without some such concept, each discourse would be an entire and self-enclosed mode of life, unable to characterize other discourses. But our contemporary, postmodern culture is defined by just such cross-characterizations, transcodings, or, as we will say, translations, of discourses. Community activists have ways of talking about the actions and language of scientific experts. Workers, blacks, and women have discourses that respond to, and characterize, the difference and defects of the discourses that attempt to pin them down. And, of course, these examples could be reversed.

This is a central difference between the situation analyzed in *Dialectic of Enlightenment* and the present debates concerning postmodernity: the discourses of opposition to performativity, technocracy, and system maintenance are now an integral part of the culture to be analyzed, though this cannot (as is sometimes imagined) relieve critique of the necessity of reflexive justification. Moreover, the new, open field uncovered in the postmodern condition has been characterized from an array of intellectual discourses with mutually antagonistic presuppositions and methods. It is in this ability to characterize the postmodern condition within a plurality of discourses, which is also the origin of the cross-characterizations of discourses and of ideologies attempting to define the totality, that we may find an emergent universality that can justify reflexive critique. By following out this possibility, this chapter outlines a concept of general rhetoric that responds to the critical task in the postmodern condition.

The postmodern condition is neither a simple plurality of discourses (as Lyotard claims) nor adequately addressed by continuing the conversation between subject positions within a discourse (as Rorty claims); it is also an open field of discursivity constituted by a mutual and continuous process of translation of discourses. The plurality of discourses can be characterized within a single discourse precisely because other discourses are not eternally, in principle, exterior to it. A contingent exteriority can always be reduced by translation into an interiority. This is not, it must be recalled, a claim that through translation a discourse appropriates all that is true or enlightening in another discourse, which would be to return to a representational theory of truth. Here, we remain firmly within the performative modification.

The notion of postmodernity as the inability to totalize a plurality of discourses must therefore be understood as a dynamic relation. It is best formulated as a continuous process of failure to establish a discourse totalizing discourses, or a metadiscourse of the whole, within an open field in which there is continuous translation between discourses. We may characterize this dynamism in the open field as a "general agonistics" between discourses.[9] This is the dynamism that general rhetoric responds to and intervenes in. Whenever a given discourse attempts to translate the others into itself in such a manner as to produce a grand narrative of the whole, it calls forth its own deconstruction. To the extent that a totalizing translation begins to succeed, it is besieged by the countermove of rhetorical criticism, which reestablishes the untranslated residue through recourse to the instituting components of the discourse in question. That is, the prospective grand narrative is retranslated into the various given discourses through which it attempted to establish its totalization. Thus, the loss of metanarrative is not a single event but an event continuously reproduced by the very attempt to establish a metanarrative. The postmodern condition is thus not a simple plurality of discourses but the unstable process of their attempted totalization and deconstruction.[10] When a given discourse translates another discourse into a theme within itself, it aims at totalization; the outside of this totalization is recovered through deconstruction, with reference to its own instituting moment.[11]

Within this open field constituted by a general agonistics between discourses, the role of rhetorical criticism of a given discourse is generalized from the persuasive component within discourse to the criticism of discourses as a whole in the new open field. Every discursive formation embodies a set of procedures that can be formalized as rules, which express the rationality practiced in the performance of utterances. The giving of reasons thus assumes a discourse within which certain statements function as reasons in given circumstances. This exchange of reasons within a discourse can be traced back to a primal image that becomes the foundation, or *archē*, for the discourse in question. A discourse is thus instituted through the metaphorical extension of an image, a figurative showing, on the basis of which a discourse takes on theoretical, universal, and rational dimensions. Such a primal metaphor is practical, particular, and imaginative. In this situation, the range of rhetorical criticism is expanded from its restricted character, in which it is oriented primarily to persuasive language events within a given discourse (though this included also the general characteristics of such persuasion). General rhetorical criticism becomes the uncovering of primal images that found and regulate discourses, the study of the metaphorical, or tropological, origination of the plurality of discourses.

Practical rhetorical criticism either sustains or undermines discourses as a whole in this type of intervention in the general agonistics. This critical and reflexive move is therefore in a complementary relationship with the instituting speech that is poetry. Therefore, the institution of a discourse must be understood as poetically enacted and rhetorically sustained rather than as founded in philosophical universality.[12] Without a grand narrative, it seems that philosophy can no longer restrict the scope of rhetoric. The discourse of truth gives way to a plurality of regimes of truth, and rhetorical criticism consists in interventions that undermine the insupportable—but nevertheless continually arising—claim of a single discourse to fix meaning within itself and thereby to substitute itself for the lost grand narrative. From this perspective, any claim by philosophy that it fixes meaning in a privileged discourse that monopolizes the activity of translation is no less an unwarranted attempt at domination of the field of discursivity than any other attempt at totalization.

The loss of grand narrative characteristic of the postmodern condition, then, is not adequately conceived as the loss of a universalizing dimension to discourse, as Lyotard's characterization suggests. If we simply had ceased to be able to totalize discourses at a given moment, we might attempt to create, or perhaps might simply wait for a higher power to dispense, a substitute. The situation is more complex because there is within every sufficiently complex discourse a universalizing and reflexive component that, in principle, can translate every other discourse, though it cannot achieve a fully universal status under which it might subsume particular cases.[13]

Recognition of the plurality of discourses therefore does

not imply, as is often imagined, that each discourse is an enclosed vessel, or that there can be no discourse spanning discourses. In fact, it implies the opposite—that each discourse spans all other discourses, or that there is no pure externality. Consequently, the move to purely internal legitimation of a discourse through continuing the conversation is not an adequate response to the postmodern condition. Neither is the reassertion of a metanarrative. From the viewpoint of postmodernity, these two alternatives can be seen as mirror opposites: the alternative of internal or external legitimation appears when the modern conception of sublation (*Aufhebung*), whereby speculative reason is both internal and external to a given discourse, has been torn into two halves. Initially, and it is here that many discussions of postmodernity are stuck, it seems necessary to decide between the two sides of this alternative. But in the present formulation, we can see that the postmodern condition is not merely an episode of skepticism—a defense of the many against the one or of the particular against the universal. It is rather a new configuration of unity and plurality, particularity and universality, and cannot be countered by simply asserting the traditional arguments concerning the self-cancellation of relativism and skepticism, the necessity of unity to the definition of plurality, claims to universality in the perception of particulars, and so forth.

The new, open field of the postmodern condition simply means that a discourse spanning, or translating, different discourses cannot be given an independent legitimation—that no one discourse can monopolize the locus of translation. Modernity, by way of contrast, consists in an unprecedented recognition of the plurality of discourses integrated with a simultaneous grand narrative of totalization. Premodern, traditional societies consist in the regulation of discourses by a grand narrative. The grand narrative does not have to be legitimated by recuperating the plurality of discourses, as in modernity, but penetrates them from the outset: a given discourse can only be legitimated in reference to the grand narrative. This thereby generates the illusion that traditional society consists of a single discourse, which, if it were not an illusion, would make impossible the emergence of modernity.

Continuous translation of discourses embodies a universalizing component that simultaneously falls back into a particular discourse. Universality fails to stand above, and order, the discourses, while particularity asserts itself as capable of incorporating other discourses. This general translatability makes general rhetoric possible, and the tendency of particular discourses to attempt to hegemonize the field of discursivity makes it necessary. Loss of boundaries between discourses inaugurates a new, open horizon for the field of discursivity. The postmodern condition can thus be defined as the continuous interplay between totalizing translation and rhetorical criticism of aspiring metanarratives in an open field of discursivity. The effect of translation is to undermine the fixity of meaning within a discourse. Aspiring metanarratives attempt to fix meaning within a higher totalization. In destabilizing attempted metanarratives, rhetorical criticism reestablishes unfixity of meaning. This continuous dynamism generates a radical unfixity of meaning within the field of discursivity as a whole. Proliferation of temporary senses continuously undermined injects madness into general agonistics. Since translation reduces boundaries, other discourses, and the discursive field itself, enter every discursive formation. Madness, which is this unfixity of meaning, invades each utterance within a discourse from its outside (cf. Felman, 1985).

General rhetoric is thus haunted by madness. Rhetorical criticism reestablishes plurality of discourses and therefore unfixity of meaning within a discourse. Unfixity pervades the field of discourse and therefore the practice of rhetorical criticism itself. Madness appears as both product and practice of rhetoric. Of course, there are many strategic compromises that keep madness at bay. Only by timidly holding back, by ceasing to follow the performative modification to its end, can a semblance of fixity, of saying what we mean and meaning what we say, be preserved. But the encounter with madness is fundamental to discursive interventions, due to the new relation between universal and particular in the postmodern field of discursivity.

The madness of the savage field is constituted by the inability of philosophy, or indeed any other discourse (including rhetoric), to monopolize the activity of translation. General rhetoric engages the continuous translation that defines post-modernity but, in the same moment, succumbs to the dynamism of postmodernity. This cannot be avoided, because of the tension encapsulated in this general applicability of rhetoric combined with its inability to master the open field (an inability shared with every other discourse). General rhetoric is at once a particular critical discourse and a theory of discursive interventions in general—a particular discourse that speaks about discourse universally—though it is not unique in this respect, since every utterance now overflows its borders into other discourses and into the open field. Nevertheless, rhetoric focuses specifically on the characteristics of discourses and, in this sense, is not just another discourse. Its overflowing consists in a certain absence of subject matter. Traditionally, rhetoric centered on the manner of presentation, of persuasion, but its generalized function implies that it is situated at precisely the moment of overflowing in translation. Its specific character consists in not being a delimited discourse and thereby in being able to thematize the procedures of delimitation. When a discourse translates other discourses, it assumes a rhetorical function. Rhetoric itself is this rhetorical capacity in all discourses. Consequently, it is not simply translating, as are other discourses now, but translating without a delimited domain into which translation can occur. This absence means that rhetoric, even though it is of universal application, cannot itself become a totalizing discourse. Because it operates at the moment of translation, it always recovers plurality (see Derrida, 1982b).

Thus, in its universal aspect, rhetoric dissolves by translation (or, we might say, by rhetorical criticism of itself) into the particular discourses it criticizes. In its particular aspect, as a specific discourse, rhetoric is characterized by a certain absence of content such that its critical activity—for example, uncovering the tropological origin of a discourse and engaging in a discussion of the "general" characteristics of tropes—cannot be sufficiently delimited to claim totalizing status. It has been argued that in the postmodern condition every (delimited) discourse involves an interplay of particular and universal—translating out and translating in. The uniqueness of rhetoric is that its universality, rather than aiming at totalization, recovers plurality; its particularity, rather than standing distinct from delimited discourses, clarifies their procedures of formation.

Since criticism recovers a plurality every time, it thereby engages in an activity with pervasive characteristics that seems to call for a universal theory of discourse but does not enjoy the delimitation necessary to develop a theory that could master the domain. We may call this dynamism an antidialectic, or, in Dennis Lee's (1977) phrase, a "savage field"—each side both requiring and repelling its other without reconciliation. It pervades every critical practice within the open field of discourse: particular critical practices overflow themselves toward a theory of discourse; a theory of discourse that attempts the justification of critical practices is never sufficiently universal—it seeps back toward a particular local intervention. This complex interplay in general rhetoric describes the postmodern condition. A characterization that begins solely from the plurality of delimited discourses will fail to thematize the activity of translation that calls forth general rhetoric and, thereby, this new description of the difference between rhetoric and delimited discourses. The madness of general rhetoric is the madness of the postmodern condition itself.

One may ask, is there any alternative to succumbing to the postmodern condition at this point? We have disqualified rhetoric, despite its strategic position, from monopolizing the activity of translation. If madness could be stemmed only by a monopolization of translation, this amounts to an admission that philosophy consists solely in a metanarrative of representation. The postmodern condition would be coextensive with the range of contemporary general rhetoric. And, in a certain sense, this is so. But unless we are to simply put aside the perennial debate between rhetoric and philosophy, we must inquire whether there is a moment in the savage field from which the philosophical life may take its departure—a moment in discourse that transforms the entire field of discursivity.

A contemporary defense of philosophy centers on whether rhetoric can adequately understand, in its performance, the condition of translatability in the new, open field in which it operates. If not, there is an opening to philosophy from within the performative modification of language. Let us seek to escape inherited notions of philosophy as a metanarrative guaranteeing an architectonic of knowledge and seek its transformation, alongside that of rhetoric, in the savage field. Whatever we may discover here, it could not entail a domination of uncertainty that would end the madness of the savage field. To put it in a slightly elliptical way, now that we have discovered the Sophists as our contemporaries, may we not discover Socrates also?

For the plurality of discourses to be characterized as a plurality requires an encounter with the postmodern savage field through a discourse. This is the moment of its totalization, when it translates the others into itself. In this moment, a discourse names the site from which it emerges. The postmodern condition is named from a discourse that emerges within it. As this totalization deconstructs, the discourse is translated into others. It ceases to name the site and becomes the site of naming, when what is said within a discourse can only be understood through a larger context in which it is placed. The dynamic switching between the naming of site and the site of naming constitutes the postmodern madness. These are not alternatives between which one might choose or which might choose oneself. They are two mutually exclusive, but coextensive, descriptions of the same territory. Translation is the border that switches the naming of site into the site of naming. It does not separate two distinct spaces but describes an ineradicable tension between them.

The madness can also be read back through the border where translation occurs, and this is the point where a philosophical critique of general rhetoric emerges. General rhetoric both navigates and succumbs to the savage field by proliferating discourses. At the border between discourses, general rhetoric encounters both babble and silence—uncontrollable proliferation of speech and a residue that will not cross. With every utterance haunted by madness, the performative feat is to design an utterance that ends itself, that calls for the silence beyond itself.[14] Philosophy can no longer style itself as the master discourse and seems to yield to rhetoric as does any particular discourse to discursive criticism. Only if philosophy is not a discourse but a type of move within discourse, a move that nevertheless modifies discourse in its entirety, can it navigate the rhetorical tide without stemming it. Thoroughly imbued with particularity, within the horizon of determinations that surround every utterance, it is a unique move to orient discourse toward its end. The practical intervention of philosophy is to design utterances, and, through them, perhaps discourses themselves, which are not oriented to proliferation but to an explicit termination. After representation, we are before Plato; philosophy is not a rule but a way of life. One among many. The one that does not seek to dominate the many.

In its Platonic origin, philosophy imagined temporarily leaving the world of discourse to encounter cosmos, world order, with a penitent awe expressed in silence (*Republic*, 518c, 540a, 585a–586a, 611a–612d); *Phaedo*, 79d, 81a, 83b; *Timaeus*, 90a–d; *Seventh Letter*, 344b). Armed with an order from beyond language, it could enter the world of discourse and rediscover order. From here emerged the possibility of philosophy as metanarrative, as the ordering of the plurality of discourses. In ancient philosophy, the permeation of particular discourses was such that they could achieve no independent legitimation. Later, without cosmos, this world order became divine, historical, artistic, and technological—each *archē* defining an epoch, in its turn. Modernity repudiated this permeation and thus released the potential of separated discourses to develop their internal resources. Nevertheless, this repudiation itself, as well as the continuing legitimation of modernity, unleashed discourses precisely because they could be expected to contribute to a general knowledge and enlightenment. The technical term for this expectation is *sublation* (*Aufhebung*); without it, there is no modernity. The complete discourse achieved through sublation was equivalent to the silence of absolute knowledge. The fortune of philosophy is entwined in silence. But in the postmodern condition, at the border, there is neither leave-taking from discourse nor a completion of discourse—only a moment of switching from silence to babble.

In pausing with this silence from within discourse, we recover philosophy as a moment in the savage field that will infiltrate its other moments. This is a performative rediscovery of the Platonic claim that rhetoric cannot know itself but is known by philosophy (*Phaedrus*, 269). Silence is no longer simply encountered but constructed. This silent, still point is the moment in translation where the residue asserts itself through the origin of a certain fixity that cannot stem the madness, but that can let it be seen as madness opening an utterance that will close itself.

This is a discovery of a moment beyond language, though the beyond of language cannot be discovered outside language but is that within language that allows its outside to appear. Silence is the outside of all discourse. It surrounds discourse as the emptiness enclosing the earth, rendering a place in the here and now to every utterance. This place will later be undone by the unfixity of the general proliferation, but it can be designed anew. Always anew, without hegemony, an utterance may design its own silence. Only with respect to this place, this siting, can the question of the relation between discourse and the world be properly posed, because only at this point would it no longer be a question of relating discourse to a world conceived as existing before discourse, positivistically. Siting is the worlding of discourse, the world founding of utterance, the coming-to-be of the world as a world within a cultural praxis that overflows language through the infiltration of silence.

This outside of discourse also appears within discourse. In this taming of silence, it appears in the pauses between utterances, and in the spaces between words,[15] to make meaning from the babble. In this way, it holds the madness at bay for a while, for the unfixity could not even be madness if it were immediate. In this way philosophy comes to the aid of rhetoric and releases its legitimate and necessary field of operation. Stalling unfixity allows temporary meaning within specific discourses, which is, in turn, undermined by the madness of general rhetoric. Within discourse, silence reverts behind pen to paper, slowing the undermining of meaning enough to allow the operation of general rhetoric. Outside discourse, through the moment of translation that peers outside, silence surrounds, and lies behind, all speech. Before and after the utterance, silence supports discourse with all that cannot be said, since saying is always underway but must both begin and end. Beginning is eruption, not only a starting

IAN ANGUS

but a closing off of the silence that reigned before. In this closing, discourse achieves specificity. The totality of what is closed off isolates a determinate discourse from other discourses by resisting translation. Practicing translation interrupts the eruption, reintroducing silence into discourse. Without silence, discourse would be without birth and death; it would have no meaning for those of us who speak, because we could not be present at its occasion. But with the incorporation of philosophical silence, rhetoric can operate with, and upon, the many births and deaths in, and of, discourses in the political world we share with others.

Philosophy, unlike religion or myth, requires a relation to something that is not itself, such as tradition, religion, rhetoric, hedonism, science, or technology—in short, nonphilosophy—and is constituted through this relation. Thus, philosophy can end from two opposite directions. It can simply historically cease as the discourse about discourse, since the gnoseological horizon that enabled this representational totalization has been circumscribed. Or it can cease through the incorporation of its outside. In cannibalizing everything, philosophy is finished. It becomes general rhetoric. Yet, if this new general rhetoric can be circumscribed, it can become the other to a performative rediscovery of philosophy.

An utterance that does not simply terminate but makes its own ending opens general rhetoric to a new performative philosophical turn that can also recuperate the silent philosophical origin in representation. The life without silence is not worth living. This is not every speech but a desire born within language, given form within language, and reaching beyond language, in the moment of calm when one finds the courage to end.

Notes

1. This notion of a gnoseological horizon is based on the work of Emmanuel Levinas (1969, 1981; see Angus, 1987). This work suggests that the notion of totality developed in philosophy through its orientation to knowledge is fundamentally solipsistic and reduces the ethical encounter with the other to a problem of knowledge. This insight has entered postmodern discussions

204

primarily through the writings of Jacques Derrida and Jean-Francois Lyotard. Their appropriation has elided an equally important element of Levinas' work—that, even throughout its epistemological-representational fixation, philosophy actually proceeded through an ethical, face-to-face encounter of teaching (1969, p. 295). These neglected components of philosophy need to be foregrounded and rethought in a postmodern context. The death of philosophy is also the possibility of its renewal.

2. The term *general rhetoric* has been used previously by others but not with this meaning. J. Dubois and his colleagues used the term to refer to a rhetoric "meant to be applicable to all modes of expression" (Dubois, Edeline, Klinkenberg, Minguet, Pire, & Trinon, 1981, p. 167) though they have acknowledged (in a subsequently written afterward included in the English translation) that the term was too ambitious, and that "theory of the figures of discourse" would be more accurate (p. 215). The generality in question in this case was that of the available theory of rhetoric, not that of the expansion of its field of applicability.

    Roland Barthes used the term to indicate the expansion of rhetorical methods and concerns from language to images (1977, p. 49). This concern has been taken up by Jacques Durand (1983). In this usage, it is an issue of the expansion of the field of rhetoric's applicability in a manner such as Saussure's expansion of linguistic concerns toward a general theory of signs. This usage is closer to my own, though still in this case it is a question of developing a suitable theory for analyzing an expanded field of cultural phenomena.

    My use of this term is directed more toward the field of applicability of rhetorical methods and concerns rather than toward a theory of rhetoric itself—though, no doubt, such an expansion of applicability is accompanied by a flowering of rhetorical methods themselves. Even further, I emphasize that this expanded applicability is not simply a matter of theoretical development but is based in a new postmodern intellectual situation. In particular, the thematic of knowledge as a production through discourse breaks down the traditional division of labor between rhetoric and philosophy and institutes the necessity for renewed thinking about their relation. This is especially important for the generality in question in this chapter. This usage is implicated in the contemporary debates concerning the end of metaphysics, since the separation of the two genres was settled by the metaphysical distinction between truth and persuasion.

3. Aristotle also suggested the compatibility and complementary

IAN ANGUS

character of rhetorico-political universality and philosophical universality (see, e. g., *Rhetoric*, 1354a, 1355b, 1356a, 1358a). But this is highly questionable, even within the terms of Greek thought. For Plato, there is a fundamental distinction between good (scientific, philosophical) and bad (merely empirical, political) rhetoric (*Phaedrus*, 269–74). Also important here is Hannah Arendt's claim that the philosophers "turned away from the polis" and refashioned the concept of the political from their antipolitical, philosophical stance (1973, pp. 17–21). Her attempt to regain a properly "political" concept of politics is very important after the end of philosophy and is congruent with what is attempted here under the term *general rhetoric*.

4. For this reason, the present discussion concerning internal legitimation of discourses through performativity is the successor of the earlier theory of the ideological significance of science and technology (Habermas, 1970). For an account that attempts to synthesize and extend the phenomenological and critical theory contributions, see Angus, 1984.

5. As Lyotard notes (1984, pp. 60, 65), Habermas' formulation assumes the validity of the metanarrative of emancipation and therefore poses the issue of consensus as an agreement of subjects who enter into discourses, rather than focusing on the subject positions constituted within discourses. Nevertheless, Habermas' basic move can be reformulated largely in discursive terms, as I have done in the text, though it will then run up against the criticism I develop there.

6. For this reason, Habermas rejects the notion of a postmodern condition in *The Philosophical Discourse of Modernity* and claims that the modern problematic of the Young Hegelians concerning the ability of totalizing reason to permeate specific discourses is still our contemporary one. This view is criticized in Angus, 1990b.

7. Lyotard's strategy of overturning the board seems to be the inverse of Baudrillard's (1983, pp. 43–44) notion of the masses as "refusing to participate." The unsatisfactoriness of this alternative as a standpoint of critical reason does not rule out its exemplariness with regard to the dilemmas of the postmodern condition. A genuine philosophical theory of postmodernity would need to overcome this alternative as well as to show why this unsatisfactory alternative continually reappears.

8. Keane also says that such institutions could never be accepted "fully" because a "universal metalanguage" could never be adopted once and for all (1988, p. 44). This does not resolve the

issue; it simply restates it on a higher level. Perhaps it is a sufficient practical stand for political intervention. If I extrapolate correctly, this implies regarding democratic institutions as a metalanguage with respect to political debates, and as institutions not finally indisputable and, in special circumstances, liable to become the subject of debate themselves, in which case we enter into some further metalanguage (whose identity Keane does not discuss). Theoretically, this requires an argument for a hierarchy of metalanguages applied in the political realm, which could gain support from some types of systems theory (see Bateson, 1972; Angus, 1984, pp. 19–40).

9. I use Lyotard's term here, since it is a good one. But as far as I can see, he applies the term solely within a discourse, though of course this includes paralogical moves (Lyotard, 1984, pp. 10, 16, 15, 57, 59). This is to be expected, since if the implications of the "general agonistics between discourses to hegemonize the activity of translation" were to be followed out his characterization of the postmodern condition would be revealed as insufficient.

10. A focus on simply the legitimation of a diversity of discourses by modernity will thus undermine the concept of postmodernity, since the present plurality will seem, in principle, to be the same as the plurality legitimated by de Tocqueville and other early modern theorists. John Keane has criticized Lyotard in this manner (1988, pp. 213–245).

11. Therefore, deconstruction is not just a theory but a world event. The work of Jacques Derrida is significant in expressing this moment of deconstructive rhetorical criticism (see especially 1982a, pp. 1–27). The significance of the outside in this moment is elaborated by Ernesto Laclau and Chantal Mouffe (1985, pp. 122–145). The other side of deconstructive criticism is articulatory totalizing translation (Angus, 1992).

12. This formulation of the relation between interpretation and poetry owes a great deal to the later work of Heidegger. For its extension into rhetorical criticism of tropes, the work of Ernesto Grassi is very important (1980, especially pp. 18–21; 1987, pp. 68–78). This basic shift is the impetus behind the recent development of a rhetoric of inquiry perspective (e.g., White, 1978). The related but not identical functions of rhetoric and poetry have been clarified by Michael J. Hyde (1983).

13. This distinction between universalizing and universal judgment is developed originally in Kant's *Critique of Judgment*. Hannah Arendt has used it to develop the idea of politics as a singular

judgment not subsumable under a rule (Angus, 1984, pp. 99–
118). Max Horkheimer and Hans-Georg Gadamer have also focused on Kant's "Third Critique" in developing the traditions of
critical theory and hermeneutics respectively (Horkheimer, 1925;
Gadamer, 1975). If we keep in mind that it was Kant's "Third
Critique" that led to the development of Hegel's notion of history, we can see in this convergence of interest in twentieth
century thought a return to, and rethinking of, the point of
self-consciousness of modern philosophy in Hegel's notion of
Aufhebung.

14. Neither of these two silences are the same as that which is
silenced, or repressed, within a given discourse—what cannot
be expressed within it—though the ability to define this silence
must also be seen as a frontier effect of the outside coming inside
due to translation. The more fundamental silence presently referred to is also explored in Angus, 1990a. This recuperation of
silence as a key moment of philosophy invites comparison with
other traditions of thought, especially Zen Buddhism (Kasulis,
1981).

15. Bernard Dauenhauer notes these two forms of silence—framing
discourse and within discourse—whereas Jacques Derrida describes only the latter, which he calls "spacing," since he has
writing in mind (Dauenhauer, 1980; Derrida, 1976, pp. 39, 68,
70, 139, 200, 203).

References

Angus, I. (1984). *Technique and enlightenment: Limits of instrumental
reason*. Washington, DC: Center for Advanced Research in Phenomenology and University Press of America.

Angus, I. (1987, June). *Self-knowledge, the Other, and the foundation of
community*. Paper presented at the meeting of the Society for
Phenomenology and Existential Philosophy, Ottawa, Canada.

Angus, I. (1990a). Crossing the border. *The Massachusetts Review*,
31(1–2), 32–47.

Angus, I. (1990b). Habermas confronts the deconstructionist challenge: On the philosophical discourse of modernity. *Canadian
Journal of Political and Social Theory*, *14*(1–2, 3), 21–33.

Angus, I. (1992). The politics of common sense: Articulation theory
and critical communication studies. In S. Deetz (Ed.), *Communication yearbook 15* (pp. 536–571). Newbury Park, CA: Sage.

Arendt, H. (1973). *The human condition*. Chicago: University of Chicago Press.

Aristotle. (1954). *Rhetoric* (W. R. Roberts, Trans.). New York: The Modern Library Series, Random House.

Aristotle. (1962). *Nichomachean ethics* (M. Ostwald, Trans.). New York: Bobbs-Merrill.

Barthes, R. (1977). Rhetoric of the image (S. Heath, Trans.). In S. Heath (ed.), *Image-music-text* (pp. 32–51). New York: Hill & Wang.

Bateson, G. (1972). *Steps to an ecology of mind.* New York: Ballantine.

Baudrillard, J. (1983). *In the shadow of the silent majorities* (P. Foss, P. Patton, & J. Johnston, Trans.). New York: Semiotext(e).

Beckett, S. (1958). *The unnamable.* New York: Grove Press.

Dauenhauer, B. P. (1980). *Silence: The phenomenon and its ontological significance.* Bloomington: Indiana University Press.

Derrida, J. (1976). *Of grammatology* (G. C. Spivak, Trans.). Baltimore: Johns Hopkins University Press. (Original work published 1967.)

Derrida, J. (1982a). Differance (A. Bass, Trans.). In *Margins of philosophy* (pp. 1–28). Chicago: University of Chicago Press. (Original work published 1972.)

Derrida, J. (1982b). White mythology: Metaphor in the text of philosophy (A. Bass, Trans.). In *Margins of philosophy* (pp. 207–272). Chicago: University of Chicago Press. (Original work published 1972.)

Dubois, J., Edeline, F., Klinkenberg, J-M., Minguet, P., Pire, F., & Trinon, H. (1981). *A general rhetoric* (P. Burrell & E. Slotkin, Trans.). Baltimore: Johns Hopkins University Press. (Original work published 1970.)

Durand, J. (1983). Rhetoric and the advertising image (T. van Leeuwen, Trans.). *Australian Journal of Cultural Studies, 1*(2), 42–53.

Felman, S. (1985). *Writing and madness.* Ithaca: Cornell University Press.

Findlay, J. N. (1942). Goedelian sentences: A non-numerical approach. *Mind, 51*(202), 259–265.

Gadamer, H-G. (1975). *Truth and method.* New York: Crossroad.

Godel, K. (1931). Ueber formal unentscheidbare satze der "Principia mathematica" und verwandter systeme. *Monatschrift fur Mathematik und Physik, 38,* 174–198.

Grassi, E. (1980). *Rhetoric as philosophy: The humanistic tradition.* University The Pennsylvania State University Press.

Grassi, E. (1987). Why rhetoric is philosophy. *Philosophy and Rhetoric, 20*(2), 68–78.

Habermas, J. (1970). Technology and science as ideology (J. J. Shapiro, Trans.). In *Toward a rational society* (pp. 81–122). Boston: Beacon. (Original work published 1968.)

Habermas, J. (1977). A review of Gadamer's *Truth and method*. In F. R. Dallmayr and T. A. McCarthy (Eds.), *Understanding and social inquiry* (pp. 335–363). Notre Dame: University of Notre Dame Press.

Habermas, J. (1979). The development of normative structures (T. McCarthy, Trans.). In *Communication and the evolution of society* (pp. 95–129). Boston: Beacon. (Original work published 1976.)

Habermas, J. (1987). *The philosophical discourse of modernity* (F. Lawrence, Trans.). Cambridge: MIT Press. (Original work published 1985.)

Hegel, G. W. F. (1956). *The philosophy of history* (J. Sibree, Trans.). New York: Dover.

Hegel, G. W. F. (1979). *Phenomenology of spirit* (A. V. Miller, Trans.). New York: Oxford University Press. (Original work published 1952.)

Horkheimer, M. (1925). *Kants kritik der urteilskraft als bindeglied zwischen theoretischer und praktischer philosophie*. Stuttgart: Verlag von W. Kohlhammer.

Horkheimer M., & Adorno, T. (1972). *Dialectic of enlightenment* (J. Cumming, Trans.). New York: Herder & Herder. (Original work published 1947.)

Husserl, E. (1969). *Formal and transcendental logic* (D. Cairns, Trans.). The Hague: Martinus Nijhoff. (Original work published 1929.)

Husserl, E. (1970). Philosophy and the crisis of European humanity (D. Carr, Trans.). In *The crisis of the European sciences and transcendental phenomenology* (Appendix 1). Evanston: Northwestern University Press. (Original work published 1954.)

Husserl, E. (1982). *Ideas pertaining to a pure phenomenology and to a pure phenomenological philosophy*, Book 1 (F. Kersten, Trans.). The Hague: Martinus Nijhoff. (Original work published 1913.)

Hyde, M. J. (1983). Rhetorically, man dwells: On the making-known function of discourse. *Communication*, *7*(2), 201–220.

Kasulis, T. P. (1981). *Zen action, zen person*. Honolulu: University of Hawaii Press.

Keane, J. (1988). *Democracy and civil society*. London: Verso.

Laclau, E., & Mouffe, C. (1985). *Hegemony and socialist strategy*. London: Verso.

Lee, D. (1977). *Savage fields: An essay in literature and cosmology*. Toronto: Anansi.

Levinas, E. (1969). *Totality and infinity* (A. Lingis, Trans.). Pittsburgh: Dusquesne University Press. (Original work published 1961.)

Levinas, E. (1981). *Otherwise than being, or beyond essence* (A. Lingis,

Trans.). The Hague: Martinus Nijhoff. (Original work published 1974.)

Lyotard, J-F. (1984). *The postmodern condition: A report on knowledge* (G. Bennington & B. Massumi, Trans.). Minneapolis: University of Minnesota Press. (Original work published 1979.)

Nietzsche, F. (1969). *On the genealogy of morals* (W. Kaufmann & R. J. Hollingdale, Trans.). New York: Vintage.

Plato. (1961). *Plato: Collected dialogues* (E. Hamilton & H. Cairns, Eds.). New York: Random House.

Plato. (1973). *Phaedrus* (W. Hamilton, Trans.). New York: Penguin.

Rorty, R. (1979). *Philosophy and the mirror of nature*. Princeton: Princeton University Press.

Rosser, B. (1939). An informal exposition of proofs of Godel's theorem and Church's Theorem. *The Journal of Symbolic Logic, 4*(2), 53–64.

Schurmann, R. (1987). *Heidegger on being and acting: From principles to anarchy*. Bloomington: Indiana University Press.

Seebohm, T. M. (1985) The end of philosophy: Three historical aphorisms. In H. J. Silverman & D. Ihde (Eds.), *Hermeneutics and deconstruction* (pp. 11–23). Albany: State University of New York Press.

White, H. (1978). *Tropics of discourse: Essays in cultural criticism*. Baltimore: Johns Hopkins University Press.

Index